Dear Reader:

The book you are about to read is the latest bestseller from St. Martin's True Crime Library, the imprint *The New York Times* calls "the leader in true crime!" Each month, we offer you a fascinating account of the latest, most sensational crime that has captured the national attention. In DEADLY SEDUCTION a prominent attorney thought he'd found the woman of his dreams, until the silky blonde society lady turned into a calculating, cruel seductress whose murderous future was about to rival her sordid past. DEATH CRUISE tells how a dream vacation in Florida turned into a nightmare of death on a tropical ocean for a mother and her two teenage daughters. Beneath one brilliant doctor's kindly bedside manner lurked an insatiable killer who lured his patients into a vicious circle of death in WITHOUT MERCY.

True Crime Library is also where readers go to find the classic tales of the most infamous crimes of our times. THE MILWAU-KEE MURDERS delves into the twisted world of savage serial killer Jeffrey Dahmer; WHOEVER FIGHTS MONSTERS takes you inside the special FBI team that tracks serial killers; BAD BLOOD is the story of the notorious Menendez brothers and their sensational trials; FALLEN HERO recounts the riveting tragedy of O.J. Simpson and the case that stunned a nation.

St. Martin's True Crime Library gives you the stories *behind* the headlines. Our authors take you right to the scene of the crime and into the minds of the most evil murderers to show you what really makes them tick. St. Martin's True Crime Library paper-backs are better than the most terrifying thriller, because it's all true! The next time you want a crackling good read, make sure it's got the St. Martin's True Crime Library logo on the spine—you'll be up all night!

Charles E. Spicer, Jr.
Senior Editor, St. Martin's True Crime Library

LOVE AND DEATH

The badly charred body of a petite woman was found slumped inside the scorched shell of the truck. Her clothing was burned off and the flesh of the trunk and upper part of the body was seared black by the flames. It appeared she had been deliberately set on fire, and the flames spread throughout the interior of the truck. There was no identification with the body, and authorities were able to determine how she died before they learned who she was. Los Angeles County Coroner's Office pathologists concluded that the woman was strangled before her body was set on fire and left inside the burning truck.

THE MAN WHO STANDS ACCUSED OF THIS GHASTLY CRIME IS GLEN ROGERS. READ ON TO FIND OUT MORE ABOUT THE TRUE STORY OF THIS . . .

SMOOTH OPERATOR

St. Martin's Paperbacks Titles by Clifford L. Linedecker

SMOOTH OPERATOR

Clifford L. Linedecker

St. Martin's Paperbacks

SMOOTH OPERATOR

Copyright © 1997 by Clifford L. Linedecker

Cover photograph by John T. Barr/Gamma Liaison.

All rights reserved. No part of this book may be used or reproduced in any manner whatsoever without written permission except in the case of brief quotations embodied in critical articles or reviews. For information address St. Martin's Press, 175 Fifth Avenue, New York, N.Y. 10010.

ISBN: 0-312-96400-5

Printed in the United States of America

St. Martin's Paperbacks edition/December 1997

10 9 8 7 6 5 4 3 2 1

Acknowledgments

I am indebted to many individuals for contributions to the writing and accuracy of this book.

Police officers, prosecuting attorneys, jail employees and members of their staffs, courthouse employees, librarians, and journalists have all had a hand in its production, from the initial concept to the completed manuscript.

Among those deserving of special acknowledgment for their help are Todd Blevins, a reporter for the *Richmond Register*; Beulah Phelps, a civilian employee at the Madison County Detention Center; and Deborah Garrison of the Department of Public Advocacy—all in Richmond; and Roger Jordan in Cincinnati.

Thanks also go, of course, to my agent Tony Seidl of T. D. Media; and especially to my editor, Charles Spicer, for suggesting I write the Glen Rogers story.

Contents

Contents

Introduction

In many respects, if Glen Edward Rogers is guilty of the dreadful crimes he is accused of, he is a classic serial killer.

Serial killers tend to focus on a specific type of victim based on such things as gender, age, physical appearance, and lifestyle or profession.

The four women Rogers has been accused of murdering were all redheads in their twenties or early thirties. He met three of them in bars, and the other while drinking beer and listening to country music at a state fair.

Attraction to a certain type of victim, and an almost ritualized method of operation, including the manner in which they are isolated and slain, are factors that can help police track a killer down. Geography is also an important factor. Most serial killers are as territorial as cougars or wildcats. They work a particular area.

Wayne B. Williams was convicted of murder after Atlanta was gripped in fear for twenty-two months during the early 1980s while a wave of black children and young men died; David Carpenter stalked and murdered women along hiking trails north of San Francisco; and Arthur

Shawcross killed prostitutes picked up in the red-light districts of Rochester, New York.

It took a while but all three of those serial killers were eventually run down and put out of business. Their territorial behavior was among the factors that helped police focus their investigation. Williams was arrested after dumping a body off an Atlanta bridge into the Chattahoochie River. A couple of police officers were hiding in brush at the base of the bridge, waiting for just such an event. Other bodies had already been pulled from the murky waters.

Shawcross left his scent and marked his territory as surely as any animal predator, by dumping most of his victims in the Genesee River. Writing about the murders before and after he was run to ground, the press dubbed him "the Genesee River Killer." Carpenter was similarly tagged as "the Trailside Killer," and police knew where to focus their investigation and search—the hiking trails in the wilderness areas of Marin County.

Rogers is a different breed of animal—a specific type of serial killer who can be much harder to catch. He's considered a spree killer, but, again, of a very narrowly defined type. Mass murderers who explode in sudden killing binges, bursting into office buildings, restaurants, or schools packing an arsenal of AK-47s, Uzis, and automatic pistols, and begin spraying everybody in sight are sometimes referred to as spree killers. They engage in killing sprees of sorts, but Rogers is a different breed.

Rogers fits into the same mold with such notorious butchers as Christopher Bernard Wilder, and Alton Coleman and Debra Brown, who kill in staccato bursts of violence separated by a few hours or a few days. In 1984, Wilder killed two beautiful women in the Miami area, then, after he learned police were closing in, he raged across the country murdering models and would-be models in a grisly four-week murder spree before he was finally shot to death by a state police officer in New Hampshire.

The same year, Coleman apparently first killed a little girl from Waukegan, Illinois, then he and his girlfriend set off on a seven-week sex-and-murder rampage through the Midwest slaughtering men, women, and children until they were finally tracked down and captured in Evanston, Illinois. The couple had traveled in a loop through Illinois, Indiana, Michigan, Ohio, Kentucky, and then back to Illinois.

Wilder, Coleman, and Brown moved rapidly, killing in one state, then selecting the next victim or victims hundreds of miles away in another state. Coleman and Brown drove in the cars of their victims, rode buses, and even pedaled bicycles during their crime spree. Wilder drove a series of cars, beginning with his own and then switching to others stolen from victims. Law enforcement authorities knew from the beginning of the manhunts exactly who they were looking for, but they didn't know where to look.

Rogers was much the same kind of killer, and police had to solve the same frustrating problem of where to look for him before they could put a stop to his deadly rampage. Based on the police reports, he was moving as fast and as erratically as one of the destructive tornadoes that regularly rip through the South and the Midwest, leaving death and destruction in their paths. Tornado trackers know exactly what they're dealing with, but it is impossible to figure out exactly where the deadly wind will materialize and touch down next while it's bouncing and whirling around.

For a while it seemed as if FBI agents and homicide investigators in six states who were trying to capture Glen Edward Rogers might as well have been trying to track a tornado. The man whom investigators began calling "the Cross Country Killer" was as elusive as a will-o'-the-wisp and behaved as if he were wearing a fairy-tale ogre's seven-league boots.

According to police, he first struck in California, then ripped through the South, riding in Greyhound buses and taxi cabs, or driving his own pickup truck and a stolen car. While police detectives were just beginning to investigate a killing in one state, he was already romancing his next victim and preparing to kill again in another state hundreds of miles away. He was charming, highly manipulative, and seemingly without conscience.

According to police accounts, the murders occurred during sudden bursts of rage, after a day or night of heavy drinking. Chillingly, once the killings began, there was hardly any cooling-off period. Most serial killers space their murders weeks or months apart, often methodically planning each slaying, carrying it out, then savoring and reliving the details in their minds until the pressures build up to the point where they are ready to strike again. The first two murders attributed to Rogers were separated by lengthy cooling-off periods, but as the pressure of the manhunt mounted, the time between slayings rapidly narrowed until they were occurring only three or four days apart.

Many questions about Glen Rogers are still to be answered. He himself denies committing the murders he is accused of. But based on information collected during the early stages of the investigation, police say it appears that the slayings were not planned beforehand. Two of the victims willingly took him into their beds, so for them at least rape was apparently not a motive. And although the car of one woman was stolen, and some money and jewelry was taken from the victims, it seems that robbery was more an afterthought than a motivation for murder.

The killings were as chillingly unpredictable as they were unplanned. For six dreadful weeks, police say he raged across the country, touching down in one state and then another. According to police, a mad-dog killer was on the loose. He was out of control, and no one knew where he would strike next.

Cliff Linedecker
Lantana, Florida
July 1996

GLEN ROGERS
CAUGHT
LADIES 1/2 PRICE
ON ALL DRINKS
—Handwritten sign posted behind the bar at McRed's

Mad dogs and Englishmen go out in the midday sun.
—*Mad Dogs and Englishmen*, Noël Coward

Prologue

He was an old-fashioned Southern-style charmer, a handsome, sweet-talking man with a fall of carefully sprayed shoulder-length blond hair, a neatly trimmed mustache, and a full beard.

It was obvious as well that he was no stranger to a barroom, or to chatting up good-looking women. He was a serious drinker who usually put away a half-dozen or more draft beers at a sitting. But he could also sit for hours tossing down Jack Daniel's neat, chasing each with a fresh Budweiser draft poured with just enough head to bring out the best of the pleasantly sour flavor, then get up and walk as straight a line as any man in the barroom.

He seemed to have plenty of money and generously bought drinks for the ladies, often for the house. He paid with crisp hundred-dollar bills that he peeled off a roll of greenbacks that he kept in his right-hand pants pocket. He was also a good tipper, especially if he was perched on one of the red vinyl-topped stools at the bar and Rein Keener poured his drinks or served them to him at one of the small round wooden tables.

Rein was a slender twenty-four-year-old strawberry blonde who worked part-time at McRed's Cocktail Lounge, a lively bar and restaurant in Van Nuys that was popular with the country music crowd. Located along busy Victory Boulevard in the San Fernando Valley a few minutes' drive north of Beverly Hills, McRed's was a good place to work. The earnings she brought home from her bartending duties went a long way toward paying standard living costs as well as the expenses of her law school studies at the University of Southern California.

The hangout was also a prime location for a woman with Rein's good looks to meet men, and it wasn't at all unusual for one of her customers to put the move on and try to date her. But few if any of her would-be suitors were as smoothly persistent and had the delight-ful line of small talk and courtly manners as the hand-some blond hunk who told her his name was Glen and behaved as if he thought she was one of the prettiest women he had ever seen. He wasn't shy about saying so. One time while he was nursing a cool one and the jukebox was blasting away she asked him if he liked country music. He smiled, fixed her with his clear blue-green eyes, and replied that he sure enough did—and he also liked beautiful women. Another time he bought her a bouquet of roses. They were the color of fresh peaches, like her hair, he said. Whenever he loped into the busy watering hole and saw she was behind the bar, he walked straight over to her, took her hand in his, and kissed it.

Glen's interest in the shapely bartender was obvious from the first day he began showing up at McRed's early in September. Rein's fellow bartender, Mike Saliman, didn't share her cautious enthusiasm for the courtly patron. The solidly built blond man was a bit too loud and pushy for his liking.

The experienced bartender tagged him for a phony the first time he got a look at him a couple of weeks earlier when Glen strutted into the bar talking big and claiming to be a detective looking for information about a woman he believed had applied for a job at the tavern. The stranger never did track down the woman he was looking for, but he took a liking to McRed's and began dropping by regularly after his first appearance there. He timed most of his visits for afternoons or evenings when Rein was taking care of the bartending duties or waiting on tables.

Sometimes he balanced for hours on one of the barstools, flirting and chatting with Rein about his mother in Ohio, and about common experiences in the Deep South. Rein had spent her teenage years in Biloxi, Mississippi, and he had traveled all along the Gulf Coast. He told her stories about his work and said he spent a few years as a cab driver. In between the Buds and the Jack Daniel's, however, he also confided that he was currently involved in more glamorous pursuits. He was a federal agent who tracked fugitives from justice, and he showed her a badge and some I.D. to prove it. He said he hunted people.

The barmaid eventually learned, however, that his job was much more mundane. After moving to Van Nuys from Hollywood, he was working as a self-employed housepainter and resident manager of a nearby apartment building in the 6600 block of Woodman Avenue. He tossed so much money around, it made her curious about the source of the housepainter's cash.

On Thursday night, September 28, McRed's was packed with people. Every stool at the bar had someone's rear end parked on it, and most of those bottoms were covered in blue jeans. The tables were full of people having a good time, and the clink of glasses, the clack of pool balls, loud talk, and occasional cackles of laughter mixed pleasantly with the crash of canned music by performers such as Clint Black, Garth Brooks, and Reba McEntire that blared from the jukebox. Thick threads of purple cigarette smoke hung low over the action. Some of the most spirited activity was focused on a spicy little woman everybody called Sam.

Most women who share her first name grow up with the nickname Sandy or Sandi. Somehow, however, people took to calling Sandra Gallagher "Sam," and she liked it just fine. It seemed to fit. That night, Sam was celebrating her good fortune in winning a $1,260 Keno jackpot in the California lottery.

It was about time that Sam got a smile instead of a frown from Lady Luck. The petite five-foot-three-inch ninety-five-pound woman with the big voice and the red highlights in her dark shoulder-length hair had absorbed more than her fair share of bad breaks and hard knocks in her thirty-four years. Some of them were her own fault. She had two failed marriages behind her, a reputation for hanging around with outlaw bikers, and a serious problem with drugs and alcohol that had landed her in one jam after another. During the past three years she piled up three drunk-driving arrests in California, served a stint in jail, and for a while was under psychiatric care that included a period of hospitalization.

She was somewhat of a rolling stone, and a bit of a maverick. She grew up in Downey and Fullerton where her father played steel-string guitar at local gigs, and she was a chip off the old block. Sam drifted around and lived for a while in Colorado, where she followed in her father's footsteps, picking up a few dollars here and there singing in country bars. At other times she climbed onto the tiny stages as a volunteer accompanist for the hired pickers or kept tune with the jukebox just for the hell of it. Then she followed her California roots back to the Golden State. Her children from her first marriage were there, and she was married in San Diego to her second husband, Navy sailor Steve Gallagher. The couple met in Jacksonville, Florida, when he was stationed there with the Navy in the mid-1980s. A decade later, Gallagher described Sam to a newspaper reporter as ". . . the type of woman who could get into your head."

Sam herself believed that was true, although when she talked to friends about it she used the term in a slightly different context. She was convinced she could peer into the minds of people and read their thoughts. The world was an adventure to her, and she danced through life like a blithe spirit, picking and singing, writing songs and poetry, piloting her prized pickup truck, and partying with her friends. She had a personality like a freshly popped can of 7-Up. Sam sparkled and fizzed, and other people felt good simply being around her.

Sam was living in a rundown area of San Bernardino that was so tough some people called it "Felony Flats," when she got entangled in her latest brush with the law. She was scheduled for arraignment in San Bernardino on drug charges that Wednesday, and when she didn't show up a warrant was issued for her arrest.

Then she got lucky at Keno, and the day after missing the court date she drove to the state lottery office in Van Nuys. She had given up on Felony Flats several weeks earlier and moved north to the San Fernando Valley, into a garage apartment a few minutes' drive from McRed's. Sam made friends easily and quickly developed a close platonic relationship with Chris Brady, a young man who was one of her neighbors. Brady lived across the street from her apartment, and they were soon sharing idle chitchat, and more serious confidences. Sam told him she had done some jail time before moving down the coast to begin a new life.

Every Sunday morning since moving in, she dressed up and left the apartment to drive to Venice, where she attended church. One day she invited Brady to go to a church picnic with her, and he was bowled over by the other members of the flock. Just about everyone there had long hair and tattoos, and they all seemed to be former outlaw bikers who were in the process of restructuring their lives. But everybody was friendly, and the food was good.

Sam didn't get her Keno winnings immediately, but signed a paper at the lottery office and was promised the check would be in the mail in a couple of days. That was good enough reason to start celebrating, and a few minutes after leaving the lottery office she wheeled into McRed's to spread the word in her surprising boom-box voice about her good fortune. Sam had friends there. She had done some singing around the area with a country music band, and had tipped a few cool ones at the popular watering hole in the past.

She was bubbling over with happiness and had big plans for her lottery windfall. She told Rein she was hoping to be able to move back to Northern California so she could be closer to her three sons, who lived there with relatives. But first there was time for celebrating. She was a woman of fire and spice who liked to kick up her heels in a bar until closing time, then head off with a group of friends to a restaurant for breakfast. Sam bought several rounds of drinks while celebrating, including a few for the handsome, hirsute stranger with the round, open face and the dreamy eyes. He bought a couple for her as well, and showered her with his light patter and compliments.

But his eye was still on the elusively desirable bartender. He had tried for two weeks to get her to go out with him, showering her with flattery and pestering her for her home phone number. Rein gave him the number at the bar, but she kept her home number to herself. Glen was a man who usually got what he wanted when it came to women, however, and he didn't give up easily. He repeatedly told her how pretty she was, and raved about how nice it would be to get to know her better. He was especially pushy that night, and insisted he had missed her because they hadn't seen each other for two days. Whenever he had a chance, he grabbed at her with his big, rough hands and tried to pull her down onto his lap, but she managed to duck or twist and turn away. Once, however, he caught up with her and pinned her against a wall. Then, with one hand against the small of her back, he leaned forward and tried to kiss her. Rein struggled and swiveled her head from side to side, while talking him down until he pulled back. It was shortly after that when he turned most of his attention to the zealously celebrating lottery winner.

Sam was busy with her friends and although she smiled and acknowledged the flood of compliments, initially she paid more attention to the pool games she was playing than to the glib, sweet-talking blond man. He was persistent, however, and eventually they became more friendly. Despite her frequent troubles she was a sunny-side-up type of woman. She had a bubbly, outgoing personality and was more likely to walk up to a stranger and introduce herself than needlessly put down even the most timidly awkward admirer. And the blond man wasn't awkward or timid. He was a good talker and a snappy dresser. Even after spending several hours in the barroom, his blue jeans looked like they were freshly pressed, his long-sleeved collared workshirt was as crisp as a cracker, and he was wearing his trademark matching cowboy boots and leather belt with the heavy metal clasp. He didn't look like the kind of man who slept in his clothes.

A couple of times while the jukebox was belting out sweet country tunes, he led Sam out onto the crowded dance floor and tried to teach her the two-step. It was a Jack Daniel's night for him, and it may have been the whiskey that caused him to repeatedly step on her toes. Even though he was a strapping, big, broad-shouldered man who was at least six feet tall and appeared to pack almost two hundred pounds on a hard body, the petite woman didn't seem to mind. She shrieked and giggled when he persistently pulled her down onto his lap at the table.

He said he was stopped by police for driving under the influence and didn't have wheels, so he needed a ride home. He had told basically the same story to the bartender, claiming he walked the mile between his apartment and McRed's. But Sam was either having too much fun to leave, or simply wasn't in the mood to climb into her pickup truck with the handsome stranger and drive off with him into the night. The old Ford, with its pitted gray and black paint, may have looked like a rattletrap to some other people, but it was one of Sam's most prized possessions. The tiny woman was a sight to see when she roared up to McRed's or some other country bar perched like a doll behind the steering wheel with the seat pulled up close to the dash so her feet could reach the pedals on the floor. She was so little she even had trouble using the mirrors to keep an eye on the traffic behind her, or to do an occasional feminine touchup on her hair and face.

Shortly before closing time, the roughhewn Romeo's persistent pleas for a ride finally seemed about to pay off. But it was Rein, not Sandra, who agreed to give him a lift. Her purse strap was draped over her shoulder, her car keys were in her hand, and she was about six feet from the front door, all ready to walk out with him, when some of her friends called to her. They talked her into sticking around and playing a few final games of darts.

Her hopeful passenger was waiting for her to finish her game when she began to have second thoughts about giving him a ride. An uncomfortable feeling that something was wrong swept over her, and she began thinking about how tiny and weak she was and how big and strong he was. She told him she was sorry, but she had changed her mind. The offer of a ride was no longer open.

He was furious and yelled at her. When he leaned over and tried to give her a kiss, she pushed him away. "Rein, I've got to tell you," he growled, frowning down at her and fixing her with eyes that were as frosty as a freshly drawn mug of draft, "I always get what I want." Then he turned and stalked away.

The next time Rein noticed him, he had calmed down. He was with Sam, who agreed to play chauffeur. She was no naive schoolgirl, and she knew better than to simply waltz off with the first stranger who gave her an admiring look and a smooth line. And even though she sometimes talked to her friends about possessing an uncanny ability to read the thoughts of other people, she played it safe. She asked a few of the regulars at the bar what they thought about the big, blond hunk who had been pestering her and the bartender for a ride, and decided that there wouldn't be any serious danger in playing Good Samaritan. He had been showing up at McRed's for a couple of weeks or so and never caused any trouble. He was courtly to the women, a friendly companion to the men, and generous with his money. Sometimes he spent as much as a hundred dollars setting up drinks for the house. Furthermore, his apartment was in Van Nuys, a few minutes' drive from the bar, and it was on her way home. Perhaps most reassuring of all, he showed up at the bar that night with a couple who were well known and liked. Since Sam trusted them, she figured there was no reason to distrust their companion.

Picking up her purse and fishing out the keys to her pickup, Sam Gallagher walked confidently into the night with the shaggy-haired Romeo. As she stepped out the door of the tavern with her handsome companion, she called reassuringly back over her shoulder to Rein: "You know me, I never leave with anyone I don't know."

Saliman was running the bar and silently watched through the window while Glen opened the door for the petite driver, then moved around to the passenger side of the truck and slid onto the seat beside her.

At almost exactly 6:30 on Friday morning, September 29, just over four hours after Sandra Gallagher left McRed's with the handsome stranger, firemen and EMTs responded to a report of a burning pickup truck behind a convalescent hospital at the corner of Morris and Victory streets in Van Nuys. The fire was quickly extinguished, but the old model Ford with the Colorado license plates was totally destroyed. Authorities had far more serious concerns than the destruction of a rattletrap pickup, however.

The badly charred body of a petite woman was found slumped inside the scorched shell of the truck. Her clothing was burned off and the flesh on the trunk and upper part of the body was seared black by the flames. It appeared she had been deliberately set on fire, and the flames had spread throughout the interior of the truck. There was no identification with the body, and authorities were able to determine how she died before they learned who she was. Los Angeles County Coroner's Office pathologists concluded that the woman was strangled before her body was set on fire and left inside the burning truck.

Four days after the corpse was discovered, investigators positively identified the murder victim as Sandra Gallagher. The combined efforts of pathologists and fingerprint experts, and plain old legwork running down witnesses and checking out the truck's registration and license plates with the state motor vehicle bureau authorities in California and Colorado, paid off. But there was no trace of the handsome mystery man who was with her when she walked out of McRed's for the last time. Police believed they knew who he was, however, and they wanted to talk to him.

A couple of days after Sandra was identified, a flyer was printed by the Los Angeles Police Department and distributed throughout the state. The flyer contained two photographs, one of the slain woman, and the other of a man with long, shaggy blond hair and a neatly trimmed mustache and beard. The word "MURDER" was printed at the top in bold, black capital letters. Immediately below that, in white print set in a black box, were the words "INFORMATION WANTED."

Prologue

A terse eight-line message was jammed between the headline and the photos. It read: "The Los Angeles Police Department is seeking your help in the murder investigation of Sandra Gallagher. Gallagher was viciously raped, murdered, and then set on fire at about 6:30 A.M. on September 29, 1995, at the rear of the convalescent hospital at Morris and Victory. The below subject, Glen Rogers, is currently wanted for questioning in this matter. They were last seen driving an older Ford pickup truck, gray and black in color, with Colorado license plates (the truck was destroyed in the fire). Anyone having any information or seeing Rogers or the victim during the early morning hours on Friday September 29th please contact Van Nuys Homicide Detectives Coblentz or Lopez at [phone number] or 'Voice Mail' at [number] mailbox #123794."

Chapter One

GLEN AND DEBI

IT MAY HAVE BEEN that there simply wasn't enough attention to go around in the troubled Rogers family when Glen was growing up as the youngest child among four boys and a girl.

He loved to tell tall tales. Whenever he recounted something he had experienced or witnessed, he could be depended on to make the story bigger, better, and more dramatic than it really was. He lied, stretched the truth, and expanded on everything with all the easy grace of a telephone marketer or a Washington politician. Even after family members caught on, the stories continued to help him attract attention at school and among others who didn't know him as well as other members of the rowdy Rogers clan.

The towheaded boy could spin outrageous lies with all the feigned earnestness of a huckster peddling snake oil at a medicine show. If he was caught in a whopper, he simply smiled and moved on to another that was bigger and better without so much as a flicker of shame in his mournful eyes.

His eyes were his most riveting characteristic. From

the time he was a little boy, some people looked at him and saw eyes that were as crystal clear and green as a fine piece of Amazon stone. Other people, however, swore his eyes were as crystalline blue as finely cut and polished sapphires. As he grew older, other dissimilarities cropped up in descriptions of his behavior and character that were equally glaring and puzzling. He would be seen by some as an angel; by others as a devil.

Even during his childhood, his eyes could be strangely mesmerizing. They were disconcertingly cold, and they didn't smile when the rest of his face did. But it wasn't until years later that neighbors and family members had reason to recall that. At the time, grade-school girls and older women who knew him were more impressed by his impish grin and his ready line of blarney.

He had a nasty skin rash that began troubling him when he was still in elementary school and stayed around until long after he reached adulthood. His mother talked later about the polluted water puddles from the old chemical plant, where he, a brother, and other neighborhood boys waded, splashed, and played before they grew up and the factory closed. The plant and other local factories produced dumps, slag piles, and pools of noxious water covered with pastel sheens of chemicals. They were the nasty by-products of the manufacturing process, but provided an exciting low-rent adventureland for small boys with imagination and a spirit of swashbuckling daring.

Young Glen had other serious problems that his teachers and classmates at school knew nothing about. According to legal documents later filed by his attorney, he ate paint, but by the time authorities learned about the disturbing childhood aberration, it was too late to figure out if it was lead-based. If it was, it could have caused a wide variety of problems, including severe brain damage. According to the court documents, the boy also had a habit of repeatedly banging his head against the wall of his upstairs bedroom at night. He explained to family members that he had to do that in order to fall asleep.

The scrappy boy, who was quick to use his fists and feet to settle disagreements he had with other kids when soft soap and snow jobs failed to work—as court documents later indicated—didn't stop wetting the bed until he was twelve. His brothers wouldn't double up in the same bed with him because almost invariably sometime during the night they would wake up to wet blankets and sheets. Another child, in different circumstances, would almost certainly have been referred to mental health professionals for evaluation and treatment after exhibiting such troubling and dangerous behavior. He fell through the cracks.

The late 1960s and early 1970s when Glen was behaving so strangely weren't the best of times in Hamilton, but they weren't the worst either. Jobs were still available in the southwestern Ohio factory town, located some twenty-five miles north of Cincinnati and twenty miles east of the Indiana line. By the time he was fourteen or fifteen, however, the working days of his father, Claude Rogers, Sr., ended and the family finances went into a slump. The family patriarch had a good-paying job for a while as a pump operator at the Champion Paper Company, but he was forced into early retirement when his health went bad. In 1979 he suffered a stroke, and for the next eight years the family reportedly had to get by largely on Social Security disability payments.

During his enforced idleness, Claude Rogers, Sr., did more drinking than was good for him, or for other members of the rambunctious young family jammed into the big old wood-frame two-story house they called home. He was generally quiet and easy to get along with until he began to drink, which was much of the time. Then he became ornery and hard to live with.

The house was constructed with a long side porch leading to the front door, and it was as solid and as well kept as those of most of the neighbors. There were plenty of bedrooms upstairs for the kids. The Rogers patriarch cared about his brood, but he didn't have the energy to carry out the role of strong father figure. So he took a backseat in the task of raising the boys and their sister, Clara Sue, until his death in 1987.

His wife, Edna, was the dominant figure in the family and most of whatever supervision the children received while at home was due to her efforts. She kept her brood clean and well-fed, even after her husband took sick and the family income began drying up. Mostly, however, based on Clara Sue's later statements and recollections, the children were permitted to make their own rules. Like Topsy, in *Uncle Tom's Cabin*, they simply "grow'd." They "grow'd" up scrappy, and most of them eventually wound up in some kind of trouble with the law.

School and neighborhood acquaintances from that time have similar recollections of lax and spotty supervision from the home. Glen was largely left to his own devices, and when other boys were concentrating on their homework or were called inside the house for dinner, Glen was allowed to remain outside doing whatever he wished to do.

The Rogers clan could be wild and rowdy, but so were some of their neighbors. They lived in a neighborhood where rusted-out hulks of cars without their wheels often rested on cinder blocks in front yards, and tires, piles of lumber, and other urban jetsam littered the curbsides. Kids ran around barefoot most of the summer, built tree houses, played in packing boxes or at factory dumps, and settled quarrels with sticks and stones.

As many of their neighbors did, the family had strong roots in Kentucky, which was barely an hour's drive almost due south. Glen was born there on July 15, 1962. It was one of the hottest days of a broiling summer when baseball enthusiasts around the country were excited over the debut of new or transplanted teams in New York, Los Angeles, San Francisco, and Houston. But the newcomer would never become a baseball fan. Even though he spent most of his youth within about an hour's drive from Cincinnati, he never traveled to the stadium to watch the Reds play.

Some of his siblings were also born in Kentucky, and he had aunts, uncles, and cousins spread throughout the ridges, hills, and hollows like the goldenrod that grows there in such profusion. The Rogers clan and others whose forebears left the bleak, stone-pitted mountains for jobs in the southern Ohio factory town were sometimes described by neighbors as "Hamiltuckians." According to some estimates, about 60 or 70 percent of the people who live in Hamilton have roots in Kentucky.

The bastardized description wasn't coined as a complimentary term, but that didn't bother Glen. He loved the green mountain solitude of the Kentucky ridges and valleys, and looked forward to the times when Claude Rogers's family packed up their old car and drove to the cabin for a stay of a few days or a few weeks. When he reached adulthood, the cabin became a personal refuge, a private hideaway where he knew he could go and wouldn't be bothered by anyone else, neighbors, family—or police. The cabin was a place where he could live cheap, easy, and private.

Like most people in Hamilton, the Rogers family lived on the hilly west side of the Great Miami River. The muddy green river split the city of some 60,000 people almost exactly in half. Almost all the factories and the slumping business area were on the east side. During Hamilton's early days, a separate town named Rossville occupied the west bank, and people moved back and forth across the river from one community to the other by ferryboat. In 1818 a toll bridge was constructed to link the two communities, and in 1854 Rossville merged with the slightly larger town on the eastern bank of the Greater Miami. By the time the seventies were winding down, the east side was already rapidly decaying, and ten years later the west side had also begun to show the serious effects of lost jobs and income from factories that had cut back production, closed down, or moved out.

Outside Hamilton, and Middletown, its slightly larger rival to the northeast, the best-known landmark in Butler County is Miami University in the little town of Oxford, almost exactly on the Indiana state line. The school name derives from the same river that runs through the center of Hamilton, and ultimately to an Indian tribe that once inhabited the area. The remainder of the county is primarily rural, an area of farms and tiny settlements with such biblical, topographical, and Anglo-Saxon names as Bethany, Jericho, Pisgah, Seven Mile, Maud, and McGonigal.

Hamilton was first established in the 1790s as the town of Fairfield. A few years later when Generals Anthony Wayne and Arthur St. Clair fortified it as an outpost for soldiers and settlers during wars with the

Indians, it became known as Fort Hamilton. Early in the nineteenth century, about the time Ohio became a state, the settlement was finally given its current name. The names of the fort, then the city, stem from Alexander Hamilton, who became the first U.S. Secretary of the Treasury. Ironically, the adjoining county to the south is named Hamilton and is dominated by the city of Cincinnati.

As a schoolboy, Glen was exceptional only for his poor performance. Much of his trouble was tied to difficulty with reading. He never did really get the hang of it, and lagged way behind most of the other kids his age when it came to figuring out the printed word. His trouble with reading affected the rest of his schoolwork, and he increasingly dropped further behind other boys and girls his age. As he neared his teens, he began slipping off with some of his buddies to a woods behind the school to smoke and drink Mad Dog, Night Train, Old Milwaukee, or whatever other alcohol they were able to obtain. The cheaper, and the more potent, the better. Years later he was remembered by his former gym teacher, Charles Bevilacque, in the Shreveport, Louisiana, *Times* as a "handsome little fellow" who was constantly "in hot water. It didn't seem there was a lot of direction in his life. There was no discipline, no love—things that young kids need. If there was trouble around, he would kind of find it," the instructor said.

Whenever Glen or one of his siblings got into a scrape and their mother was called to the school for a talk, her reaction was predictably consistent, according to the recollections of former principal William Warman. She would blame someone else for the trouble.

Glen got into a few fights as an elementary school student, but most little boys do. For the most part, he got along well with his classmates during his early school years. He had stopped eating paint, but he had substituted drinking and smoking. And according to motion papers later filed by his attorney, shortly after he began his adolescence an older brother shot him up with speed. By the time he entered his teens, he had picked up a reputation for an explosive, violent temper.

He was also building a reputation as a ladies' man. He liked girls, and they liked him. Glen seemed to have an instinctive knowledge of exactly how to make fourteen- or fifteen-year-old feminine hearts flutter and melt. He had been working on his line of Hamiltuckian flapdoodle since he was a little boy, and when he took a shine to a girl all he had to do was focus his soulful eyes on her and shower her with some of his ready line of blarney. It worked like a charm, and he could coax or wheedle girls into doing just about anything.

The handsome youngster didn't perform nearly as well with his formal education, however, and by the time he was sixteen he was already a year or two behind most of the classmates he began school with. He was in the ninth grade on March 2, 1978, when he was expelled from Wilson Junior High School. He had been kicked out of another junior high school earlier. Nearly twenty years after his formal education ended, and the old Wilson Junior High had long ago been torn down, details of the expulsions were hazy. School authorities weren't positive about the reason he was kicked out, but indicated it may have been truancy. Whatever the reason was, after he was sent packing for the second time he never returned to the classroom.

He was seventeen when his fourteen-year-old girlfriend, Deborah Ann Nix, told him she was pregnant. Deborah lived with her parents, three sisters, and a brother just over the Hamilton County line in the north Cincinnati suburb of Lockland. Glen didn't get around to marrying her until about a year later, on January 2, 1980. Like her new husband, Deborah was a poor student and frequently failed to show up for some classes or skipped school altogether. Also like him, she dropped out of school while she was still in the ninth grade. She left an unimpressive scholastic record behind her that ranged from a B in math, and two incompletes, to an F in civics. By the time Deborah and Glen repeated their vows, her first son, Clinton, was already four months old. The boy was named after one of Glen's brothers, and he was a healthy baby.

If Glen's family, or his new in-laws, had hoped marriage would settle him down and end his wild-and-woolly ways they were in for a big disappointment.

A few weeks after the young parents belatedly tied the knot, the bridegroom logged up his first arrest in Hamilton as an adult. The eighteen-year-old was charged with aggravated menacing. That was the most serious of the charges tied to the five different arrests he logged in Hamilton before he was nineteen. One time he was ticketed for failure to have a muffler on his rattletrap car.

Then the arrests stopped. The wild, hell-raising Hamilton teenager's name suddenly dropped off the local police blotters. When they had reason to look into the matter years later, Hamilton Police figured out that he left town. Rogers moved across the country to Southern California and got a job at the Highland Press Printing Company in Pasadena. Deborah, the baby, and one of Rogers's brothers followed several weeks later, and he moved his family into a duplex on Olive Avenue in the town of Monrovia. He was still working in the printing plant about two weeks before Christmas in 1981 when his wife gave birth to a second son, Johnathon C.

If the child bride journeyed to California anticipating a sunny new life next door to Hollywood, with fancy restaurants, white-sand beaches, and garden apartments surrounded by weeping jacaranda trees, she was sadly disappointed. Geographically, that vision of California was within easy reach. In every other respect it was a world away. She and her husband were teenagers who ended their formal education before they were ready for high school, and they were already saddled with two small children. Their star-crossed marriage was rocky, violent, and brief.

Glen was drinking before he was old enough to drive, and he never slowed down or stopped. He already had an explosive temper, and booze made it worse. Just about anything could set him off: burned bacon, a whining kid, or a barking dog. Deborah took the brunt of his abuse. When he was angry he didn't slap or push. He smashed her in the face and body with his closed fists, and kicked her with his feet.

The young mother was also showered with curses and threats. If she was late with a meal, or Glen didn't like what she set on the table, she was cursed or beaten. If the toddlers bothered him when he wanted to be left alone, he pounded her again. Sometimes she and the boys didn't have to do anything at all. He would just bust inside the door reeking of booze, feeling mean and ornery, and begin beating her up and tossing their things around. Deborah told her father, Clifford Nix, horror stories about the beatings and about being locked in a room by her husband. The young woman was no match for the brutal bully she married. He was big and mean, and he liked to hurt her. She was banged around by her husband so many times she lost count. He beat her in California, and he beat her in Ohio. For a while the couple wandered back and forth between the two states, dragging the little boys with them, while the marriage limped painfully along toward a predictably miserable conclusion.

Deborah was back home in Ohio with her husband when he beat her so severely she was hospitalized. It was August 6, 1982, her birthday. It was a hot and muggy late summer day, and her father and stepmother bought some T-bone steaks and corn-on-the-cob, then took the food to Glen and Deborah's home for a barbecue and celebration. Glen was on pretty good behavior during the barbecue. He was enjoying himself and everyone had a good time.

Soon after the Nixes returned to their home early that evening, however, they answered the telephone and learned that Deborah was in the hospital. Their eviltempered son-in-law had flown into one of his rages, knocked her down, and kicked her in the crotch with one of his steel-toed workboots. He was like that; good-ole-boy friendly one moment, and a brutal bully the next. He hurt Deborah so bad that time she curled up on the floor, unable to defend herself and bleeding like a stuck pig. When paramedics arrived at the house there was so much dried blood on her they had to cut her pants off before they could begin treatment, her dad later said. She spent four or five days in the hospital, and her father and stepmother never saw their son-in-law again.

A warrant was sworn out for his arrest, and southern Ohio suddenly became too hot for him. Glen returned to California, switched his birth date around, and went back to work. Relocating to another state when he got in hot water for beating a woman or for some other problem with the law would become a habit for him. He learned that when he got into trouble all he had to do was head for the tall timber and wait for things to cool down. It was a ploy that worked to keep him out of the courtroom and out of jail repeatedly over the next few years.

Most of the offenses he was accused of were relatively minor missteps in the eyes of the law, compared to serious felonies like rape, robbery, and murder that were jamming the criminal justice system all over the country. People, frequently including the victims of his outbursts, tended to lose interest and the charges were dismissed, or over time the cases simply died on the vine.

Early in 1983, about nine months after Rogers left Ohio, his wife filed for divorce. In the legal action, filed in the Domestic Relations Division of the Butler County Common Pleas Court, she accused him of "Gross Neglect of Duty and Extreme Cruelty." Deborah asked for custody of the boys and "reasonable support" for their care. In related documents, she stated that she was unemployed, and had no funds of her own to pay for the costs of the action. She signed an "affidavit of indigency" as "Debi Rogers."

Finally, she went to the Butler County Welfare Department on Maple Avenue and signed up for benefits. She didn't have a job, and was approved for food stamps and $263 a month in Aid to Dependent Children. Her rent for a modest Sycamore Street apartment in Hamilton was $175 a month and ate up most of the welfare payments. The court meanwhile issued a temporary order granting custody of the children to their mother, and directing her estranged husband to pay $30 per week for their support as well as any extraordinary medical expenses they might incur.

Glen was mad as a hornet over the breakup, and

wasn't willing to admit that his wife was gone for good. He had her nickname, DEBI, tattooed across the knuckles of his right hand. It was one of the same fists he used to beat her with so viciously, and she wasn't impressed. In August, about ninety days after Deborah filed the initial paperwork, her divorce was granted. The Butler County Domestic Relations Court awarded custody of the boys to the mother, and Glen was instructed to pay $35 per week for their support. The court also continued the earlier stipulation that he would be responsible for any "extraordinary" medical expenses for the children, and expanded the original order to include dental care. In the order dissolving the troubled two-and-a-half-year union the court concurred that the husband was guilty of "Gross Neglect of Duty." There was no mention of the accompanying allegation in Deborah's divorce petition accusing him of "Extreme Cruelty."

Glen made a few payments, and he paid for some school clothes for Clinton, but soon fell behind and Deborah went back to court for help in collecting the money. By that time she was living on Glen Rose Avenue in Cincinnati, where she was on food stamps and receiving $295 per month from the county in Aid to Dependent Children.

Legal Service Lawyers filed the new action in the Hamilton County Common Pleas Court in November 1985 under the Ohio Uniform Reciprocal Enforcement of Support Act. The act was set up to deal with matters of support when one of the former partners lives out of state. The rowdy printer was again living in an Olive Avenue apartment, and the action in California was processed through the Uresa Division of the Los Angeles County courts.

The petition didn't tell the whole story. In January

1984, a few months after the divorce, the boys moved in with their father in California. Deborah remained in Ohio until July, when she followed her sons to the West Coast to bring them home. Glen wasn't ready to give up the boys, so she moved in with him and waited. It was about a week before he left the apartment one day, and she fled with the boys to a nearby Roman Catholic church. She didn't have any money, so a priest provided her with enough cash from a church fund to pay for some food and buy bus tickets back to Ohio for her and her sons.

Court authorities took the six months Glen cared for the boys into account, and several hundred dollars was subsequently trimmed from the amount of back support payments Deborah asked for in the original petition. There was no indication in the records to show if the absent father paid the final $1,400 he was said to be in arrears.

According to other documents filed with the action, additional important developments had occurred in Glen's life. Deborah claimed he fathered another son by a woman named Katherine, and he might have remarried. Once more, the documents didn't tell the whole story, but they provided some solid clues. It was true Glen fathered another son with a woman named Catherine, although she spelled her name with a "C" rather than a "K." Glen's sister later told reporters the Southern California woman was Catherine Kopoian. Clara Sue, whose friends and family generally referred to her by her middle name, said Catherine was different from most of the women her little brother became involved with. She was a few pounds heavier, but importantly she was also quieter and more reserved. Clara Sue said her brother and Catherine had married, and described her former sister-in-law as, "like a schoolteacher type."

Journalists were unable later to run down any marriage records in Los Angeles, or in Hamilton County, Ohio, for the couple, but reported that the boy, Marc, was born on September 8, 1983. Marc's mother was also said to have eventually filed documents in a domestic relations court against Glen asking for child support.

Deborah drifted around the country for a while after breaking up with her first husband, and eventually moved to Houston, Texas, with the boys. Eventually she gave them up to foster care, and they wound up living in Corpus Christi.

In California, Glen was also getting itchy feet again. One day in 1986, he was working at his usual tasks in the printing plant when he laid down his tools and walked out, right in the middle of a job. He had worked for Highland Press off and on for almost six years, and that would become the longest period he ever held the same job. A short time after picking up his final paycheck, he packed a suitcase with some clothes and a few other personal items, then climbed aboard a Greyhound bus to begin the long ride back across the country to Hamilton. Glen Rogers was returning to his roots. He was coming home.

Chapter Two

LOW-RENT ROMEO

WHEN ROGERS LIMPED BACK into town he headed for the shabby, run-down streets of the East Side, where the action was.

Long before he pulled up stakes for California, leaving his young bride behind, Hamilton's job and economic base was shrinking and drying up. The formerly broad-shouldered and vigorously dynamic steel and heavy manufacturing center was becoming a classic rust-belt city. Factories were shutting down and crumbling into disrepair, moving south, where wages and other operating costs were lower, or drastically cutting back production and trimming jobs. The plants were becoming as dead as the section of the old Erie Canal a few miles from the city which barely a century earlier was plied by rugged, hard-drinking flatboatmen and river pilots who helped make Hamilton a booming center of trade and commerce.

During Rogers's early childhood in the 1960s, men like his father who settled their families in modest homes, constructed side by side on small lots on the West Side, could still find good-paying jobs in a wide range of heavy manufacturing plants and collateral industries.

Many of the local working men carried their lunch boxes through the gates at a big General Motors transmission assembly plant that was constructed in a sprawl of buildings nearby. The safe company that built the main vault at Fort Knox is still located in the southwestern Ohio industrial city. But Hamilton's biggest single employer was Armco Steel, which operated a huge sheet steel rolling mill and provided jobs for thousands of men.

Then the domestic steel business began contracting; combining some operations, and totally shutting down others. Workers at the rolling mill and a passel of other industries, who figured they were set for life with dependable high-paying jobs, suddenly found themselves on the unemployment line with nowhere else to go. Laid-off workers who did manage to find other jobs, were likely to be hired at half the pay or far less than they previously earned. The steel rail train tracks that crisscross the city were rusting with disuse, and Hamilton was on a downhill roll that didn't begin to show any positive signs of change for at least two decades.

The largely residential west side of the onetime canal town and industrial center slowly began falling into decay. It was even worse on the east side of the river. Huge areas of the once thriving shopping and business area began crumbling and changing into an inhospitable wasteland of empty storefronts, warehouses, and broken dreams. The drab gray streets became mean and dangerous; the haunt of dope dealers, con men, petty thieves, prostitutes, and other down-on-their-luck men and women.

When Rogers returned to Hamilton, however, the

dingy East Side with its store windows boarded up with plywood, iron grates over doorways, broken-down side-walks, and brazen street whores who waved and called to passing motorists was where he wanted to be. He fit right in, and made it his personal turf.

More than a decade after he rode back into town, peo-ple were still sorting out some of the details about his activities. But he left enough of a trail behind him, in betrayals, broken hearts, and police arrest records to re-construct a depressing picture of his behavior during those years. His rap sheet reads like the pathetic pedigree of a classic small-time hoodlum, and is speckled with entries for such crimes as assault, breaking and entering, forgery, theft, and arson. Police records in Ohio and Cal-ifornia show that during a period of about thirteen years beginning in 1982 he was picked up or indicted at least ten times on felony charges, fifteen times for misde-meanors, and was named in criminal and civil courts eleven different times for physical assaults on women.

Rogers shuttled back and forth between Hamilton and California for a while, prowling the grimy underside of society in two states while fitfully working at a series of catch-can, dead-end jobs. When he had money he flashed it around and spent it like water in the tough, seedy bars in which he hung out. When he had spent everything he had on booze, or hadn't worked for a while and was broke, he leeched off of other people. Eventually, after he was back in Hamilton for a few years and some old emotional hurts had time to begin healing over, he even moved in for a while with Debi and a new boyfriend she was living with. Rogers could be incredibly persuasive and convincing when the chips were down and he wanted something.

He was especially adept at wooing, then using,

women. According to accounts of fellow workers at the taxi company, he sometimes beat up hookers who refused to willingly hand over their earnings to him, and took the money away. Always, he did a prodigious amount of boozing, and also played around with drugs.

During one standoff with police he held officers at bay for four hours before they finally overpowered him and quieted him down. He was charged with aggravated menacing after the confrontation. Several years later he was charged with inducing panic as a result of one of his rampages when he smashed up his furniture, then tossed it into the backyard and burned it. But most of his brushes with the law involved nickel-and-dime traffic offenses, or were booze-related. In 1986 he was ticketed for driving without a license and for obstructing official business. He was arrested several times on booze-related charges.

Angel Wagers, who endured a near two-year relationship with him while she was in her late twenties, was repeatedly beaten. During one period in 1989 and 1990 the scrappy blonde with the red highlights in her hair filed charges of assault against him with the Hamilton Police Department at five different times. She knew firsthand the kind of violence he was capable of. In one of the filed complaints, she declared: "He is very violent. I am terrified of him. He has threatened to kill me and my family. I am afraid for my life, especially after the beating he just gave me." After that beating, Rogers was ordered by a judge to move out of the house he and the woman shared.

Threats were as much a part of his style as beatings. He used both to control his women and to keep them in a constant state of fear. One time he busted down the door of Angel's mother's house, yelling demands to talk with her. After she finally had enough of being batted around by him and left for good, Rogers memorialized his lost love with another tattoo. He had the name "AN-GEL" etched on his right shoulder. The left shoulder was already taken by the first and most important redheaded woman in his life. The word "MAMA" was tattooed there.

Like Debi, Angel at last learned that there was no future with the quick-tempered macho man whom she had been unable to break her ties to for so long. But the petite woman finally learned her lesson, and refused to allow herself to be wooed back into the arms of her brutal onetime sweetheart by a tattoo.

Angel wasn't the only woman in Hamilton who felt the bone-crushing jar of his thick fists. Like Angel, most of them were little, slender women who were a good six or eight inches shorter and about half the weight of the strapping bully they were in love with. They were more likely to run for safety if they could than to stand their ground and try to fight back.

Despite the brutality and his mean and nasty reputation, Rogers always managed to keep at least one woman around, sometimes two or three at a time. It didn't matter if he was in Ohio or in California, his good looks, charm, and rough masculinity provided lures that certain foxy women simply couldn't resist. Most of his girlfriends had red hair or reddish tints to their hair, like his mother. He also found many of them while he was trolling bars with names like the Caboose, the J & J, the Right Spot Cafe, and the Choo Choo, which was built next to the railroad tracks that snaked through the town. A woman who used to drink and dance with Rogers at the Choo Choo later described it as a ghetto bar "for the lower-crust."

She had fond memories of him. Every time he walked into the bar and saw her there, he gave her a kiss. If she needed a fresh drink or cigarettes, he took care of it for her. Rogers loved "lower-crust" honkytonks with dark corners and soft-eyed, pliant women, where the drinks were cheap, the whiskey was served in plastic cups, and the beer was drunk straight from the bottles or cans.

Jimmy Bowman, who also grew up in Hamilton and knew Rogers for years, hung around with him for a while. During a period when Rogers was keeping company with Bowman's sister, Pearl, the man and the boy were especially close. Bowman was impressed by the older man's amazing ability to walk into a bar, order a beer, eyeball the gals, and unerringly zero in on a woman who was vulnerable to the attentions of a good-looking, silver-tongued rascal. Rogers sometimes gave his young admirer rundowns on exactly how to look the women over and decide which of them were deserving of time and attention.

If a woman was drinking by herself, it meant she was down on her luck and drowning her troubles, Rogers instructed. Most likely they were tied to a man: a failed romance, runaway husband, or a hit-and-run affair that hadn't worked out. A woman like that was ripe for his kind of sweet talk. There were other women he didn't waste a second glance on. He studied the clothes women wore, their body language, and the way they talked. If there was so much as a hint of too much self-assurance or confidence, he usually moved on to a more promising prospect, especially women who had red highlights in their hair, or were strawberry blondes. He wouldn't settle for a woman who wasn't good-looking. But they had to be his kind: a woman who was properly grateful for a handsome man like him, who knew her place, and was obedient and obliging.

Even Rogers miscalculated once in a while and hit on women who turned him down. Usually when that happened, he shrugged his shoulders and turned his attentions toward a more promising candidate. He knew as well as anyone could that there was more than one fish in the pond. Occasionally, if the reluctant woman was inordinately attractive or especially struck his fancy, he pursued her with single-minded determination. He could charm the horns off a heifer, and most of the time he got his way. Watching him work women in a bar was an educational experience.

He reveled in his reputation as a ladies' man, and was almost as apt to boast about the women he loved and lost as about new conquests. He loved the title of George Strait's popular country tune, "All My Ex's Live in Texas." Sometimes he tried his hand at crooning the song title while he was sitting in a bar with an audience, but he always fiddled with the words and personalized them, substituting "Ohio," for "Texas."

The friendship between the man and the boy lasted longer than Rogers's relationship with his drinking buddy's sister. Almost as soon as the petite blonde hooked up with the ham-fisted boozer and woman beater, she started getting a first-hand look and close-up taste of the total Glen Rogers. "He likes to beat women," Bowman told the *Los Angeles Times* of Rogers. "That's his thing."

He was a bad influence on the younger man. Years after they hung around together, Bowman told the *Times* that Rogers taught him to steal. He recounted a time when Rogers instructed him to climb through a warehouse window and open a door. When another accomplice backed their truck too far into the warehouse for them to load the loot, Rogers beat the man up for making the mistake.

Rogers had a knack for causing trouble. He could spread misery like a destructive fungus, spitting out noxious spores and infecting everyone around him. But lonely, vulnerable women were his specialty.

Once Rogers reeled a woman in with his sweet-talking ways and his courtly attentions, he revealed the other, nasty side of his personality. Vicki Lakes was Rogers's girlfriend for a few months in 1989, and later talked about his easy ability to make a woman feel special. He knew how to caress a woman, and always seemed to know exactly the right things to say to melt her heart. Like her sisters in sorrow, the shapely strawberry blonde also knew about the mean side of the ill-tempered Lothario. He was as smooth as a quart jug of clear Kentucky moonshine, but his kick could be hangover-mean.

His masculine charm gave him an advantage over other cabbies while he was driving for the Ohio Red Top Taxi Company. He wasn't on the job very long before women customers began telephoning for rides and specifically requesting that ''Glen,'' or ''the good-looking blond guy'' be sent to pick them up. He met a lot of women that way, and dated a few of them. Rogers already knew his way around his hometown, but his fares could take him as far north as Middletown or Oxford, south to Cincinnati, or around the Queen City into Clermont County along the north bank of the Ohio River.

He liked driving a cab and he was good at the job, but worked only a few months in 1991 before his fledgling career was interrupted by a major fracas with the law. It wasn't unusual for police to be called to quiet him down when he was raging or beating one of his women, and some of his most memorable battles were with Cora McKnight. He won some of the showdowns, she won some, and others were pretty much of a draw.

Rogers was alternately driving a cab, and drinking and fighting with Cora, when police responding to a domestic disturbance call showed up at the couple's home on Ludlow Street and were confronted with a madman. He beat Cora before barricading himself inside, then held police at bay for two hours while he raged through the house, snarling threats to shoot them if they tried to haul him out. The high point of the tense standoff occurred when he fired up a blowtorch, aimed it at a police officer through the keyhole of the front door, and set the wood framing on fire. After police finally managed to take him into custody without serious injury to themselves or to the raving drunk, he spent several days in jail.

The fight was apparently tied to an earlier confrontation between the battling couple that briefly left Cora in the winner's circle. They were at the home of her mother, Mildred McKnight, quarreling over a mutual friend when Rogers grabbed Cora's arm and clamped down. In pain, she swept up a butcher knife that was lying on the coffee table and stabbed him in the elbow. Rogers wasn't used to his women drawing blood, and he turned and ran out of the house.

Then he filed a complaint with the police against Cora for stabbing him. The feisty twenty-seven-year-old woman didn't deny she went after him with a knife, but said it was self-defense. He had already beaten her up several times, and she was afraid he would do it again. That was the first time she ever complained to the police about his abuse. But he was much bigger and stronger than Cora, and she lost most of the physical battles.

The wife of one of Rogers's fellow cabbies was dispatching for Ohio Red Top one time when she saw him apparently break Cora's arm during a tussle in the company parking lot. Cora wound up with her arm in a cast, but she never filed charges against him for this attack. Another time he tossed her out of the house, heaving her all the way across the front porch. Cora's mother later told reporters about the brouhaha and said her daughter's former boyfriend could be talking real friendly, then suddenly seem to become another person. No one wanted to be around when that happened. Mrs. McKnight said her daughter finally left Rogers for good after about two years.

His friends at the cab company marveled at the way he was able to attract and control women, and at the abuse they accepted from him. Some of the women were lonely shopworn females who, although they were still in their late twenties or early thirties, had already seen their best days. Others were undereducated single mothers on welfare or women stuck in dead-end, minimum-salary jobs whose romantic prospects and expectations were pitifully bleak. A few were hardcore hookers whose lives were so blighted by alcohol and drugs that they were reduced to walking the streets. Rogers specialized in rejects and retreads, and he expected his hooker girlfriends to hand their earnings over to him. If they refused, he beat them and took their money anyway.

He liked to hang around with hookers when he was drinking in local watering holes, and sometimes he gave them free cab rides. That wasn't unusual. Other cabbies also provided free transportation on occasion for working girls. Rogers even tried to get a few of them jobs with the cab company but was unsuccessful. He was always ready to provide whatever it took to insinuate himself into the confidence and life of a desirable female. He loved the challenge of attracting the attention of a good-looking woman, setting the hook, then reeling her in.

Doug Courtney, who owned the cab company, didn't know about all his driver's unusual extracurricular activities and considered him to be a good employee. Courtney was aware of some of Rogers's flaws, such as his flares of temper.

About the only predictable thing about him when he was drinking was his temper. Sometimes all it took was a couple of beers, then just about any little thing could set him off. He turned into a wild man. As soon as he had a half-dozen Buds in him, or a shot or two of Jack Daniel's, he might begin verbally abusing people. If he couldn't pick a fight right away, he might fly into a rage and smack someone, preferably a woman. Several times when a woman wasn't handy and he tangled with men, he got the worst of it.

One time he got so down in the dumps that he swallowed a bottleful of the over-the-counter anti-inflammatory and pain-relieving pill, Motrin, then injected alcohol into his veins. A doctor tried to have him involuntarily committed to a psychiatric facility after that caper, but was unsuccessful. As soon as Rogers was on his feet again, he headed for the streets to pick up where he left off.

On the positive side at Ohio Red Top Cab, he was punctual and did the things a good employee is expected to do. He brought in considerable repeat business and made a lot of money for the firm. Rogers could be good company when he wanted to be, and sometimes when another driver or some other fellow employee invited him home for fried chicken or a plate of spaghetti he behaved like a perfect gentleman. He always showed up clean, neatly dressed, and was especially courteous to the wives or girlfriends. His friend Mark Crouch took him home one time to show off his pair of Boston terriers, and Rogers was all smiles. He acted like he was crazy about the dogs.

Often, if he was at work and other employees were hungry he would pick up coffee or sandwiches for them. When a fellow driver at Ohio Red Top who was one of his drinking buddies died suddenly, Rogers organized a funeral cortege of taxi cabs.

Both McKay and Crouch, who drove cabs with him, talked about the medication he took. According to Crouch, who was in his fifties when the men were driving cabs together, Rogers carried around a bottle of Ritalin. The medication is commonly used to treat children who are hyperactive or have been diagnosed with behavioral problems like the condition known as Attention Deficit Disorder, ADD. The doctor who was Rogers's personal physician during that time said later that he never prescribed Ritalin for him.

The cab company boss apparently never witnessed any of the violence the randy driver inflicted on his women, but other employees did. Dispatcher Chuck Spahn watched one time when Rogers viciously beat a one-armed woman in front of the cab company offices. The blond bully hit her in the face and knocked her down, then leaned over and ripped at her clothes until he found the money he was looking for. He stalked away with the cash, and left the woman stretched out and moaning on the sidewalk with a bloody face and torn clothes.

He worked for the cab company for a few more months before finally quitting for good. This time he quit because he didn't want to submit to a drug screening test. Even after leaving his job, however, he continued to show up at the offices now and then to touch base with friends. Sometimes he told them he had been in California, or worked awhile in Louisiana, Alabama, or some other state, or had spent some time in Kentucky.

His real roots were in Kentucky, and he loved the state of his birth. Once a year or so when he was still a boy, his parents packed up sandwiches and cold drinks, then loaded the kids into the family car, and Claude Rogers drove almost straight south across the Ohio River into Kentucky. They rode over the rocky ridges and looked down on quiet hollows where rickety shanties with stacked stone chimneys or dust- and dirt-mottled trailer homes sprawled among a scattering of outbuildings and rusted-out trucks or cars in the yards. Their destination was a dilapidated cabin a few miles outside the Daniel Boone National Forest near Beattyville in the mountains of East Central Kentucky. Claude Rogers's father built the shanty years earlier and the family kept it as a refuge where they could refresh themselves and escape the factory grime and clatter of the industrial city where they lived.

Even after Claude Rogers's health failed and the children grew up, the baby of the family continued to make pilgrimages to the deserted cabin on his own. Glen wasn't a hunter of wild game—he did his hunting on street corners and in no-name bars—but if he had been, the forests and meadows around the Beattyville shack would have offered golden opportunities to indulge the hobby. The area teemed with whitetail deer, wild turkeys, partridges, pheasant, rabbits, raccoons, and squirrels. During the fall and spring months, mushrooms sprout up in profusion, and the woods and hollows are filled with wild berries, sassafras, and other edible plants and roots.

Rogers didn't spend much time poking around in the woods, but he roamed all over eastern and central Kentucky, moving from east to west and north to south, stopping at one place for a while, then loading up his car and driving on to another. For about six months during the spring and early summer of 1993, he rampaged through Winchester, a city roughly fifty miles northwest of the Rogers family cabin. Winchester is a normally quiet community of about 16,000 people just off Interstate 64 almost midway between Lexington and Mount Sterling at the edge of the fertile bluegrass country.

He found work for a while as a driver for City Trucking in Winchester. But he didn't hold onto that job very long. He had other interests that were more important to him. He was a lover, a fighter, a drinker, and a drifter.

Anna Means was one of the first Winchester residents to form a friendship with him. She first met him when she served him a beer at the Lost Canoe Bar, a popular watering hole in the downtown business district, and she was impressed. He was polite, and had the kind of warm, trustworthy smile that could have fit on the face of a preacher—or a door-to-door salesman. He didn't have a job or a place to live, but he was cleanly dressed and was so downright charming that she let him move in with her for a couple of weeks. He even baby-sat for her little girl.

Rogers found himself another redheaded girlfriend in Winchester and livened things up while he was in town. He left a record of his stay there on local police blotters, at the Clark Regional Medical Center Emergency Room, and on the psyches of other people whose paths he crossed. Sometimes people called police to protect them from him. At other times, while he was drinking and fighting, he telephoned police and warned them he was going to kill somebody.

The center of local government for Clark County (named after Revolutionary War General George Rogers Clark), Winchester is a marketing center for locally grown wheat and corn, and for the rich burley and dark tobaccos Kentucky is so famous for. Winchester also supports small industries tied to the coal and gas fields. On broad, magnificently kept estates and horse farms a few miles out of town, handsome Thoroughbreds, Stan dardbreds, and saddle horses graze on the magnificent blue-green grass. Rogers didn't show any interest in Winchester's rich history, topography, or the production and movement of commodities. He wasn't a historian, horseman, farmer, or a man who had even the slightest concern over the quality of tobacco, its growing seasons, or drying techniques.

He was far more interested in the rich, mellow brown sour mash whiskey Kentucky and its neighboring state, Tennessee, are known for; its captivating honey-toned women; and in brawling. Rogers worked fitfully at a variety of unskilled jobs, usually just long enough to pay his bar bills and provide for a few other basic needs. He spent more of his time balancing on bar stools in local watering holes beside other men dressed in dusty jeans and heavy boots, whose work-roughened hands were marked with the nicks, creases, and stains that came with spending long hours planting and cultivating the tobacco crop, then baling and hauling it to the Winchester tobacco market to be displayed, inspected, and auctioned off.

The only local crop Rogers showed interest in was hemp. He was charged with possession after police walked into his apartment on North Maple Street and found a plastic bag of marijuana sitting in plain sight on a table. The officers drove to the apartment after he made several calls to the police station earlier that day threatening to kill somebody.

Rogers spent the night at the Clark County Detention Center, and was released the next afternoon. He was eventually sentenced to twenty days in jail on the marijuana possession charge, and an additional ten days was tacked on for his failure to appear on the charge. His behavior in Winchester was about the same as it was in Hamilton. He would no sooner get out of one jam with police before he stumbled into another.

Local youngsters were still lighting sparklers and shooting off leftover firecrackers around town on July 5 when Winchester Police Patrolmen Frank Doyle and Raleigh Craig linked the Ohio drifter to a car that belonged to another man. The white 1979 Mercury was owned by Russell E. Wright of Hamilton and still carried the Ohio license tags when the officers spotted it in the rear parking lot of the Eight Knights Motel on Mount Sterling Road. Wright had reported his Mercury stolen on June 30.

Rogers had the car keys, and he was booked on a felony charge of receiving stolen property. Cash bail of $5,000 was established during a hearing in Clark District Court. On August 4, less than one month after Rogers's arrest, the charges were dismissed without prejudice.

But Rogers's nasty temper and bullying ways got him back into serious trouble again the same day when he punched a fifteen-year-old Winchester boy in the chest so hard that he bruised the teenager's heart. John

McQueen was taken to a hospital where an X-ray disclosed the injury, and he was placed on a heart monitor for about an hour. Most of Rogers's fights were with people he knew he could beat: women or smaller, physically weaker men.

Four days after punching the teenager, and before he was picked up for the assault, Rogers was arrested for public intoxication. He was already locked in the Clark County Detention Center the next day when he was formally arrested on felony charges of second-degree assault for his attack on the boy. Cash bail was set at $2,500. He eventually plea-bargained the charge down to fourth-degree assault, and was ordered to serve thirty days of a ninety-day sentence. As part of the sentencing agreement, he was placed on probation with the stipulation he have no new criminal offenses for two years. He was also directed to stay away from young McQueen and his kin, and to pay them $702 in restitution.

Almost every time he got in trouble with the police, Rogers listed a different address. When he was arrested for punching the boy, he gave a private address on East Broadway. The Eight Knights Motel was listed as his home when he was booked on the stolen property charge. He was living on North Maple Street when he was nabbed on one of the marijuana charges. He moved around constantly, renting cheap rooms and apartments by the day, week, or month, or squatting with girlfriends and other acquaintances until his welcome wore out and it was time to pull up stakes and break camp.

By the time Rogers first blew into Winchester he was experiencing blackouts and seizures. One moment he would be drinking and carousing and the next moment he would be on the floor, flopping around and foaming at the mouth. Twice during the late 1980s and early

1990s he was treated at hospitals after collapsing with fits.

Long periods sometimes went by when he had no memory of where he had been or what he was doing. He was in the Butler County Jail in Hamilton in April 1991 after one of his run-ins with the law when he told authorities some of his blackouts lasted for as long as four days. A couple of months after he was locked up, authorities described him in records as "somewhat paranoid." Rogers was nervous and shaky, and one entry on Butler County Jail records quoted him as saying he felt he got "out of control and things happen to him."

His wild and woolly ways led to frequent head injuries. He hurt his head in car crashes, his skull was battered with clubs, and he was bashed over the left eye with a tire iron. Those were just a few of the more violent incidents in which he was injured. Half the time he couldn't remember what happened. He simply noticed that he had some new cuts, bruises, or broken bones.

He was constantly on the move, sometimes packing up a suitcase and traveling hundreds of miles, and at other times traipsing no farther than the next county. But wherever he went, trouble followed him. He was driving on the wrong side of Third Street in Richmond, Kentucky, on July 31, 1987, when he was stopped by local police. When they administered a Breathalyzer test, his blood-alcohol content was a whopping .14 percent. A reading of .10 percent can lead to a drunk-driving arrest in most states, and it's lower in some. Rogers, who listed a rural Beattyville address, was charged with driving-under-the-influence and with not having an operator's license.

Richmond is the Madison County seat, just south

of Clark County, and Rogers was released from custody when a Winchester woman appeared at the jail and posted a $500 surety bond. The next week he failed to show up for a scheduled appearance in Madison District Court on the DUI charges. By that time he was long gone from Richmond, doing his drinking and brawling elsewhere, but local authorities hadn't seen the last of the cantankerous bail jumper. The next time he turned up in the Madison County-seat city, he would be in more trouble than anyone could have dreamed of.

At least once, the Ohio wild man ranged into Lexington in Fayette County, the county northwest of Clark, and got his name scribbled on the police blotter there. According to police records another drifter was allegedly beat up and robbed by Rogers. The reputed victim left town soon after the incident and couldn't be found, so police didn't waste time looking for the reported assailant. But Detective Larry Etherington didn't forget the case.

After Rogers got out of the Clark County Detention Center on September 7 following his punch-out of the teenager, he skipped town without paying the court-ordered restitution to the injured boy's family. Four days later a Clark District Court Judge issued a bench warrant for his arrest.

But Rogers had finally cleared out of Winchester for good, after hanging around and livening things up for about a year. Most people who knew him, including police, were probably glad to see him go. His friend at the Lost Canoe bar wasn't one of them. Whenever he showed up at the Lost Canoe and she was working the bar, he behaved himself. She never saw him get drunk or get into a fight.

Once he was back in Hamilton, he was the same old

Glen Rogers, however. Some of the time he was likable as could be. At other times he was mean and acted as nutty as a peach orchard boar. But women loved him, despite his orneriness and the element of danger that followed around behind him like a dark cloud.

Some of Rogers's drinking friends got the clear impression that he enjoyed hurting women. It made him feel good when he could make them cry. Even his sister was deathly afraid of him. She knew about the vicious beatings he inflicted on his girlfriends, and according to her later statements he threatened to kill her and her children. "He was a scary person," she was quoted later in an Associated Press report. "He scared me."

Beating up his women and getting into one minor scrape after another with the law had become a way of life for Rogers, when his streak of good luck finally snapped. On a late autumn day in November 1987, when his mood was as dark and gloomy as the heavy slate-gray clouds that hung close over the shabby city, he went on a toot and tried to ram his car into the plateglass window of a Midas Muffler Shop on Erie Avenue. He stole a blank check, filled it out for $450, and cashed it early the following month.

On December 15, four days after passing the bogus check, he was picked up by the Hamilton Police, charged with forgery, and locked up. They also charged him with burglarizing the muffler shop. Both offenses were fourth-degree felonies, which could bring fines and prison time, depending on the whim of a judge.

Locked in the Butler County Jail, Rogers talked with his lawyer, Patricia Oney. Two days before Christmas he appeared in the Butler County Court of Common Pleas and pleaded guilty to both charges. This time he didn't walk away after a tongue lashing, slap-on-the-wrist fine, or order to serve probation. He was sentenced to an eighteen-month term at the Ohio State Reformatory in Mansfield on the charge of breaking-and-entering for the muffler shop burglary, and another six-month term for forgery. The judge ordered that the sentences were to be served consecutively.

The respite in prison offered the advantage of professional medical attention, a luxury that Rogers largely ignored during his tumultuous, violent life, except for instances when he was patched up in hospital emergency rooms after suffering beatings in barroom fights or was banged up in various car crashes. At Mansfield he was diagnosed with porphyria, a relatively uncommon ailment widely identified in the tabloid press as the "vampire disease." The mainstream press and some popular television shows have also linked the ailment to ancient reports of vampires and werewolves, however, because of some of the symptoms.

An inherited enzyme disease, porphyria is a collective name for seven separate ailments that manifest themselves as metabolic disorders and have been pinpointed in some scientific papers as the source of vampire and werewolf legends. Biochemist David Dolphin, of the University of British Columbia in Vancouver, suggested the legendary children of the dark who attacked and drank the blood of their fellow villagers may have been motivated by a desperate effort to get healthy hemoglobin in their systems. Porphyria is caused by a defect in the bone marrow that interferes with the oxygen-carrying cells in the blood.

One of the keynote characteristics of acute porphyria is excessive sensitivity to light, and direct sunlight can cause sores to erupt on the skin. The skin around the mouth can become hard and the gums recede so that the teeth look reddish and take on the appearance of fangs. During the acute stages of the disease, the face can become hairy, and other symptoms similar to leprosy can lead to horrid disfigurement, including the loss of fingers, eyelids, or the nose. Stress can bring on attacks.

Although apparently no one bothered to check back into his childhood and earlier adult years, it seemed the pools of industrial chemicals Rogers played in as a boy may not have been the cause of his longstanding problems with skin rashes and sores. It was also interesting that the sores at last went away after he grew up and began spending more time in darkened barrooms than outside in the direct sunlight.

Despite the seemingly stern sentence ordered by the judge in stacking one term onto the other, Rogers stayed out of trouble while he was imprisoned, and with time off for good behavior, he was released on parole after serving only a few months. But staying out of trouble when he was locked up, and walking the straight and narrow when he was outside and free of the disciplinary restraints of prison were two different stories.

It seemed that the prison term made a deep impression on him. He had spent a night or two in local lockups on occasion, but never previously put in any serious time behind bars. At Mansfield he was locked up with people like himself, or worse, and it was a miserable experience.

That didn't mean his prison episode rehabilitated him. He was still a vicious drunk who beat up on women, occasionally fought with other men, and existed on society's sordid criminal fringe. The day after he rode a bus back to Hamilton from the reformatory he was driving Angel Wagers's car when she said something he didn't like. According to Angel, he pounded her in the face with one hand while he steered with the other.

Angel stuck with him longer than some of the other women and was horribly battered by him. He chipped a tooth of hers during one of his outbursts, and once when they were feuding, he reportedly threatened she would blow herself up if she tried to start her car.

Unless Rogers made a miraculous turnabout, it seemed it was only a matter of time before he got into another jam with the law and was sent back to prison. So he began working as a snitch for the Hamilton Police Department. Since that time, Hamilton Police haven't had much to say about how he was recruited. Although every police department of any size needs informants, snitching on fellow criminals can be a dangerous business. Police naturally and properly are extremely protective about details. Snitches often take risks that cops won't, or are prohibited from doing by laws, departmental regulations, or other circumstances. But the relationships between police and their informants are marriages of necessity and convenience that are established on shaky foundations.

Police must deal with certain dangers and other special problems that go hand in hand with relying on snitches. Snitches may lie, exaggerate, and use every opportunity to manipulate police as well as other criminals on the street. Longtime convicts have been freed from prisons and convictions overturned because informants have changed their stories or been proven by others to have lied to the police and prosecutors. The stories of police snitches must be carefully checked, and preferably substantiated by other sources.

Police informants come in different shapes and sizes. Some are upright citizens who share information with the police because they want to chase crime and criminals out of their neighborhoods or workplaces. Sometimes people become informants in order to get revenge against someone they blame for a wrong. But the most common and the most consistently valuable informants are people like Rogers. They are bottom-feeders, without conscience or ethics, who are willing to doublecross anyone for a few dollars or some advantage.

In bygone days other criminals called them "canaries," "stool pigeons," "rats," "squealers," and worse. Today they're called "CIs" (confidential informants), "snitches," or "mouths," and they provide dramatic examples of the widely accepted lie that there is honor among thieves. If the old saying was ever true, those days are gone forever. The expression is as outdated and worthless as a two-dollar bill issued by the Confederate States of America.

Rogers was typical of many CIs. He was a small-time criminal who was a known liar, exaggerator, and manipulator, but those qualities also helped make him a perfect candidate for the role of police snitch. He was firmly accepted among the whores, pimps, and petty criminals who prowled the underbelly of the city's shabby East Side, and he knew many of their secrets. He knew who used drugs, who dealt them, who the pimps and hookers were, and who committed burglaries and other petty crimes.

The inner workings of Glen's alcohol-sodden mind were known only to him, but it seems reasonable that the opportunities to put cash in his blue jeans by informing on his friends was as appealing as the opportunity to build a semifriendly relationship with individual police officers. He liked being a mouth, and he enjoyed making the rounds of the bars with undercover Hamilton Police Detective Daniel Pratt and other vice cops, drinking and setting up deals. Ironically, Pratt went to school with Rogers, and his first arrest when he was a rookie cop occurred when he put the collar on his former schoolmate.

Pratt, who later moved into the job as the HPD's media chief, was impressed with the informant's glib tongue and smooth manner. They were helpful traits for a cab driver—or a CI. Snitching also gave Rogers a chance to learn some of the secrets of how police operated. And there was pleasure to be had in gaining the confidence of the other slicksters he ran with on the street, and outsmarting them. Finally there was the added appeal of earning a few dollars while being treated specially by the very people who had always been his adversaries, and the implied promise of being able to get away with things he wasn't permitted to do in the past. The law needed him, with his contacts, street smarts, and information.

Rogers had always been able to manipulate and lord it over women, but ratting on his friends gave him a measure of control over people he had never before been able to influence, even though it exacted a price. He was bedeviled by paranoia, and sometimes became so terrified he telephoned Pratt from whatever bar he happened to be drinking in and begged the detective to come and get him.

Police began picking up the cronies and other assorted riffraff who hung around with their industrious CI, or operated along the edges of his circle, with increasing regularity. He got away with it for a while, but the rumors that he was a police snitch burst into full bloom in 1991 when Hamilton Police rounded up more than forty people on an assortment of drug charges. Almost every one of the suspects sold drugs to Rogers at one time or another, and when they realized he somehow escaped arrest or indictment in the sweep they put two and two together and figured out he was the snitch.

Rogers got into fights, with women and with men, but increasingly often he began showing up stumbling along the streets with his face looking like he had just spent sixty seconds in a boxing ring with Mike Tyson. Like some of Tyson's opponents, half the time he couldn't remember where the lumps and bruises came from. One morning friends found him unconscious on the street in front of the cab company. Someone had given him a savage beating, and his right eye was swollen to the size of a hen's egg.

About three months later police and EMTs were called when he went into convulsions. The attack eased off, but he still had trouble communicating. About the only information he was able to get across for a while was that he was scared to death.

He finally left town, but he couldn't stay away. A few weeks later he stopped into the Caboose and telephoned a former girlfriend, Vicki Lakes. He said he was in Hamilton, but he was disguised and didn't want anyone else to know he was there. He wanted Vicki to come and meet him, but she prudently decided she had other things to do. True to his character, Rogers persisted, and continued phoning every fifteen minutes for an hour, alternately wheedling and threatening, determined to get his way.

Vicki had listened to the silver-tongued heartbreaker's sweet talk before, and this time she didn't budge. Rogers was in a rage when he hung up the phone after the last call. He hated it when a woman he figured he had under his thumb broke away and turned him down.

Rogers had outlived his welcome in Hamilton, and

people who drank and hung around with him in the past didn't want to have anything to do with him anymore. It was dangerous to be his friend. Even if someone did indicate their old friendship wasn't affected by the big drug bust and the sinister stories about him, Rogers couldn't be sure how safe he would be if he went out drinking with them. It was time for him to move on.

Chapter Three

CARNIES AND A MISSING MAN

AFTER SERVING SERIOUS PRISON time for the first time in his life, and with his reputation firmly established on the street as a police snitch, Hamilton lost some of its luster for Rogers.

He left town and moved onto the carnival circuit, working county fairs and similar events. Most of the time he set up and broke down rides or peddled caramel corn, cotton candy, or cheese dogs at the food trailers that carnies call "grab joints."

Rogers's primary employer was the Farrow Amusement Company, a Jackson, Mississippi–based concern that provides carnival rides. At other times he worked for Charles Productions, a traveling entertainment company. The pay was low, barely enough to keep his shirts pressed, to occasionally hole up in a cheap motel room, and to pay for a few six-packs of Bud, a bottle, or a sodden fling in some seedy saloon near the fairgrounds.

He traveled to states from Tennessee to Oklahoma, and Louisiana to Minnesota, but he wasn't much of a tourist. Most of the sights he saw were dusty fairgrounds, highways, and the insides of barrooms, including some that were so roughneck-tough that the operators put up chicken wire between the tables and the stage to protect local pickers and singers from tossed beer bottles.

There wasn't much of a future for him in carny work, but there were other important advantages. If someone like Rogers knew even a little bit about how the business ran, there were almost always jobs available somewhere on the circuit. Unskilled laborers like himself were always crawling too deeply inside a bottle to work anymore, or wandering off for some other reason and quitting in the middle of a show. There was a constant need for strong backs and practiced hands. A poor work record, alcoholism, fighting, and other shortcomings that normally adversely affect someone's employment opportunities don't always apply to the rough, down-on-their-luck men known in the business as roustabouts and "ride jockeys."

Traveling with carnivals also kept him on the move, and for someone with his uneasy ability to constantly get into trouble, the nomadic life was perfect for him. Even when his runaway drinking and vile temper led to brawls with some of his fellow carnies and brushes with police, he was never in town long. It wasn't unusual for authorities to simply release carnies and skip or drop prosecution once the show moved on. The prevailing attitude held that there was no use wasting time and the taxpayers' money tracking down or prosecuting small-time troublemakers who were already hundreds of miles away somewhere in a distant state.

County and state fairs to many Americans mean 4-H Club exhibits, livestock barns where prize animals are pampered and shown off, or craft and homemaking pavilions where sewing, canning, and baking skills are put on display and rewarded with ribbons and writeups in local community newspapers. Rogers carried out his working, drinking, and carousing only a few hundred yards away from the wholesome, squeaky-clean environment of 4-H and Future Farmers of America, but it was a completely different world. His world was firmly tangled in the cheap glare and glitter of neon lights, the hum of powerful generators, the repetitious, amplified recorded blare of talkers, merry-go-round music: all the raucous hurly-burly of the midway—and of the canvas, ropes, coiled electric lines, and human detritus that made up the seamy, depressing life that lurked just behind the scenes.

Rogers fit in among the rejects and peripatetic peons who did the carnival grunt work. But he and his sidekicks didn't mix with the more professional carnies, who included some people who could trace family participation in the business back three or four generations. Freaks like Emmitt the Alligator Man, the Lobster Boy, the Bearded Lady, the Pretzel Man, and the Quarter Man, along with sword swallowers, fire eaters, and magicians, were carnival royalty. They were people with special talents or special conditions that could be exploited and made them unique and valuable.

As a ride jockey with no special skills, Rogers was merely a part of the support staff, one of the rootless people without any particular attention-demanding condition or abilities who traveled with them for a time. He couldn't swallow swords, make rabbits disappear, or bite the heads off chickens and frogs. He didn't even have the kind of motormouth to qualify for the ''dunk-the-clown'' game, where a man sat on a flat paddle over a pool of water and flung a solid stream of insults at the crowd while young men pitched baseballs at a trip-lever to dunk him and give him his comeuppance. Rogers had the gift of gab, but his spiel was more personal and one-on-one persuasive. He could promise a woman the world by moonlight, get what he wanted, then slip away in the harsh light of day and disappear forever. But he didn't have what it took to be a successful carnival talker.

His kind were a dime a dozen on the carnival circuit: alcoholics, speed freaks, ex-convicts, and sometimes people who were simply defeated by life and so down on their luck they desperately needed any kind of a job. Being a ride jockey, hauling all that iron, putting it up and taking it down, then starting all over again, was hard, unrewarding work. The composition of the crews that worked the rides was fluid, constantly changing.

The carnies lived in trailers, motor homes, and in the backs of trucks. Everything had an air of the communal about it. The toilets tended to be dirty, littered, and smelly holes where long, open metal urinal troughs hung haphazardly against the walls, and a few booths held stools that were almost always clogged with toilet paper, trash, garbage, and worse. The cement or dirt floors were littered with more toilet paper, beer cans, crumpled cigarette packages, and the eye-stinging odor of stale urine was everywhere. The mess on the floor was slippery and could get ankle deep. The toilets were, nevertheless, prime locations where roustabouts and drifters hung out to drink beer or swig from half-full pint bottles of Mad Dog, to argue and fist-fight.

Sometimes roustabouts and casual day workers recruited from the local community ate communally at long tables in big tents. Most often they snacked from the leftovers at the food trailers and booths they ran or worked at themselves. Rogers quickly became familiar with the mind-numbing routine, and was as at home on a carnival lot as he was on the streets of Hamilton; or in Pasadena, Monrovia, and in other towns that were part of the disorganized urban sprawl radiating out from Los Angeles on the West Coast. When he was setting up equipment for the Ferris wheel, tilt-a-whirl, or merry-go-round, he knew without asking that the kiddie rides went up at the entrance with the grab joints. The games were set up in tents and under canopies along the midway, the shows were at the back, and the rest of the rides were scattered here and there throughout the area. It was a tough life, but a certain camaraderie developed among the men who shared the experience.

Carnies are the ultimate outsiders. In many ways they're like classic Gypsy nomads: constantly on the move, and when they settle into a community for a few days, they're there to take all the money they can from the locals, then leave. Fairs and carnivals are popular and an entertaining staple of the American way of life, but the people who work them are more tolerated than appreciated when they move into a town. There is an attitude of "them against us—townies against the carnies," and vice versa. Rogers and his rough carnival kindred seldom moved out of a town without a few of them logging up arrests for drunkenness, fighting, or some other minor altercation with the law.

Despite his wretched drinking habits, Rogers was husky and strong. But camping for three or four days or a week at a fairgrounds on the edge of a city or small town, then breaking up the equipment, loading it into trucks, and moving on to begin the job all over again was excruciatingly hard work. His transportation was like his life, basic and without frills. When the carnival moved, Rogers rode along in one of the equipment trucks, or climbed in one of the fleet of dilapidated cars and pickup trucks driven by some of the other carnies for the drive to the next site. For a while he drove his own rattletrap flivver, but it was old and it was difficult to keep it in running condition. He scooted under a few cars in his life, but he was more a tinkerer than a mechanic.

Carnies who followed the circuit for a while had their own special skull orchards where they drank and brawled that were in or near most of the larger cities they set up in. The husky, young roustabout with the long, dirty-blond hair tipped drinks and eyeballed or hustled the female clientele in many of them. He spent a few months in Gibsonton, Florida, a lickspittle Hillsborough County town of about 2,500 people at the edge of Tampa Bay that is known as the winter home for many carnies. Most people who live there or nearby, call it "Gibtown," or Showtown. Active and retired carnies and circus performers are scattered throughout the area. Riverview, which is only a few minutes' drive from Gibsonton and is so small most tourists don't even realize they're there when they pass through, is the site of the Showman's Retirement Home. A few more minutes' drive south along U.S. 41, Gibsonton's larger neighbor, Sarasota, is home to yet more retired performers, freakshow exhibitors, and various lesser members of the traveling amusement community.

The late John Ringling made the Gulf Coast city the winter home of the Greatest Show on Earth when he settled there in the 1920s, and the roustabouts eventually followed but formed their own low-rent colony a few miles north. A few other carnies also settled in Gibsonton, including a fire eater or two, grab-joint operators, and a handful of tired talkers who had lured their last wide-eyed townie into a girlie show or poisonous snake exhibit.

For the most part, however, the carnival community in Gibsonton attracts men who have never stood out from their peers for much of anything except their failures. While wintering a few minutes' drive from the glistening white-sand beaches, $125-per-night motels, and fine restaurants of Florida's Gulf Coast, they live in trailer parks, or in rust-streaked RVs with names painted above the doors like "Heartbreak Hotel" and "Possum Plaza," or in cluttered, cramped rooms in run-down motels where they can pay by the week or by the day.

Only one thing differentiated Rogers from most of his colleagues. He was tied to a hard, dirty job, with living conditions that were often primitive, and many of his cronies seemed never to wash off the road dirt. Nevertheless, day and night, he was almost always neatly dressed and clean. His blue jeans were pressed, his crisp workshirt was open a couple of buttons down from the collar to show off a clean, white T-shirt, his long dishwater-blond hair was sprayed and carefully combed, and his face was freshly shaven.

He met a lot of women working as a carny. He also got into lots of fights and other scrapes. In March 1992, just as show operators were preparing to move out to begin the summer circuit, Rogers told Hillsborough County Sheriff's deputies that he was held up by a friend and robbed of his cash and car. He said he was at a BP gas station parking lot when a friend turned on him, and stuck the muzzle of a .38-caliber revolver to his neck. The friend pulled $104 from his pants pocket, then climbed behind the wheel of Rogers's beat-up '79 Chevrolet Caprice and drove away, the complainant added.

Rogers didn't stick around Gibsonton or anywhere in

Hillsborough County to follow through on his complaint. He left the area with the carnival for Minnesota the next day. Sheriff's deputies ran down a witness to the incident, and, after talking to him, decided that the robbery report was unfounded.

By January 1993, Rogers's name showed up again on a Florida police blotter. This time he was in the county just to the southwest of Hillsborough, in the St. Petersburg area, when he got into a fistfight with a coworker at the Wagon Wheel Flea Market. Police were called by the boss of the combatants, George Curran, manager of Charles Productions. Both men were given their pay and left the area before police arrived.

Three months later, a couple of uniform cops were on patrol in Shreveport, Louisiana, when a man with fresh blood crusting on his face and hands flagged down their squad car. It was Rogers, and he complained one of his fellow employees beat him with a metal pipe and stole his billfold. The employee was charged with aggravated battery as a result of the fracas. Both he and Rogers listed the same home address on the police report—250 Farrow Drive, in Jackson, Mississippi. The Jackson address belongs to Farrow Amusement.

The two men were in Shreveport for the "Holiday in Dixie" riverfront festival, an annual affair that draws thousands of people to the northwest Louisiana metropolis every April while the magnolias are in bloom. One of his fellow employees with Farrow Amusement was an attractive redhead from Shreveport, Laura "Lori Mae" Bonneau. Ms. Bonneau had traveled with Farrow Amusement, and was back home for the festival when she suddenly dropped from sight. Her mother, Jean Huggins, talked with her by telephone on April 21, and could hear music and other festival noises in the background, but never heard from her again. A fisherman discovered the young woman's body a few days later floating in the Red River which flows between Shreveport and Bossier City. The mysterious death is still under investigation by the Caddo Parish Sheriff's Department. (Rogers has never been named as a suspect by police.)

Working the carnival circuit for Rogers was becoming too much like being a grunt in an Army rifle company. Danger and violence lurked around every corner. Trouble popped up around him like mushrooms pushing through the moist gray soil of the central Kentucky cave country. His boozing and his darkly feral temper were the fecund compost that nurtured it until it burst into full bloom. There was an air about his life of living in a combat zone. But it was combat without honor or medals.

Near the end of the year, while many of his fellow carnies were holing up for the winter in Gibsonton and bringing a renewed rush of business to some of the rougher walk-in, limp-out bars there, Rogers showed up back in Hamilton. He was tired, broke, and unemployed. He didn't even have a place to live.

He had long ago worn out his welcome with a string of live-in girlfriends and casual acquaintances in his hometown. They were fed up with his beatings, lies, and vagabond wanderings, and wrote him firmly out of their lives. His first wife, Deborah, had remarried once after their breakup, given birth to another son, then divorced again, and was living in Lockland. There was a new man in her life, who also fathered a child with her, but that child died in infancy. Both Clinton and Johnathon were in Texas, and there was no longer room in her life for Rogers. He was nothing more than a bad memory.

Hamilton is located near the far southwestern edge of

Ohio, and the winter temperatures are a far cry from the bone-chilling cold of Maine or Minnesota, but the local weather can nevertheless become chill and nasty. Rogers might be able to curl up in a woodlot on a December or January night somewhere in Hillsborough or Pinellas County, Florida, and safely sleep off a drunk with no harm to himself. But Hamilton, Ohio, was no place to be stranded outdoors and on the bum during a winter cold snap.

It was true that Rogers had other family in the Hamilton area, including his mother and siblings, but they either weren't able or weren't willing to take him in. Clara Sue, by her own later account, was afraid of him. His widowed mother still lived in a neatly kept home on Hamilton's west side and she talked with an old friend, Mark Peters, about her homeless son's need for a place to stay. Mrs. Rogers and Peters knew each other from shared activities at the Fraternal Order of Eagles and she explained that her son had a wife in Texas who was getting a divorce, and he needed help.

Peters was a good man who had worked hard as an electrician for several local companies before retiring. He was a widower, and he and his late wife, Clara, raised five boys and two girls. A daughter, Joan, was married to a Hamilton firefighter, John Burkart, and lived about six blocks away from the old man's home on Fairview Avenue in the same Lindenwold neighborhood. A couple of his boys also lived in Hamilton.

In retirement the elder Peters was able to spend time at his hobbies, collecting and repairing antique clocks, refinishing furniture in his garage workshop, and developing his reputation as a neighborhood handyman. Peters loved to putter around and fix things that didn't work: to make a long-silent clock tick again; to silence a dripping faucet; and to fill in the scratches and scrapes in a fine old maple cabinet or stand, then cover it with a new coat of varnish that brought out the natural rich, brown beauty of the wood and the pleasantly flowing patterns of the grain. He picked up some of his broken or damaged treasures at flea markets, and found others at public auctions and yard sales. Once a week or so, neighbors could peer out their windows and watch him drive up to the garage in his battered blue 1981 Chevrolet LeBaron and begin unloading the day's harvest.

He was a nice man, and if he had any serious faults they weren't tied to any deficiencies of character. Peters had a tendency to be too trusting and open. He had a soft spot in his heart for people who were down on their luck, and the seventy-one-year-old man opened his home to his friend's son and set about the task of helping him find a job. Rogers packed up his suitcase and moved into the Peterses' white wood-frame house.

A certain type of person equates kindness with weakness and vulnerability, and if later accounts are true, Rogers was one of those people. He settled down among the soothing ticking of a dozen or more ancient clocks and neatly kept clutter that held the memories of the old man's lifetime. He didn't bother finding a full-time job. Instead, he began taking advantage of his unsuspecting benefactor.

While Peters was puttering around in his garage workshop or away from home picking through flea markets, Rogers was inside the house helping himself to his host's cigarettes and beer. He also went through Peters's personal belongings and private papers. Among the valuables the sticky-fingered houseguest helped himself to were a copy of the birth certificate and the Social Security number of his host's son, James. Some of the antiques that Peters collected and so lovingly refinished or repaired also turned up missing after the freeloader moved in. Much later it was learned that they were stolen and sold.

At other times, Rogers stuck close to Peters. He talked him into chauffeuring him around town, or simply climbed into the decade-old Chevy and rode along in the shotgun seat while the old man visited, ran errands, or poked around at flea markets. Sometimes when Peters stopped at the fire station to talk with his son-in-law, Rogers sat outside in the car by himself patiently waiting for the driver to return.

The freeloading boarder also tried to capitalize on his relationship with Peters by wooing one of the old man's customers. Elizabeth Whitman and her twenty-year-old daughter, Michelle Von Stein, sometimes stopped by Peters's house and workshop. After meeting Rogers there, they got together with him a few times at local diners to share breakfast or lunch.

Rogers was as attentive to the older woman as a cat watching a mousehole, and as smooth as fresh cream. His conversation was uniformly courteous and speckled with "thank you's" and "pardon me's." He opened doors for the ladies, held their chairs at the restaurants, and was as polite, considerate, and helpful as he could possibly be. He was being Glen Rogers at his best. That may have been what scuttled his romantic scheme. He poured on so much syrup that it made Ms. Whitman suspicious, according to her daughter. Ms. Von Stein later recalled that all those good manners made her mother leery of him. The personality he presented was simply too good to be true, and despite his carefully practiced efforts nothing developed. But Rogers had cast out lines before and reeled them in without a hit. He was aware that no fisherman lands a prize catch every time out.

The women weren't the only ones with misgivings about the courteous freeloader. Peters was apparently aware that his trust was being betrayed, and he didn't quite know what to do about his shifty houseguest. He talked by telephone with his son, James, in California, and asked him to come stay with him awhile. But James Peters couldn't get away at that time. The old man's unease grew, and he continued to fret. He was an Army veteran who served in the Philippines during World War II, but getting rid of a shifty houseguest who had overstayed his welcome posed an altogether different sort of survival problem. The retired electrician had grabbed the proverbial tiger by the tail when he invited the younger man into his home; and he couldn't figure out how to let go.

Brisk mid-October breezes were already chasing scrap paper across the littered sidewalks of East Hamilton, and the tree-lined streets on the residential West Side were flushed with radiant reds, oranges, and yellows when Peters's daughter, Joan Burkart, and her husband left town for a vacation that would last until the end of the month. When they returned home, one of the first things Joan did was to check in on her father. She lived the closest to him of any of the children, and talked with him regularly, frequently took meals or favorite foods to him, and generally looked after his welfare.

Mark Peters didn't answer her phone calls, and when she and her husband drove to the house to look for him, he didn't answer their knocks on the door. They walked around the house, and checked out the workshop, but there was no trace of him or his trusty old flivver.

She was worried, and her unease deepened after she

talked with one of her brothers and learned that he also hadn't heard from their father for several days. The sudden vanishing was frighteningly out of character for their father. It wasn't at all like him to simply climb into the ancient Chevy and drive away from his house, workshop, family, and friends without telling anyone where he was going and when he would return home.

Mrs. Burkart and her husband drove to the Hamilton Police Department headquarters downtown, and reported her father missing. It was November 1. Initially, it appeared that police weren't taking her fears all that seriously. After all, her father had taken pretty good care of himself for seventy-one years, his mind was still good, and his physical condition was about as good as it could be expected considering his age.

Then she mentioned that her father might be with Glen Rogers. There weren't many street cops or plainclothes officers on the Hamilton Police Department, if there were any at all, who didn't know about Rogers and his hair-trigger temper and reputation for violence. He was especially dangerous, they knew, to people who were weaker than he was.

Hamilton Police began looking for the missing man. They checked out his house and workshop, talked to neighbors, made the rounds of street people and informants asking about Peters—and about his sinister houseguest. No one knew anything that was helpful, or if they did they weren't talking about it.

When the mystery of Peters's whereabouts was finally solved, it was due to a tipster who telephoned the Hamilton Police early in January of the new year. The caller indicated that Peters was somewhere in the rugged country of Lee County, Kentucky, just outside Beattyville. When news reporters later asked about the caller's identity, police played it close to the vest and declined to reveal a name immediately. But information gradually leaked out, indicating it was a man and he may have been a close relative of Rogers'.

The Hamilton Police passed the information about the retired electrician, his suspected whereabouts, and the younger companion he was last seen with to authorities in Lee County. Sheriff Douglas Brandenburg and Beattyville Police Chief Danny Townsend started poking around, asking questions. They located a rugged, sturdily built man who seemed to fit the description provided by police in Hamilton and had a talk with him. He didn't know anything about the old man from Ohio, and was quickly cleared of involvement.

The law officers also learned that Rogers had stopped in at the Bear Claw Grocery, about a mile from the cabin, several times over a period of about one month. But he hadn't been seen around the area lately. That wasn't unusual for Rogers, who had drifted in and out of the isolated mountain community from time to time since he was a teenager.

But the two small-town lawmen had the scent, and according to information passed on to them, there was a good chance that a body might be hidden somewhere on a forty-acre spread of scrub pines, scraggly oaks, shale, and dirt trails four or five miles out of town. The lawmen agreed among themselves that there was justification for calling in a search party to look over the isolated patch of land known locally as "the Old Rogers Place." No one had lived on the spread for years, although Rogers family relatives were still scattered throughout the area, including a couple of elderly sisters who were distant cousins and lived in a mobile home within sight of the farm.

But there was no reason to rush. Beattyville is in East Central Kentucky about an equal distance from Virginia to the east and Tennessee to the south. Even in good weather during the year-end holiday period, the early winter sun is too weak to burn off the bitter cold in the middle of the day. And the weather was bad, with cutting winds that swept across the peaks of the lumpy Appalachian foothills, up from the hollows and through the bare branches of the ragged oaks and scrawny maples. In fact, it was bone-chilling. It might be good weather for hunting wild turkeys, but it was no time to be digging through the frozen rocky soil while temperatures were icy cold and the wind chill was in the single digits. The law officers decided to wait for the weather to break.

Early on Monday afternoon, January 8, sheriff's deputies, Beattyville city police officers, members of the Lee County Rescue Squad, and game wardens gathered near the junction of Kentucky Highway 52 and Old Landing Road about ten miles north of town. About 100 feet up a steep ridge, the Old Rogers Place overlooked the junction. The desolate farm, with its dilapidated cabin, was the targeted area for the conscripts and volunteers.

Dressed in uniforms, or hunting jackets and blue jeans, caps with earflaps, and solid hiking boots, the heavily bundled members of the search team didn't have to brave the harsh weather very long. Barely a half-hour after they formed up and began moving out over the rugged terrain looking for bones lying atop the gray rock-strewn dirt, or suspicious mounds of earth, Game Warden Larry Hagen signaled that the search was over.

Hagen had pushed his way into a weatherbeaten clapboard shack at the top of a hill overlooking the junction of Lee County Road 52 and Old Landing. Inside the littered old house, a human skull, a leg, and a few other bones were partially wrapped in a blanket and lying at the bottom of a pile of discarded wooden furniture, beer cans, rope, and other garbage. The rope was knotted and appeared to have been used to tie the body to one of the straightback chairs, before time, weather, and other forces of nature loosened the bindings. There were indications the victim may have been gagged. The eerie scene in the murky interior of the silent house was like something lifted from a cheap Hollywood horror movie.

There was no sign anywhere near the shack of the old blue Chevy that belonged to the man whose remains were presumably inside the shack. Peters's car was never found.

While Hagen and a handful of his appalled colleagues spread out to complete the search of the littered house, other members of the search team working under the twilight gray skies began locating additional bones scattered here and there on the barren hillside. Some of the bones were scarred with toothmarks, and police surmised they were carried out of the house by dogs.

Sheriff Brandenburg notified the Kentucky State Police, and Detective Floyd McIntosh hurried to the cabin with a KSP colleague to take over the homicide investigation. It was common practice for law officers in small or isolated Kentucky communities to step aside for State Police and adopt secondary roles in investigations of certain homicides or other major crimes. The state law enforcement agency has the numbers and specially trained manpower, as well as physical resources such as an up-to-date crime laboratory, computers, and other state-of-the-art crime-fighting equipment that a small police or sheriff's department simply can't match.

Importantly as well, since July 1, 1948, when the old Kentucky Highway patrol was given a new name as the Kentucky State Police, the KSP was also charged with expanded responsibilities. Equipment and staff were upgraded and the KSP was empowered to provide full police services to everyone in the state outside a few major municipalities such as Louisville and Lexington. The KSP continued to patrol highways, but criminal investigation became an important part of its official role.

With discovery of the human remains in the shack, there was no question that the KSP would be called in. The Sheriff and the Police Chief continued to provide support, but the State Police spearheaded the rapidly burgeoning investigation.

Even though the ominous circumstances surrounding the gruesome discovery seemed clearly to point to foul play, the remains were in such poor condition that authorities weren't able to determine the cause of death. Consequently, authorities were unable to rule the death a homicide and follow through on a full-scale murder investigation. It required more than two months of study and analysis by experts before the bones could even be identified as those of the missing Hamilton electrician.

Near the end of March, Lee County Coroner Emmitt Daugherty disclosed that identification was confirmed. The bones were those of the missing Hamilton grandfather, Mark Peters. Elizabeth Murray, a forensic anthropologist and professor of biology at the College of Mount St. Joseph in Delhi township, assisted in the identification process.

Kentucky authorities released Peters's remains to his family in April, and they were returned to his hometown. Family members and friends traveled to Hamilton from all over the country to attend a memorial service. Then he was finally laid to rest in St. Mary's Cemetery beside his wife.

Identification of the victim also added fuel to the desire of Kentucky State Police investigators, along with their brother officers in Hamilton, to talk about the case with Peters's former houseguest. Although the Hamilton Police checked all Rogers's usual hangouts in his hometown, he hadn't been seen recently on the street and hadn't gotten in touch with any of his cronies there. The Hamilton Police told Peters's daughter and son-in-law they were prepared to drive or fly anywhere in the country to question his former freeloading houseguest.

But they had no idea where he was. Glen Rogers seemed to have disappeared without a trace.

Chapter Four

MARIA

WHILE POLICE IN OHIO and Kentucky were looking for Rogers to talk with him about the tragic death of his benefactor in the isolated mountain cabin, he was up to his old tricks in California, boozing, brawling, romancing, and messing up the lives of redheaded women.

He was also making use of the identification documents and information stolen while he was rifling through his former host's home in Hamilton.

Mark Peters's children and other family members were still puzzling over his baffling disappearance and praying he would miraculously show up alive, while Rogers was in Los Angeles, applying for a California driver's license. In documents made out for the permit, he listed James E. Peters's Social Security number. The name and documents were handy identification to have, and Rogers would use them more than once before the unsuspecting owner learned what was going on.

The drifter had pulled on his cowboy boots and neatly put more than 2,500 miles between himself and the twin police investigations in Ohio and Kentucky. But nothing else in his life changed except the places and faces. He was still living on the edge, frequently drinking until he blacked out, then waking up unable to remember where he had been or what he had done, and plunging into one jam after another. His favorite combination of drinks remained the same as it had been for years. When he had the money, his drink was 86-proof Jack Daniel's, black label, chased by a full glass of Budweiser. The Tennessee sour mash whiskey and the beer were a potent combination. Just one of those concoctions could explode in a man's brain and deliver a kick like a Kentucky mule. And Rogers never drank just one.

His drinking problem flared so out of control for a while that he was admitted to the Acton Rehabilitation Center in Los Angeles to dry out. A few weeks after Rogers's release from the rehabilitation program, James E. Peters got a collection agency bill in the mail at his home near San Diego. The agency was demanding $2,816, which it claimed was owed to the County of Los Angeles for drug treatment provided to James E. Peters.

While the real James E. Peters was trying to sort out the tangle with the collection agency over the bill, Rogers was settled into a North Hollywood apartment with a fellow patient from Acton, Julio Clark. Later in the summer when he applied for a loan, James Peters was confronted with an unpaid $300 telephone bill for service at the North Hollywood address.

The North Hollywood bunkmates meanwhile teamed up on housepainting jobs in the area, but Rogers was hitting the bottle as hard as ever. Sometimes he showed up for work drunk, and sometimes he left drunk. It didn't take Clark very long to realize that he had teamed up with an undependable coworker and a scary roommate who was a mean-tempered bully. One moment Rogers would be as friendly as could be, and the next moment he seemed to turn into a monster.

Despite his almost nonstop orneriness and reputation for violence, Rogers once stepped briefly into the role of neighborhood hero. A pervert had been hanging around the area exposing himself to women and children, when he crossed paths with the hard-drinking housepainter and his sidekick. The two roommates spotted him in action, and Rogers punched him in the face. The flasher tried to get away, but the roommates chased him down and held him for police. Rogers's hero role was out of character, and it didn't last long. He went right back to his old ways, continuing to build on his reputation as a man whom it was best for everyone to avoid.

When he first slipped back into California after leaving Kentucky, he was clean-shaven and his thick mop of hair was cut short and looked more light brown than blond. The short hair made his ears stand out from the side of his head, Dumbo-style. There were also times when he was on a prolonged toot when he neglected to shave for a day or two, and the light-colored stubble sprouted on his cheeks and chin like a haze of dirty mold or tired fuzz on a peach that was beginning to rot. But when he was spruced-up, clean-shaven, and fixing his captivating eyes on a woman he was still a handsome man.

While Rogers was alternately fighting the battle of the bottle and playing neighborhood hero in California, his former teenage bride was back in Ohio losing her personal struggle against the demons that had pursued her all her adult life. Deborah was eight months pregnant and living in Lockland on March 22, 1994, when she died. Complications from diabetes mellitus was cited on the death certificate as the cause of death, but cocaine abuse was also noted as a contributing factor. Her two boys were in Texas, still in foster care.

Rogers didn't make it back home to southern Ohio for the funeral. He was still making his presence known in the Los Angeles area where police were becoming reacquainted with the Ohio bad boy under his own name, while following up on a scattering of complaints— most of them tied to domestic dust-ups. They were called to his apartment, and to taprooms where his new girlfriend worked as a bartender. Rogers was in the habit of following her to work and kicking up a fuss.

He struck up a romance with Maria Gyore soon after settling again into the suburban sprawl that meanders through the San Fernando Valley north of the Southern California megapolis. The glamorous redhead was a Hungarian-born single mother of two children. She was in her mid-forties, a few years older than the women Rogers usually set his sights on, but she had kept her shape and had a sparkling personality and zest for life that made her appear younger than her chronological age. She was also lonely, vulnerable, and ripe for plucking: exactly the kind of woman he was at his best with. Rogers swept Maria off her feet, and into a shared apartment in Van Nuys.

Rogers was comfortable in Van Nuys and the San Fernando Valley. There was a bit of Kentucky in the Valley, with mountains, large areas of wide-open spaces and forests, and it was so vast that there was a serious political move afoot to break the area off from the rest of Los Angeles County. With a population of more than 9 million, the county had nearly three times the number of people as the entire Commonwealth of Kentucky. If the Valley seceded and became a city it would have a population of about 1.2 million, almost exactly one-third as many people as the Bluegrass State.

Among those 1.2 million people there were a lot of sassy redheaded women, and a profusion of blue-collar and country music saloons and lounges where a good-looking man could meet them. Rogers didn't know much about demographics or have any serious interest in city or county politics, but he could hardly have been more comfortable or at home trolling the Valley and seeking new romantic conquests like Maria.

The Midwestern Romeo relied on his tried-and-true method to woo the new woman in his life. During the initial stages of the courtship he was excessively courteous and considerate to her, and he showered her with attention. He wrote her long love poems, and elevated her to a special place of honor in his life along with Debi, Angel, and his mother by having her name tattooed on one of his beefy arms.

It wasn't until after the hook was firmly set that Rogers revealed his true character in all its sordid violence. As he had done after luring other women with his courtly manners and attentive ways, he allowed the nasty side of his dual personality to click in. The Eastern European siren's fairy-tale romance with her exciting new macho American boyfriend metamorphosed into a nightmare.

Maria's dangerous boyfriend was a fitful worker. He picked up occasional work in construction, as a handyman, housepainter, apartment manager, and whatever other jobs he could find that didn't require much special training or concentration. Mostly he drank. If Rogers was awake and wasn't working somewhere under the watchful eye of a boss, he was usually boozing—bending his elbow inside a darkened saloon somewhere with fellow barflies or privately sharing a twelve-pack with a friend.

When he finally passed out or dropped off into a fitful, sodden sleep after a day and night of drinking, the only thing his girlfriend could be certain of was that he would wake up feeling mean. Rogers could put away huge amounts of alcohol without showing the effects, but eventually it built up in his system until he got roaring drunk. That was when he usually began wanting to hurt Maria and anyone else who was around him.

He would storm into the apartment yelling threats and curses, then begin pounding her with his big fists and feet. Rogers still had his first wife's name tattooed across the knuckles of his right fist, but it wasn't Debi he was punching. It was Maria. He smacked her against the walls, tipped over furniture, and destroyed her clothes and anything else she owned and cared about.

One night in August 1994 was especially memorable for his use of fire as a feature of his violence. He set fire to Maria's clothes closet, and after police were called to the couple's modest apartment Rogers was processed into the jail under his own name on preliminary charges of arson. Police in Los Angeles turned on their computers and plugged into California's statewide police computer system in Sacramento and National Crime Information Center computers to check out the accused arsonist. They learned their prisoner had a lengthy rap sheet, including a string of arrests in his hometown in Ohio. California officers telephoned the Hamilton Police, told them they had Rogers in custody, and asked for background information.

The disclosure seemed to be the kind of break Ohio detectives investigating the mysterious disappearance and death of Mark Peters were waiting for. Soon after the exchange of information, Homicide Detective James Nugent made arrangements to drive across the Ohio River to Kentucky, board an airliner at the Greater Cincinnati International Airport, and fly to Los Angeles. Local law enforcement authorities were all set to meet him there, and drive him to the jail so he could have a sit-down talk with Rogers about Mark Peters. Nugent never boarded the flight. At the last minute, Chief Simon Fluckiger called off the trip. Hamilton was a cash-poor city, and the police department operated on a razor-thin budget that didn't leave much room for detectives to fly around the country chasing chimeras. A round-trip cross-country flight, coupled with the costs of hotel accommodations and meals, was too expensive.

Furthermore, the motormouth who had worked as a snitch for the Hamilton Police and spun tall tales to anyone who would listen to him when he was drinking at shabby East Side bars always experienced a sudden change of character when he got into personal trouble with the law. He became uncharacteristically close-mouthed. Overall, Rogers had already been arrested at least twenty-six times, and he never gave a single statement to Ohio police. He knew when to talk, and he knew when to balk.

Mark Peters's family was heartsick when they learned of the lost opportunity. For months Joan Burkart had pestered authorities in Hamilton and in Kentucky, trying to stir up interest and get them to do something about her father's macabre death. No one seemed willing to pursue the kind of aggressive investigation it was going to take to bring any official closure to the mystery, however. Finally, she tired of butting her head against a brick wall, and gave up—for the time being. But she and her husband were shocked and outraged when they learned of the lost opportunity to talk to Rogers about the mystery. Talking to the press months later, John Burkart said of Rogers: "He didn't fall through the cracks. Police just didn't do their jobs."

Spokesmen at the Hamilton Police Department responded by explaining they believed their colleagues in Kentucky were actively pursuing the Ohio bad boy. Instead of going after Rogers, however, Kentucky authorities dismissed old burglary charges that were pending against him.

The good luck that surrounded him in Ohio and Kentucky continued in California. Maria refused to testify against her rowdy boyfriend, and the charges were dismissed. Rogers walked away from the Van Nuys courthouse a free man. The troubled couple moved back in together, this time into the Excalibur Apartments on Woodman Avenue in Van Nuys. It was looking more and more like he was a man who could get away with anything. He didn't even have to go out of his way to beat the system. It wasn't necessary for him to bring into play the sinister manipulative skills he honed and perfected so well over the years. He had merely to stand passively by, and the system would beat itself.

A new generation of police officers in the Los Angeles suburbs were becoming reacquainted with the Ohio-born ruffian under his own name, while following up on a scattering of complaints, most of them tied to domestic dust-ups.

Near the end of April 1995 he was kicking up a ruckus in a bar when another man smacked him over the head with the butt end of a pool cue, shattering the bone around one of his eyes and fracturing his skull. Rogers was patched up in the emergency room of a nearby hospital before limping away under his own power.

But it wasn't until June 6 that he got into trouble that was serious enough to at last convince authorities it was time to put him behind bars for a few weeks. He was in one of his drunken rages, beating on cars in the underground garage of an apartment building in Hollywood when a security guard ordered him to stop. Rogers pulled a knife, chased down the frightened guard, and slammed his head against a stone pillar. Then he turned on a building resident, and chased him into an elevator where he held the long blade of the knife to the man's throat for several minutes, before finally backing off.

When police finally collected him after the terrifying incident, they hauled him off to the Los Angeles Police Department's Hollywood District Station and booked him on charges of assault with a deadly weapon. A few days later Rogers appeared before Municipal Judge Michael Mink and pleaded no contest. Judge Mink ordered him to serve six months in jail, and three years' probation.

Rogers was behind bars for forty-two days, including time served awaiting his bench trial and sentencing. On July 17 his civilian clothing and other personal effects were returned, and he was freed as part of a work-release program designed to ease overcrowding in jails, detention centers, and prisons in Los Angeles County and throughout the state. Although his crimes were frightening and serious, they were misdemeanors, and that meant he was eligible for work-release. Over a period of thirty-six days, he was assigned to a variety of menial jobs from washing cars, painting over graffiti, and cutting weeds until completing his work-release obligations on September 7.

Threatening someone with a knife is a serious crime, even in Los Angeles. But people are locked up for far worse offenses, so many in fact that there isn't room in the jails to keep everyone who is sentenced behind bars for the full length of their term. According to local court and police records at the time, Rogers was convicted of two offenses, and both were misdemeanors. His bunk was needed for felons arrested for drive-by shootings, drug executions, and a ghastly witch's brew of mindless violence that is such a sad fact of daily life in the Los Angeles area. It was common practice for someone like Rogers to be released after serving no more than about one-third of his sentence.

Prison and jail overcrowding was especially acute at the time because California state legislators had crafted and added a tough new habitual-offender stipulation to the criminal codes which directed that mandatory terms of from twenty-five years to life in prison be ordered for anyone convicted of three felonies. Signed by Governor Pete Wilson, the new so-called Three Strikes Law also significantly hiked the time required to be served by one- and two-time convicted felons. One of the immediate effects of the stern new law was jails and prisons that were bursting to the seams with especially dangerous criminals. Compared to some of the rapists, stickup artists, and killers he was locked up with, Rogers was considered to be small-fry—the kind of bothersome roughneck who might be jailed in June, freed in July, and dropped completely from supervision in September.

Rogers wasn't mellowed either by the time served behind bars or by his good fortune in receiving an early release. He was meaner than ever, and apparently tormented by jealousy of his girlfriend. He stormed like a wild bull into the bars where she worked and created troubles with her boss.

One time when she was at work, Rogers began screaming at her, and one of Maria's fellow employees, Paula Clark, stepped into the dispute. He was making a scene and she tapped his shoulder, telling him to calm down. He hurled her onto the bar, and began lumbering toward her with his fists clenched and his pale blue-green eyes blazing. Instead of cowering in fear, she straightened up and started yelling at him. The plucky woman's surprise counterattack stopped him in his tracks. His fists uncurled, he shrank back and quieted down.

There may or may not have been a valuable lesson to be learned through the experience. The swaggering bully had retreated at least once before, years earlier when he tangled with Cora McKnight and she went after him with a knife. He also retreated when he was faced down by Ms. Clark, who was armed with nothing more than her anger and with sharp words—although the confrontation occurred in a crowded tavern. But he had beaten other spunky women to within an inch of their lives when they tried to stand up to him. Although Rogers left Ms. Clark alone after the embarrassing face-off in the barroom, he didn't stop abusing his girlfriend.

She was working at a sports lounge owned by Oscar Rozsa in Van Nuys when Rogers flew into one of his rages and began breaking beer bottles. Rozsa threw him out. The next day Rogers returned, sober and seemingly contrite. He apologized, but Rozsa told him he wasn't welcome there anymore. The bar owner ordered him to get out and never come back.

Rozsa also reluctantly fired Maria from her bartending job. He hated to do it, because he liked her and he liked her work, but her surly boyfriend simply caused too much trouble. And regardless of how awful Rogers treated her and behaved around her friends, she always took him back. Nothing seemed to be too outrageous for her to forgive, and she stuck with him even when her friends began writing her off because they couldn't stand her cantankerous trouble-making sweetie. Rozsa continued his friendship with his troubled former bartender after he had to fire her, but later told reporters that even her brother stopped talking to her for a while.

Rogers was unfazed by the fuss he was causing. There were lots of saloons in Van Nuys where he was unknown and still welcome to drink, including McRed's, a pleasant laid-back watering hole about a mile down the road where the crowd favored cool draft beer and loud country music. He reluctantly crossed Rozsa's sports bar off his list and never returned. It wasn't the first time he had been kicked out of a place.

In late August, almost a year to the day from the time Rogers set fire to Maria's closet, he flew into another of his rages and threw her out of their apartment in Van Nuys. He tossed her clothes and other personal possessions outside after her. Maria and her brother, Laszlo, who was concerned about her tempestuous relationship with the brutal drunk and worried for her safety, went to the Van Nuys police station the next day and filed a complaint. A short time later a pair of uniformed officers arrested him on suspicion of spousal battery, and transported him to headquarters.

Rogers was still on probation for threatening his neighbor with the knife and it may have seemed that he was in serious danger of being returned to jail to serve out the remainder of the earlier sentence for violating the terms of his probation. But Van Nuys was still in

Los Angeles County, and the courts were overwhelmed with the crushing workload, funding for the criminal justice system was in short supply, and the jails were as crowded as they were when he was released about six weeks earlier.

When misdemeanors are involved, justice in the Los Angeles courts can move with warp speed. Glen faced just such production-line justice when he appeared before Van Nuys Municipal Court Commissioner Rebecca Omens. He wasn't a celebrity defendant, no O. J. Simpson; not even a Lyle or Eric Menendez, who would eventually be convicted after more than six years and two trials of the double murder of their parents. He was a nonentity, who again pleaded no-contest to the charge against him.

Commissioner Omens was a dedicated professional who handled cases involving traffic violations and misdemeanor pleas. The proceedings in her courtroom weren't generally the type that made headlines or attracted attention on the local 6 o'clock news. Her job was important, but it was grunt work, and like other bench commissioners it was common for her to hear as many as 300 to 400 cases every day. She couldn't personally read every legal document and delve deeply into the background of every defendant and every case. By necessity she had to depend on other professionals in the system, such as sheriffs' investigators, attorneys, or assistant DAs to red-flag anything that was especially serious or unusual. Apparently no one noticed Rogers was already on probation ordered in another courthouse only a few minutes' drive along the freeway, and red-flagged the battery case.

Commissioner Omens ordered him to spend two days in jail, but he had already served the time while waiting for the hearing. In addition, he was ordered to pay a hundred-dollar fine, to enroll in a domestic violence program, and to stay away from Maria. The Commissioner could have revoked his probation and returned him to jail to serve out the remainder of his term for pulling the knife on his neighbor if she had known about the earlier offense and court appearance. Or she could have stunned him with a total of two and a half years of jail time if she had chosen to stack maximum penalties for probation violation and the new spousal battery charges.

Based on the information she was aware of at the time, however, as well as the crowded condition of the jails and prisons, it would have been difficult to justify such a severe penalty. Maria reportedly picked up only one new bruise in that particular beating. There were no broken bones. Richard Schmidt, supervisor of the city attorney's office in Van Nuys, later told the *Los Angeles Times* he didn't know if the Commissioner was aware of Rogers's criminal record. "It was a low-level violation in terms of the kinds of spousal abuse cases we get here," he said. Rogers's good luck was holding up, and he walked out of court a free man.

The sentence ordered by Commissioner Omens was standard for that particular offense, but Laszlo Gyore was shocked and worried by Rogers's lenient treatment. His sister was scared to death. Both the sister and brother knew Rogers's reputation for refusing to play by the rules, and there was no guarantee he would heed the order to stay away from her. He was a dangerous man, and there was every reason to believe that his anger would continue to be focused on his estranged girlfriend. Laszlo said he telephoned the Van Nuys deputy city attorney to warn about Rogers's potential for more violence, and he pestered the police with additional warnings. Maria left the country, fleeing all the way back to her native Hungary to escape the frightening, brutish man she had once thought of settling down with into a serious romantic relationship. Her rustic Prince Charming had turned into a monster, and was making her life a nightmare.

Rogers didn't know his frightened girlfriend was in Hungary, but the idea that she was hiding out somewhere poured new fuel on the flames of his white-hot anger. He had beaten her up before and she had taken him back. It was a pattern established with most of his women, and when one of them like Debi, Angel, Cora, or Maria finally broke away it turned him into a raging maniac.

Rogers grew his beard and mustache and set out to look for his woman or a replacement, while the anger generated by her disappearance simmered and cooked. He did most of his looking in saloons, and bartenders and other taproom employees who weren't already familiar with his nasty reputation quickly learned that the Jekyll-and-Hyde character was a troubling customer to have around. When he had swallowed enough drinks to ensure he would be in his usual bad mood, he insulted people, started fights, and broke things. One of the bars in which he looked for Maria was McRed's.

Chapter Five

FLIGHT

IT TOOK FOUR DAYS for authorities to figure out that the woman whose strangled and charred corpse was discovered in the burned pickup truck was Sandra Gallagher, a single mother of three.

Identification was made and confirmed through the combined efforts of pathologists working for the Los Angeles County Department of Chief Medical Examiner–Coroner, and by homicide detectives assigned to the case. Crime-scene technicians and detectives carefully combed through the devastation of the truck cab looking for clues: anything that may have survived the flames. Even as seemingly insignificant an object as a cigarette butt, a swatch of material torn from a shirt, a stray fiber from a blanket, or a foreign hair could help solve the puzzle. Arson specialists studied the body and the cab interior as well for traces of an accelerant, any kind of fuel that might have been used to ignite the flames and encourage burning.

Other detectives checked the serial number of the truck and the out-of-state license tag number with the Colorado State Department of Motor Vehicles, and began interviewing neighbors in the area where the truck and body were burned. Downtown at the office of the Los Angeles County Medical Examiner–Coroner, pathologists and a team of forensics technicians and laboratory specialists concentrated on the grim task of lifting the body's secrets from the corpse itself.

To most people it may have seemed that the pathologist and his assistants didn't have much to work with when they gathered around the blackened corpse stretched out on the stainless-steel body tray. But the coroner oversees more than 6,000 autopsies every year, and a startlingly large number of them are performed on bodies that have been horribly damaged.

Some are mangled in traffic accidents on the thousands of miles of city streets and freeways; washed ashore when gases formed by the decomposition process finally pops them to the surface of lakes, rivers, or the Pacific Ocean; torn to bits by blasts from the deadly machine guns known as "street sweepers" during gang and drug wars; buried in the Angeles National Forest above the city by rapists or professional hitmen; or mutilated and ruined in myriad other ways.

The bodies of some, like those of the mystery female found in the burning truck, have been horribly charred or nearly destroyed by fire. Even those bodies can sometimes yield valuable clues to the identity of a victim, and to the exact cause of death as well.

A fingertip may have survived the flames and provide a usable print to be matched through local police computer checks, the U.S. Justice Department's massive database available through the NCIC, or the state-of-the-art supercomputer and identification system operated by the California State Department of Justice. Manufactured by the Nippon Electric Company, the NEC computer has the capability of searching through 650 fingerprints per second, and can even read samples that are distorted or smudged. That's important, considering that Los Angeles County has fed more than 1.5 million fingerprint cards into the system, and additional millions are on file from other areas of the state.

Other valuable clues are also available through the autopsy process. Evidence of old injuries, operations, or of child-bearing can all contribute to solving the puzzles and moving an investigation forward.

Working quietly and efficiently among the odors, the pans, and scalpels and scales, the pathology team determined that the woman on the table was strangled before the body and the interior of the truck cab were set afire. Samples were taken from the vital organs, from other body tissues, and of the blood, bile, and urine, all to be submitted later to careful examination in sophisticated laboratory tests.

Pinning down solid information to show if she was raped posed even more difficult problems than ferreting out her identity. Normally when conducting an autopsy where there is a possibility sexual assault was involved, swabs are taken from the vagina, rectum, and mouth to be examined for traces of semen or other evidence of rape or consensual sexual activity. Evidence of rape disappears within a few hours, however, and consequently in most jurisdictions specialists make visual observation of sexual organs and surrounding areas, and collect samples before the full post-mortem examination.

Despite early police reports that the burned woman was raped, pathologists were unable to positively conclude that she was involved in sexual activity around the time of the murder. The body was too badly damaged by the fire. Investigators had better luck following up other aspects of the probe, however.

Once Sandra was firmly identified as the victim, it was a relatively easy job for homicide investigators to follow her trail to McRed's and to the strapping big-talking braggart with the bedroom eyes with whom she walked out of the taproom on the last night of her life. A couple of homicide detectives stopped in at the honky-tonk and showed a photograph of a slender-faced woman with shoulder-length reddish hair to Rein Keener. They asked if she knew who it was.

The shocked bartender immediately realized she was looking at a picture of Sandra Gallagher. When she learned that Sandra was a murder victim, she was also faced with the dreadful realization of how close she may have personally come to being killed. There was good reason to believe that Sandra died in her place. Rein hadn't spent much time worrying about the big blond man's reaction after reneging on her promise to drive him home from the bar a few nights earlier. But now the chilling memory of the awkward scene flooded back.

"I know that was supposed to be me," she later told a reporter. "It was going to be my night."

News that the murdered woman was Sandra flashed through the local bar scene like wildfire, especially at McRed's, where the men were outraged and the women were scared to death. The big-talking free-spender with the dishwater-blond hair whom patrons at McRed's knew as "Glen," was identified by several people as the hell-raising rowdy who had lived with Maria Gyore before the couple broke up and he had scared her so bad she fled the country. He was a devastatingly frightening man. Maria knew it, and now Rein Keener knew it.

Throughout his violence-speckled career as a small-time criminal and woman beater, Rogers was more lucky than smart. While he was making the rounds at McRed's and other taprooms in Van Nuys and Pasadena, he didn't even take the precaution of covering himself with the handy alias he picked up before clearing out of Hamilton.

By the time Van Nuys police had a firm I.D. on the suspected killer, however, he was hundreds of miles away from Los Angeles County. The same day Sandra's pitiful remains were carried from the burned interior of the ruined truck cab and transported to the morgue in downtown Los Angeles, Rogers bought a one-way ticket and climbed aboard a Greyhound bus to begin a 2,000-mile ride across country. He did the same thing after Mark Peters disappeared, only this time when he stowed a bundle of clothes in the overhead compartment and slid into his seat for the exhausting ride he was going in the opposite direction. He was headed almost due east to Jackson, Mississippi.

Whenever Rogers got into a serious jam, he cleared out and hotfooted it for other familiar surroundings, far from police investigators and anyone else who was looking for him. Too many people connected to the law were already anxious to talk with him in Ohio and Kentucky, so he lit out for the Mississippi capital city he came to know so well while he was traveling with the carnivals. He had roamed some of the shabbier neighborhoods there, drank in no-name bars, and there was always the possibility that if he was out of money and desperate to keep on the move he could hire on again with Farrow and move out onto the carnival circuit for awhile.

Once police in Los Angeles County had checked the suspect's known haunts in the San Fernando Valley, talked to regulars in barrooms, and neighbors near his apartment in Van Nuys, and assured themselves he was apparently gone for good, they notified federal authorities. A federal warrant was filed at the U.S. District Court in Los Angeles against Rogers for unlawful flight from prosecution. Authorities correctly figured he was probably up to his old tricks, and crossed state lines in a desperate move to put as much distance as he could between himself and the troubling questions waiting for him in California. Law enforcement agencies had looked for Rogers before, but he finally made the big time. He was wanted by the FBI.

The Hamilton Police put out their own alert for the local desperado. He had fled to the familiar surroundings of his hometown before when he got into trouble, and there was a good chance that unless he stepped widely out of character he would be showing up again. About the same time the Hamilton Police stepped up their vigilance, Jimmy Bowman received a telephone call from his former drinking buddy and criminal mentor. Rogers said he needed money, and he asked if he was "hot" in Hamilton, Bowman later told reporters.

The Hamilton Police alert was a few weeks premature. Rogers was in Jackson, Mississippi, where he first checked into the Holiday Motel, then moved on to another moderately priced hostelry. He stayed longest at the Sun 'n' Sand motel downtown, and when he checked in on the night of October 4, he impressed manager Sam Boone with his pleasant manner. Rogers was also impressive when he pulled out a thick wad of money and peeled off bills until he had enough for his first week's stay in a thirty-dollar-a-night room. He checked into the Sun 'n' Sand the day after the charred body pulled from the pickup truck in Van Nuys was at last identified.

Jackson was familiar territory, and there was a sense

of security for him there in the heart of the Magnolia State. He was comfortable in the sprawling, vibrant city at the southern matrix of the huge finger-shaped Ross Barnett Reservoir. Two major highways, I-20 and I-55 bisect in Jackson, and he could easily travel by car or Greyhound to just about anywhere in the country he might want to go. Interstate 20 runs almost exactly east and west through the city, and can be followed east all the way to South Carolina. To the west it continues on across the Mississippi border, and through the twin river cities of Bossier City and Shreveport, Louisiana, into West Texas before finally petering out. Interstate 55 extends to the north on an almost straight line past St. Louis, all the way to Chicago. To the south, it runs through Louisiana and ends after skirting the west edge of Lake Pontchartrain just outside New Orleans. Rogers had traveled both highways dozens of times while hanging around Jackson and working with the carnivals.

He was also comfortably at home moving among the rednecks and roughnecks in certain Jackson honky-tonks where country music blared from jukeboxes and the crash of broken bottles and tipped-over stools were known to mix at times with the thump of fists on flesh and the roars of drunk and angry men.

Rogers even knew where to find work if he wanted to stick around town instead of returning to the carnival circuit. There were opportunities to get a few days' or a few weeks' work on some of the construction jobs that were constantly underway in and around the city. He also had a valid Mississippi Class A commercial driver's license, and if he wished he could probably hire on with a cab company or do some truck driving.

In the meantime, while he was looking things over and checking out opportunities, the Mississippi State

Fair was scheduled to open in a few days. The spacious fairgrounds were located at the eastern edge of the city where Interstate 55 drops down and cuts through Hinds County on the way to New Orleans. He had been to the fairgrounds before.

Chapter Six

LINDA, TINA, AND ANDY

"How can they catch me now? I love my work."
—note to Scotland Yard from
Jack the Ripper

LINDA PRICE WAS A pretty, sparkling woman with long, lush auburn hair and an irrepressible zest for life. From the time she was a teenager, she looked for adventure.

In those days she apparently didn't give a second thought to the danger she was courting when she stepped out alongside a highway, stuck a thumb out, and climbed into the cars or truck cabs of strangers to ride off into the unknown. Sometimes the free-spirited girl was gone for months, but she eventually showed up back home, seemingly no worse for the wear and brimming over with exciting stories of her exploits to share.

Linda became a mother for the first time when she was barely sixteen. At twenty she had her second child. And she had just celebrated her thirty-second birthday when she became a grandmother.

But at the ripe old age of thirty-four, the Jackson, Mississippi, retail saleswoman and part-time house-cleaner was lonely. She was never able to form the kind of loving, lasting relationship with a man that could provide her with the lifelong companionship she so desperately yearned for. She had three divorces behind her, and another relationship with a man in 1994 that turned so stormy and sour she filed for protection under Mississippi's Domestic Abuse Act.

Then she drove across town with a group of family members to the state fairgrounds and coliseum just off I-55 to attend a country music concert. The Mississippi State Fair was in full swing and it seemed her most optimistic romantic daydreams had at last come true when she met Glen Rogers at a tent sponsored by the local newspaper, the *Clarion-Ledger*.

Linda had never been accused of being shy, and when she saw the good-looking man sitting by himself sipping a Bud in the music and beer tent, she walked over and asked him to dance. Moments later they were in each other's arms, scooting around the wooden dance floor to the sweet country rhythm of a group of pickers and singers on the bandstand. The man Linda cut out from the herd was handsomely debonair, wore his blue jeans well, had plenty of money, and was generous. By that time the former carnival roustabout had been in town nearly two weeks, bought a sleek, burnt-orange-colored 1987 Datsun pickup truck with an extended cab from a man he met drinking in a bar, and was looking for romance.

Rogers made his interest obvious from the first time he laid eyes on the trim, five-foot-four-inch 110-pound thirty-four-year-old grandmother. She looked as softly sweet and succulent as one of the persimmons that swelled and ripened on backyard trees in the Mississippi capital city. The vivacious beauty also looked a lot like one of his former Hamilton girlfriends, Angel Wagers, whose first name was still tattooed on his shoulder. Rogers showered Linda with compliments, bought her popcorn at one of the grab joints, and a couple of Old Milwaukees in the beer tent.

For Linda, it was love at first sight. She spent the rest of that night with the exciting, attentive macho man in his motel room. The only blemish on the enchanted evening occurred when someone stole his pickup truck. It was an ironic turnabout for someone who spent much of his life stealing from other people and conning them out of their possessions.

Nothing could dim Linda's enthusiasm, however, and she could hardly wait to show off her catch to the rest of her family and friends. The day after meeting the rustic Prince Charming, she told her mother, Mrs. Carole Wingate, all about him. He was her dream man, she bubbled. Everything from then on was going to be fine, she assured her mother. It seemed that it was about time Linda started living a dream with a man instead of a nightmare. She was Mrs. Wingate's baby, the youngest of five children, and she had already packed a lot of disappointments and hard knocks into her thirty-four years.

Her first husband committed suicide in 1988, and she had had problems with men ever since. Most recently, a boyfriend she broke up with shortly before meeting Rogers beat her up. And that wasn't the first time a man knocked her around.

Kevin Smith, a forty-year-old family friend, was at Mrs. Wingate's when the cheery redhead dropped in early one night in October with her new boyfriend in tow. Mrs. Wingate was impressed, and later said he was so good-looking that he was "beautiful," even though that wasn't usually a word used to describe a man. It wasn't just his looks that were appealing, however. As soon as he met her, he gave her a big hug and said, "You're the prettiest mother and grandmother I've ever seen." Mrs. Wingate understood perfectly why her daughter was so taken with the audacious flatterer.

There wasn't a lot of conversation about his work, but there seemed to be little doubt he had a good job. He had enough money to buy a used Ford Mustang for the woman he was already calling "my little angel." They moved from the motel they were originally staying in, and set up temporary housekeeping at the Tarrymore Motel on U.S. 80. They only stayed at the Tarrymore a few days, before he shelled out a fistful of cash to rent a $385-a-month two-bedroom apartment on Rainey Road. Smith got the impression that the sturdy blond stranger who swept Linda off her feet was a truck driver. Truck driving was a profession Linda had a special affection for. She hitched rides with dozens of truck drivers when she was on the road, and she was working toward qualifying for her own commercial license. She was hopeful of getting away from freelance housecleaning and beginning to collect a more regular and fatter paycheck.

Being treated so well by someone she had just met was a novel experience for Linda. She was the one who had the reputation for going out of her way to help a friend or a neighbor when they needed a ride to the store or a few dollars to buy milk for a baby.

Linda had been staying by herself at the Briarcliff Apartments before packing up and moving into the new love nest with her generous sweetheart. Her boyfriend didn't have much personal property except for his clothes, and had lost some of his few possessions when his pickup truck was stolen, so she busied herself redecorating the cozy home on Rainey Road with personal treasures and knickknacks she had with her in the motel and others that she stored with family or friends until she got a place of her own. The apple of her eye was a china cabinet, which she filled with her doll and Marlboro collections, and a trove of Harley-Davidson motorcycle accessories and other biking mementos.

Family pictures of her eighteen-year-old son, fourteen-year-old daughter, two-year-old grandson, and her mother were also elevated to places of honor on shelves and stands. Her personality and tastes dominated the apartment, but overall it took on a cozy and homey look. Both Linda and her handsome boyfriend acted as if they were happy to be out of motels and firmly settled down in a place of their own. Linda was convinced her fondest dreams had come true, and she was so proud of her home she planned to bring the manager of the apartments around to take a look at the decorating.

Her boyfriend even helped her cut down on her drinking. Instead of her usual daily intake of two quarts of Old Milwaukee, she tapered back to two twelve-ounce cans a day. But it was a "do as I say, not as I do," situation. He continued drinking as much as ever. When he was living at the Holiday Motel, and for a while after he moved out, his favorite hangout was the Sportsman's Lounge. It was just a few minutes away from the motel, along U.S. 80.

Whenever Rogers loped into the lounge, regulars knew there was going to be some action. He insisted on being the center of attention, and would sometimes shout loudly across the room to order his first drink before he reached the line of stools in front of the bar. Most of the time he would pull a roll of cash from his pocket, slap a hundred-dollar bill on the bar, and order drinks for the house. One Monday night he drank for four hours, setting up drinks for everyone in the saloon and paying for everything in cash.

Rogers couldn't have been nicer, but he didn't want anyone else paying for anything when he was drinking and in one of his expansive moods. If someone ordered a bag of peanuts or pretzels, he insisted on paying for it. No one else paid, and no one else outdrank him. He drank faster than anyone else in the bar, and when he finished a beer and was ready for another, he told the bartender to set up a fresh round for everyone.

The other patrons had trouble keeping up with him, but if they were still nursing the last brew when he ordered a new round, he wouldn't let the bartender keep the fresh bottle on ice. He ordered her to pop the cap and place it on the table in front of the customer. When Rogers finally walked out of the lounge that night, most of the other people still sitting at tables or at the bar had four or five open bottles of warm beer still lined up in front of them.

Some of the barflies and casual drinkers at the Sportsman's wondered about the source of all the cash the big-hearted spender so lavishly spread around. He didn't look like a John Moneybags, but he acted like it. When police around the country later began looking into his movements and behavior, they were equally mystified by his free-spending ways. After leaving his first serious job with the printing company in Pasadena, he never stuck very long with a single employer and didn't earn the kind of money necessary to account for the thick wad of hundred-dollar bills he always seemed to have stuffed in his jeans pocket. In Jackson he worked for a while in construction, but he didn't have the specialized job skills to earn really big money. The question of his ready cash source was a puzzle.

Late in October the couple's fortunes took another promising turn when the Jackson Police notified them they had recovered his pickup truck. Mrs. Wingate drove him to the police impound lot to pick it up. She waited while he showed a copy of his driver's license and other identification to a clerk, before being allowed to climb into the truck and drive out of the lot.

When Rogers reclaimed his truck, police missed what could have been a golden opportunity to take him in custody. On October 17, Van Nuys Municipal Judge Alice E. Altoon issued a murder warrant for his arrest as a suspect in the Gallagher slaying, and the information was available in national police computers. All the Jackson Police had to do to match the sturdy, bearded vehicle owner with the warrant was to call it up on a screen, but people reclaiming stolen vehicles are understandably presumed to be victims, rather than perpetrators of crimes. Consequently, the Jackson Police don't check the background of owners before releasing their vehicles to them.

Rogers's phenomenal good luck was continuing to hold, even after a second warrant was issued in Los Angeles County for his arrest. When he failed to show up for a probation violation hearing tied to his sentencing for threatening his Hollywood neighbor with a knife, Judge Mink revoked the probation order. Mink issued a new warrant on October 25, only eight days after the murder warrant was sworn out. By that time the rambunctious probation violator was halfway across the country, taking his peckerwood pleasures in the Deep South and practicing his charm on unsuspecting women.

Linda's mother wasn't the only family member who was taken with Rogers's charm. Linda's older sister, Kathy Carrol, was impressed with his pleasant manner, polite talk, and smiles. As soon as he walked into a room where any of Linda's family or friends were around, he started off with the smooth talk and the blarney. He told everyone he had a cabin in the mountains of Kentucky, and planned to take them there before long to spend some time relaxing in the outdoors. For all his expansive good-time-Charlie behavior, there was also an attractive air of mystery about him. He confided to one of Linda's nieces that he used ten aliases. It was difficult to tell if he was joking or not, but the boast nevertheless made a good story.

Rogers couldn't charm every member of his girlfriend's family, however. Her older brother saw through the bluster and phony geniality. From the first day they met, Chester Wingate, Jr., distrusted Rogers. He didn't feel at all good about Rogers, and wouldn't even shake his hand. There was something forced about the boyfriend's hearty gregariousness and the overwhelming attention he paid to the women in the family. The suspicious brother picked up other disturbing hints that a few ignition wires were crossed somewhere as well. Sometimes, Rogers dropped the folksy friendliness, and revealed a more ominously disturbing side to his personality. It was almost like he flicked on some kind of a switch in his brain.

"He would act like he had something against somebody, like an evil spirit to him," Wingate later recalled to a newspaper reporter.

One night before Linda moved out of the Briarcliff, she invited her brother over for a spaghetti dinner with her and her boyfriend. If Wingate had needed any confirmation for his bad feelings about Rogers, Wingate said the Ohio drifter provided it that night. Rogers wanted Linda to put pornographic videotapes in the VCR, Wingate later reported, but she refused because her brother's five-year-old son was present. But her boyfriend didn't want to take "no" for an answer, and kept pestering her to turn on the dirty movies. He used blunt, ugly language to describe just exactly what it was he wanted to see.

Linda's brother saw a bit of the real Glen Rogers that night, and even though it was the barest possible glimpse and didn't come close to touching on his full capacity for evil, it was enough to make Wingate even more uneasy than ever. He talked to his sister, cautioning her that she didn't know Rogers all that well. There was something about the man that wasn't right, Wingate warned. But Linda shook off her brother's reservations. She had found the man she wanted, and she was convinced he wouldn't hurt her.

"She was lonely," Linda's mother later told a *Clarion-Ledger* reporter about her daughter. "She was searching for love that she never had, that she needed to find somewhere in this world."

Rogers wasn't totally settled down. After getting his pickup truck back, he left town at least once, while Linda stayed in Jackson clerking, cleaning houses, fussing with the apartment, and sharing confidences with family and friends about life with her new boyfriend and her plans for the future. Rogers retraced some of his earlier travels from his days with the carnivals, driving almost straight west, past Vicksburg, and into northern Louisiana. Following the broad highway past old-time cotton plantations and a patchwork of small dirt farms, he moved into the Pelican State's Thoroughbred country, and on to Bossier City a few minutes' drive from the Texas border. The Louisiana State Fair was underway at the fairgrounds in its sister city, Shreveport.

In some ways, Bossier City has a lot in common with Hamilton. Like the two sides of the Ohio town, Bossier City and Shreveport are twin communities separated by a river. On the southwest side of the Red River, Shreveport, the larger of the two Louisiana cities, is a busy center of commerce and culture. The Shreveport Opera, Shreveport Symphony Orchestra, R. W. Norton Art Gallery, and the Strand Theatre are famous landmarks and sources of great civic pride. Generations of country music fans grew up listening to "The Louisiana Hayride" broadcast weekly across much of the country by the powerful radio signals of studios located in Shreveport. The late Hank Williams and Elvis Presley were two of the more famous performers who appeared on the show.

Like the rowdy east side of Hamilton, the community in Bossier Parish on the northeast side of the Red River is better known for its wild and woolly ways and low-class amusements than for its sophistication and cultural amenities. When stories are recounted about famous sons, they are likely to focus on rascals such as John A. Murrell, one of America's first and most ruthlessly prolific serial killers, and train and bank robber Jesse James. Both men once roamed both sides of the Red River. Born into relative privilege during the late eighteenth century, Murrell was a Tennessee plantation owner who began his criminal career stealing slaves. He then progressed to the robbery and wholesale butchery of travelers stalked along the Natchez Trace and farther west in Louisiana. His favorite means of getting rid of bodies was to slit open stomachs, fill them with rocks, and submerge them in rivers, lakes, or swamps. No one knows

A nationwide manhunt nears a dramatic conclusion as fugitive Glen Rogers speeds through a state police roadblock in the tiny mountain hamlet of Waco, Kentucky, in a battered white Ford Festiva. Minutes later the stolen car driven by the suspected serial killer was forced off the road and he was captured. *(AP/Wide World Photos)*

A Kentucky State Police officer inspects a damaged police cruiser that forced Rogers off a winding mountain road near Waco, Kentucky, during a high-speed chase. The white Ford Festiva that Rogers was driving is in the background. *(AP/Wide World Photos)*

Kentucky State Police Detective Bob Stephens puts Glen Rogers into a police cruiser after the shaggy-haired fugitive was arrested. Rogers was suspected of leaving a trail of bodies of redheaded women behind him in four states during a bloody six-week orgy of violence. *(AP/Wide World Photos)*

Kentucky State Police Detective Nolan R. "Skip" Benton talks to reporters at the KSP Post in Richmond about Glen Rogers, shortly after the capture of the suspected "Cross Country Killer." Police travelled to the KSP Post and to the nearby Madison County Detention Center from several states in hopes of questioning the suspect and to compare evidence. *(AP/Wide World Photos)*

Rein Keener may have narrowly escaped with her life after changing her mind at the last moment as she was leaving McRed's Lounge in Van Nuys, California, with Glen Rogers. Rein stayed behind to play darts with friends and another woman died horribly that night after offering Rogers a ride from the bar to his nearby apartment. *(AP/Wide World Photos)*

Reputed "Casanova Killer" Glen Rogers is charged or convicted in the murders of four women, including Sandra Gallagher of Van Nuys, California *(pictured)*, and has been investigated in the mysterious death of a retired man who befriended him. *(AP/Wide World Photos)*

During a court hearing in Tampa, Florida, reputed serial killer Glen Rogers glares at Public Defender Joan Corces. *(AP/Wide World Photos)*

Madison District Judge William G. Clouse addresses the court before talking on closed-circuit TV with Rogers, who was being held at the adjacent Madison County Detention Center in Richmond, Kentucky. *(AP/Wide World Photos)*

FBI Agent Joe Errera points out blood spots on a pair of dungaree shorts to jurors during Glen Rogers's first-degree murder trial in Tampa. The bloody shorts were taken from Rogers after his capture in Kentucky. *(AP/Wide World Photos)*

Glen Rogers sits with his attorney, Nick Sinardi *(left)*, during jury selection in his murder trial at the Hillsborough County Courthouse in Tampa, Florida for the slaying of Tina Marie Cribbs. *(AP/Wide World Photos)*

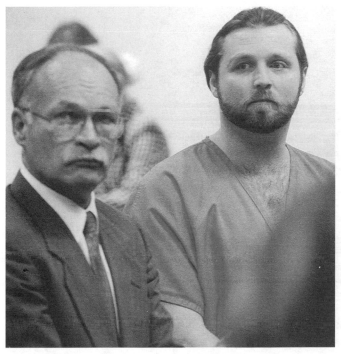

Rogers stands next to his attorney, Bob Fraser, during a pretrial hearing in Tampa, Florida. *(AP/Wide World Photos)*

Glen Rogers's mother, Edna Rogers, during her son's trial for first-degree murder. *(AP/Wide World Photos)*

the exact number of his victims, but he may have murdered as many as 500 people, and some of them were dumped in the Red River.

More recently, Danny Rolling and Henry Lee Lucas left the bloody imprints of their passage on the twin city area. Rolling was a stickup man and the ne'er-do-well son of a Shreveport police lieutenant who drifted to Gainesville, Florida, and butchered five college students in a series of particularly ghoulish attacks in 1990. After his conviction in Florida, where he is on death row, authorities in Shreveport quietly closed the case on the 1989 slash-and-stab murders of a Southern Hills man, his daughter, and grandson.

Lucas made headlines in the 1980s when he was arrested in Texas and confessed to hundreds of killings during a decade-long cross-country murder orgy. He has been charged with, or is a prime suspect in, eighteen Louisiana murders, and a Bossier Parish grand jury indicted him in two slayings. Although he eventually retracted his confessions, he was convicted of a Texas murder and is on death row in the state prison at Huntsville.

Of the two sister cities, it is Bossier City with its history of cathouses, gambling dens, rotgut booze, riverboat toughs, strong-arm robbers, and assorted desperados that has held onto a reputation as a playground for the rough-and-tumble set over the years. In recent times, the bars and easy women in the seedier areas have drawn airmen from the sprawling Barkesdale Air Force Base at the edge of the free-wheeling river town who drink, play, and occasionally mix in dust-ups with homegrown roughnecks.

But the old heady violence and easy communion with ways of the flesh have been muted today and airmen and others who are so inclined can drink in relative safety, if they behave themselves. They can do their gambling at the nearby Louisiana Downs Racetrack on East Texas Road. Bossier City even has its own smaller, less-heralded version of the "Hayride." Once-a-month the "Ark-La-Tex Roundup" is broadcast from the KWKH studios there, featuring performers from a three-state area.

Nevertheless, Bossier City was still Rogers's kind of town. The engine on his pickup truck had barely started to cool after the long drive from Jackson before he was oiling his parched throat inside the twilight darkness of some of the bars in a rough section of town known to police and other locals as "Podunk." It wasn't an area generally frequented by the carriage trade.

Rogers swapped some tall tales with a few barflies, shot some pool, and danced with some women. One of his dance partners was Andy Lou Sutton, a good-looking strawberry blonde with a sunny personality and a taste for Miller Lite. The couple met at the Touch of Class lounge on U.S. 80, the same highway he lived alongside of when he was staying with Linda at the Tarrymore Motel. But the Touch of Class was 220 miles almost due west of the Tarrymore, a few minutes' drive across the Red River from the Louisiana State Fairgrounds. Andy was a local girl, a southern beauty who grew up in Bossier City, graduated from Airline High School, and had a Louisiana drawl that was as alluring and sweet as the odor of magnolias in full bloom. Rogers was impressed, but he didn't stick around.

A short time after arriving in the river town he climbed into his Datsun and began the long haul past the Spanish moss–covered cypresses, the myrtles, maples, and ash of Louisiana, all the way back to Jackson and the comfortably warm apartment he shared with Linda. Only Rogers knows the reason for his rapid return: if he was sincerely fond of his new roommate, or if some other motivation drew him back. According to police, whatever the reason for the decision may have been, his return would ultimately cost Linda her life.

The idyllic relationship Linda's mother later recalled as making her daughter happier in one month than she ever was before in her life, began to fray around the edges. One night they were bending their elbows at a local taproom with one of Linda's relatives when the lovebirds got into an argument and her new boyfriend whacked her around. A couple of days later a childhood friend ran into her while they were grocery shopping, and Linda told her she had moved into an apartment with a handsome man. But Linda was nervous and didn't prolong the chitchat. She explained she had to get back to the apartment and cook supper before her boyfriend returned home "and kicks my ass."

Linda had the fearful, nervous look of a woman who was spooked and had the self-confidence and vitality sucked out of her. It was often a condition that went with the territory when a woman became Glen Rogers's girlfriend or wife. All it took was a few Buds or a couple of shots of Jack Daniel's, and the easy graciousness and country charm that attracted them to him was replaced with sudden bursts of rage and brutality. Many of his relationships with girlfriends and wives were poisoned by violence. He browbeat women, slammed them with his fists, kicked them with his cowboy-booted feet, and kept them in a state of fear. Living with Rogers could be like spending the rest of your life with a bad hangover that wouldn't go away.

On Monday night, October 30, Linda and her sister,

Marilyn Reel, were out with Rogers when the women went to the restroom. Linda confided to Marilyn that she was afraid of her new boyfriend. There was a lot that needed to be told about him, but she couldn't go into it in detail at that time, she said. Linda had less than one week to live.

Linda had missed work, and wasn't making her regular telephone calls to her mother to talk about the new boyfriend who was making such a big difference in her life. Despite the reservations that had begun to creep into her reveries, sparkles still danced in her eyes like diamonds when she talked about him. And she talked about him every time she called her mother. He was her favorite topic of conversation.

Mrs. Wingate began worrying about her daughter when the telephone calls and conversations suddenly stopped. Linda didn't call for a couple of days, and when the concerned mother tried to reach her no one answered the phone. On Friday evening, November 3, Jackson police officers knocked on the door of the silent apartment. After repeated efforts to rouse someone, the officers directed a maintenance man to unlock the door. Then they walked inside, cautiously calling out their presence while moving slowly past the potted plants, family pictures, and mementos placed so lovingly on shelves and walls.

Linda was in the bathroom. The naked body of the generous, trusting woman was stretched out facedown in the tub, with four ragged slashes in her back and chest, and her throat slit. There was no sign of her purse or of her handsome boyfriend. The tub was not filled with water, but it appeared the shower had been turned on so the killer could wash the body. The woman's face was lying on a soggy washcloth.

Despite the ferocity of the attack and the terrible damage inflicted on the body from the deep, broad slashes, there was very little visible blood at the crime scene. The apartment the woman decorated and fussed over so lovingly had been given a quick scrubdown, apparently by the killer. Before or after tidying up, he left a cryptic message scrawled with lipstick on the bathroom mirror. It read: "Glen, we found you."

There was no sign of the murder weapon, but Mrs. Wingate provided investigators with a good lead to help identify the exact type of heavy, sharp instrument that was used to butcher her daughter. A machete once owned by the victim's father was missing from the apartment.

The time of death still had to be determined by the Hinds County Coroner after an autopsy, including examination of her stomach contents, tissue decomposition, and other clues that would be given up by the corpse. Old-fashioned police footwork, including interviews with neighbors and family members and friends of the victim would also be used to narrow down the time window.

Mrs. Wingate and neighbors of the former couple told police the boyfriend who was missing, along with the machete, the purse, and a small amount of jewelry, was Glen Rogers. The Jackson Police tapped his name and birth date into NCIC computers in Washington, and turned up the warrants issued in Van Nuys.

The same day the gruesome discovery was made at the apartment in Jackson, Rogers was miles away in Louisiana saying a temporary good-bye to Andy Lou Sutton, the strawberry blonde he met during his earlier stopover in Bossier City.

The high-spirited woman with the taste for Wrangler

jeans, cowboy boots, and country and western music may have had a name that is generally associated with males, but there was nothing masculine about her. She was completely and softly feminine. Andy was also a party girl, who loved to drink, dance, and kick up her heels with her friends. Sometimes she drank too much, and she was arrested once for driving with a blood alcohol level that was a whopping .216 percent. She didn't bother to renew her driver's license when it expired.

Andy was born in 1957, and even as the mother of four children ranging in age from nine to nineteen, at five-foot-six-inches tall and a trim 120 pounds she had a showgirl's shape. The thirty-seven-year-old woman lost custody of her minor children during a recent divorce, but was looking around for a job and had her heart set on getting her two youngest back.

Andy had just broken up with a boyfriend in October after keeping up an off-and-on relationship for about a year and a half. They developed a pattern soon after beginning to keep company with each other. They would get together for a while, then tangle over something or other, and one of them would move on. A few days or a few weeks later they would be lovey-dovey again. This time, Andy insisted to friends, the breakup was permanent. The old love affair was finally over, and the spunky strawberry blonde was footloose and fancy-free. There was room for a new man in her life.

Rogers spent a night with her at the Port Au Prince Apartments at 400 Preston Place, where she had moved in with a friend, Teresa Whitehead. But he was jumpy and had itchy feet, so the next day the two women drove him to the bus station, where he boarded a Greyhound cruiser headed for Tampa, Florida.

In Jackson, Mrs. Wingate was grieving for her daughter when she answered the telephone and a man identifying himself as Glen Rogers's brother said he had a message for her.

"My brother's momma and daddy are in the Mafia and anybody that has been connected with him the last two years is dead. I'm not surprised your daughter is dead, but he didn't kill her." Mrs. Wingate had never talked before with the brother of her daughter's boyfriend, but the voice on the telephone sounded an awful lot like Glen Rogers himself.

The claims that Rogers's family had Mafia ties were characteristic of his behavior. References to being "connected" or of actually being a Mafia wiseguy were among his favorite barroom boasts, even though it was probably difficult for even the most gullible barflies to believe. He didn't fit the ethnic image. And Mafia wiseguys and button men weren't known for moonlighting as cabbies and carnival roustabouts, or for hanging around country music bars trying to impress barmaids with their big talk about being mobsters.

If the mystery voice was indeed Rogers's, the call apparently represented one more clumsy attempt, like the lipstick message on the bathroom mirror, to deflect suspicion from himself as Linda's killer. But the ruse was amateurish, shallow, and unconvincing. It failed to deflect suspicion from him, and rubbed salt in the emotional wounds of Linda's family. It cruelly dredged up the personal pain and horror.

At about 11 o'clock Saturday morning Rogers stepped out of a taxi cab and walked out of the midday Florida sunshine into the cooling false dusk of the Showtown USA cocktail lounge in Gibsonton. The Showtown is a local landmark, and carnies eat there, drink there, and hook up with jobs by checking out listings on bulletin boards there. Like lots of other Gibsonton taprooms and clubs, it was busy. Business always picked up during the winter months when carnies were in town sitting out the bad weather up north and waiting for the new season to start.

The short ride in the back of the taxi was like sitting in an oven, and coupled with the walk of a few steps through the blistering Florida midday sunshine from the cab to the door of the tavern had left a shine of sweat on his forehead and temples. When he slid onto a bar-stool, he ordered a cola, heavy on the ice. The drifter balanced on the same barstool throughout the afternoon, switching his drinks to draft beer. He exchanged some idle chitchat with bartender Lynn Jones, and joked and kidded with other drinkers, keeping the conversation light and friendly. When a group of women walked in at about 2 P.M., and sat down at a nearby table, he sent over a round of drinks. When the first round was gone, he sent more. He also ambled over to the jukebox, turned, and asked the ladies what tunes they would like to hear, then shoved in a stack of quarters.

The bearded backwoods Beau Brummel with the shoulder-length hair was neatly dressed in a pair of crisp shorts with a tucked-in collared shirt, carefully arranged to obscure the gentle bulge that was providing the first hints of someday turning into a full-fledged beer belly. At the moment it served to show off the handsome, heavy metal buckle on the leather belt that circled his waist. He looked like a construction worker.

The six women at the table were friends and cowork-ers who were on the housekeeping staff at the Ramada Inn in nearby Apollo Beach. The motel was full and they had spent an exhausting day making beds and cleaning toilets and tubs before stopping in at the Showtime to relax. Thirty-seven-year-old Ruth Ann Negrete later explained to a newspaper reporter that they didn't plan any serious drinking. "We had no intentions of getting plastered," she was quoted in the *Los Angeles Times* as saying. "We just wanted to have a drink."

The generous stranger acted like his pants pockets were stuffed with hundred-dollar bills, and flashed a few of them around when he was ordering drinks. He was as smooth as fresh cream when he introduced himself to the women, and whirled them one at a time out onto the dance floor while country tunes blasted nonstop from the jukebox. He started off introducing himself as "Brandon," but after awhile began using a different name, "Randy." That should have set off a few warning bells, but no one seemed to mind. He was generous, charming, and a good dancer. Entertaining company on a hot Sunday afternoon.

"Brandon" or "Randy" went around the table asking each of the women if they had husbands or boyfriends. He finally settled on thirty-four-year-old Tina Marie Cribbs, and began focusing the lion's share of his attention on her. Tina was on the plump side, wore glasses, had a missing upper front tooth, and at the time was romantically unencumbered. However, she may have seemed especially appealing to the curious stranger because of the dark hair that she wore short with an auburn tint.

There was also an air of vulnerability about her that would be instantly recognizable to an experienced predator like Rogers. She had the look of a woman who was as defenseless and ripe for plucking as a bird with a broken wing. Mrs. Cribbs was basically a beer drinker, but she was tired and the tips from the tourists that day were good, so she knocked back a couple of shots of whiskey. It was an indulgence she seldom permitted herself.

She was going through a difficult period of her life. She had just busted up with a longtime boyfriend, and was living with her twelve-year-old son, Damien Vandemark, in the Alafia Mobile Plaza, a trailer park a few miles down the road on Gibsonton's south side. Her mother, Mary Dicke, lived a few doors away in a mobile home in the same park. Tina supported herself and her son with her work at the Ramada, as well as two more full-time jobs as a short-order cook at the Tropical Restaurant and as a cook and waitress at a Steak 'N Shake. She was buying her own trailer and trying to catch up on a pile of debts.

Her first full-time job after moving to Florida was as a cook at Sue's Country Kitchen in Gibsonton. She also took care of the books and taxes for the owner and built up a reputation as a trustworthy, hardworking employee during three years with the restaurant before finally quitting in October. She completed a college course in computer science, and was willing to work at about any kind of job necessary to support herself and the boy.

By necessity and by choice, she was a woman who filled her life with work and with other activities. She attended St. Anne's Catholic Church in the hamlet of Ruskin on Tampa Bay, and was an active member of the Riverview Women of the Moose Lodge 1031; American Legion Alafia Post Number 148; and of the Veterans of Foreign Wars Post Number 6287. When she had an opportunity she enjoyed sitting down at a piano and picking out a few sentimental tunes, or working the business end of a guitar and doing some picking and singing. She taught herself to play both instruments.

Despite troubles with men and marriage and a host of

other disappointments in her life, she managed to remain upbeat most of the time, and had a reputation for going out of her way to help others. She was a good-hearted soul whose standard greeting to men or to women was, "Hello, Darlin'." When she smiled, unlike most people with a missing front tooth, she didn't pull her lips protectively over her teeth to produce a thin, cautious grin. She greeted friends and strangers with a ten-gallon smile that spread all over her face. Even her eyes smiled, beaming out warmth, friendliness, and trust at everyone around her. Considering her setbacks and defeats, Tina was amazingly open and ingenuous. With one glaring exception, she shared some important life experiences with Linda Price. She hadn't had much luck with men.

Ray Cole, Jr., a longtime live-in boyfriend who fathered a son with her before the couple split up in the middle of the 1980s, was an exception. After ten years apart, they were still friends who could count on each other. Their fourteen-year-old boy, Raymond, lived with his father in Oklahoma City and in Cortland, New York.

After breaking up with Cole, Tina was never able to keep a relationship with a man on track for more than a few years at the very best, and some of her romances were hardly more than a few days old before they began turning into appalling ordeals of emotional and physical abuse. A boyfriend in Oklahoma City turned so mean and violent that she and her sons wound up living in her car.

Tina had put on some hard mileage, but she was still on the sunny side of middle age and there was plenty of time for romance in her life if she could ever manage to find her "Mr. Right." In the meantime, she worked, fussed over her boys, kept busy with her church and her clubs, played music, and read historical romance novels by the stack. The heroines in the novels weren't beat up or abused by their boyfriends and husbands, and even if there were hints that was about to happen she could toss the paperback aside and replace it with another that had a happier theme.

It may have been the tough times Tina endured, but something convinced her that she would never live to see her thirty-fifth birthday. Sometimes she talked to the people who were close to her, including her mother, about the eerie presentiment of an early death. The dismal foreboding was so uncharacteristic of Tina, and she seemed to be so certain of its validity, that it frightened the older woman. So on August 30, 1995, Mrs. Dicke threw a birthday party for the fretful daughter she called by the pet nickname "Girl." The festivities were at the Showtown USA.

Girl spent her childhood growing up with three siblings in Cortland, but as an adult she moved around the country for a while and she made friends easily. She was so good-hearted that she would use her last gallon of gas to give a lift to someone in need. So it wasn't surprising when she agreed to a polite request from the handsome stranger for a ride back to his motel to pick up his car. Tina was expecting to meet her mother at the bar in a few minutes so they could share a drink then leave together for a family barbecue. But she lived by the elevating motto that if you did good to others, good would come back to you. She had time to do a favor.

Sipping the last of her drink, she pushed back her chair, stood up from the table, slung the straps of her patchwork-style fabric purse over her shoulder, and walked outside with the handsome stranger just before Mrs. Dicke arrived at the country and western bar. Mrs. Dicke was a few minutes late for their meeting, and Tina left word for her to wait. "Tell my mom I'll be right back," she told the bartender, as she left to drop off the stranger at his motel about ten miles away in East Tampa. On a lazy, late sun-splashed Florida afternoon with no rush-hour traffic to deal with, it was a thirty-minute round-trip drive, forty-five minutes at the most.

Rogers courteously helped Girl into the driver's seat of her white 1993 Ford Festiva, then walked around the car, past the broken right front headlight, and slid in beside her. It was about 3:45 P.M. when Tina Marie Cribbs guided her battered compact away from the Showtown while the courteous stranger sat beside her peering past the stuffed dinosaur and hippopotamus figures on top of the dashboard toward the highway in front of them. She would never see another sunrise.

Mrs. Dicke waited at the bar, at first enjoying the company of her daughter's friends, then becoming increasingly apprehensive and fretful as time passed. Every time the front door opened and someone walked into the barroom gloom she turned and looked, squinting her eyes against the sudden blast of sunlight, hopeful Girl would be hurrying toward the table full of apologies and excuses for being so tardy. Girl never showed up, and her friends eventually drifted uneasily out of the saloon to drive to their homes and waiting families.

At last, the worried mother contacted the Hillsborough County Sheriff's Department to report her daughter missing. But it was too early to file a missing persons report. Girl was an adult, she hadn't been gone long enough, and there was no evidence of forcible abduction or any other suspicious circumstance that might meet the criteria for launching an immediate missing persons investigation. She had merely driven away with a handsome man she met in a bar. People do that every day.

Rogers had checked into Room 119 at the Tampa 8 Inn on East Columbus Drive earlier Saturday after arriving in the bay area, and paid for three nights. He didn't have a speck of luggage with him, and he claimed to be a trucker. About nine o'clock Monday morning, a motel employee noticed the strapping big man with the shoulder-length blond hair driving away in a little white Ford with tinted windows and a thin blue-and-red stripe on the driver's-side door. No one cleaned or changed the linen in Room 119 that day. A makeshift hand-scribbled "Do Not Disturb" sign was hanging from the outside doorknob.

It was about 10:30 Tuesday morning when a housemaid finally let herself into the quiet, darkened motel room to clean. It was a routine Tina Marie had gone through hundreds of times herself in another motel. But when the maid at the Tampa 8 walked into the bathroom to clean up and collect soiled towels, she was confronted with the naked body of a heavyset woman slumped face-down in the bathtub.

The woman was dead. There was no water in the tub, but her pasty-gray flesh was clammy and cold. The body was mutilated with ghastly stab wounds and deep, ugly slashes that appeared as if they might have been inflicted with a big butcher knife, or something even heavier.

When homicide detectives arrived at the brightly painted pink and green motel near the Fiftieth Street exit of Interstate 4, they secured Room 119 and roped off the parking lot. Before the body was lifted from the tub and transported to the morgue at the Hillsborough County Coroner's Office, detectives were already turning to the task of identifying the victim. There were indications that the shower was turned on and the body was washed before the water was allowed to drain from the tub. Investigators didn't have much to work with at the scene.

Based on their observations, and later determinations of Hillsborough County Coroner's pathologists, the victim was five-foot-six-inches tall, weighed 170 pounds, and was about thirty-five to forty years old. She was missing an upper front tooth, and had a tattoo of a cross on her left shoulder. Following the autopsy, the pathologist estimated the woman had been dead about thirty-six hours before her body was found.

When the blond man paid for the room the previous Saturday, he indicated he would be the only occupant. The dead woman's name was not on the motel register, and no identification was found in the room to indicate who she was. But the man who rented Room 119 signed the motel register as "Glen Edward Rogers." Detectives talked with one of the clerks who remembered the guest because he asked for a "Do Not Disturb" sign, and when he was advised there weren't any available, he made one of his own and hung it on the front door of his room.

When Mrs. Cribbs's dead body was discovered in the motel room, Rogers was already behind the wheel of her little hatchback, driving north to Tallahassee, then west across the southern tip of Mississippi, and through Alabama on his way back to Louisiana. According to later police statements, he placed a long-distance call from Louisiana to a family member in Hamilton and made the chilling boast that the body count was going to grow.

He was in Louisiana the evening that television stations in the Tampa Bay area were reporting on local newscasts that the body of an unidentified woman was found stabbed to death in the Tampa 8 Inn. As soon as she heard the description of the victim, Mrs. Dicke knew she would never see her daughter alive again. The shaken mother contacted the Tampa Police and identified the mystery woman with the tattoo of a cross on her shoulder, missing upper front tooth, and auburn hair. It was Girl. Mrs. Dicke had been widowed about a year earlier, and since then had grown especially close to her daughter. Now both her husband and Girl were gone.

Police still had a lot of questions to be answered, but based on information gathered during the early stages of the investigation, they theorized that the suspect may have pulled a gun 'or a knife on his Good Samaritan chauffeur while they were in the car, then forced her into the motel room. But of the only two people who really knew for sure, one was dead and the other was missing and presumably on the run.

Just as police in Jackson did after tying Rogers to Linda Price's grisly slaying, when Tampa homicide detective Randy S. Bell typed the suspect's name into the NCIC computer he came up with the murder warrant in California. Glen Rogers is a relatively common name, and Bell also collected several combinations of matching or near-matching first, middle, and last names. The entry for the Glen Edward Rogers he finally settled on was accompanied by a couple of aliases—Glen Roger, with no "s" at the end of the name, and James Edward Peters.

The Florida detective also obtained a photo of the Los Angeles Police Department's wanted flyer on the suspect from the Associated Press in California, and copies of affidavits and other documents filed by authorities there as part of the request for their murder warrant. The California documents listed the wrong Social Security number, and a birthdate of July 15, 1960 that was two years before Rogers's real date of birth.

When a Tampa detective dialed investigators in Van Nuys, the California officers were already talking by telephone with Chuck Lee at the Jackson Police Department. As the detectives from three states swapped information back and forth, the similarities in the murders and events leading up to the latest slaying were obvious. They realized they were almost certainly looking for the same man.

The day after Girl's body was identified by her mother, police carried a copy of the AP photo into the Showtime and asked Lynn Jones if she recognized it. She said it was the same man who sat at a table in the corner of the bar Sunday afternoon, drinking and flirting with the women from the Ramada. It was the man she saw leaving the bar with Tina Marie Cribbs. Bell also carried the copy of the flyer he obtained from California to the Tampa 8 Motel to check out the suspect's picture with two women employees there. Before showing the photo to them, he carefully folded back areas of the flyer that identified Rogers by name and gave other pertinent information about why he was being sought to hide it from their view.

Some of the same rules that govern conduct of police lineups also apply to situations like Bell was facing, and investigators aren't allowed to give hints or help potential witnesses make identifications. Straying over the line even slightly could have disastrous repercussions after a case moves into the courtroom. Under ideal conditions, police would be able to use at least two different photographs of a subject without the potential contamination of extraneous information being included. But Bell didn't have any other pictures of the suspect at that time, so he did the best job he could with the material on hand. The women looked at the photo and said it was the man they saw at the motel.

By the time the women at the motel viewed the picture and Lynn Jones identified it as the man with Girl when she rode off to become a murder statistic, Rogers was back at his old tricks. He was living it up in a busy Bossier City honky-tonk, named the It'll Do. As usual, the free-spending drifter seemed to have plenty of money. Mrs. Cribbs had nearly $300 in her patchwork purse, and was wearing a gold watch and three rings with a variety of precious and semiprecious stones in them when she was murdered. The money, the purse, and the jewelry were all missing when her body was discovered in the motel room.

The purse was ultimately found discarded in a trash container at a highway rest stop along Interstate 10 in Tallahassee. The fastest interstate route from Tampa to Louisiana would take a driver north on I-75 to I-10, then west across the Florida Panhandle through the state capital.

Outside the It'll Do, Rogers was the object of a rapidly expanding manhunt. He was already wanted on a federal warrant issued after Sandra Gallagher was killed in Van Nuys, and a murder warrant was sworn out for him by police in Jackson. Police in Tampa were picking up his trail, and authorities in Ohio and Kentucky were suddenly showing renewed interest in Mark Peters's apparent murder. But law officers who were working together on the cross-country search for the fugitive didn't know yet that he was in Louisiana. He was moving so fast, and seemingly so erratically, he could be almost anywhere.

Disappointingly, although local media in states where Rogers was believed to have struck were getting the message out, huge areas of the country were unaware that a spree killer was on the loose. Neither ABC, CBS, nor NBC television had broadcast a word on their nightly national network newscasts about the rampage of the man who was suspected of being responsible for the so-called redhead murders. The pages of major daily newspapers with national circulation, including *USA Today*, were devoid of stories about the slayings. At least three women were dead, apparently at the hands of the same killer, and the suspect was on the loose and moving fast. The murders were committed hundreds of miles from each other, and there was no telling where the next victim would be lured to her death. The FBI and other investigators were desperately looking for a pattern to provide clues to his whereabouts or where he might strike next. They also needed help from the media in spreading the word, informing the public of his suspected crimes, of his description, and broadcasting and printing copies of his mug shots.

The tabloid press, both electronically and in print, along with local media in areas where murders occurred, stepped into the void and were taking the lead in alerting the public to the danger. A WorldWide Web home page called "Internet Crime Archives Digital Home of the Mass Murdering Serial Killer" also added Rogers's name and his perceived body count to its listing. But the home page was not likely to be widely read by the people who were most vulnerable. Cyberspace was too exotic and of dubious popularity among the people who hung out in the saloons and carnivals Rogers was attracted to.

Large numbers of Americans had never heard of Glen Rogers, or the nickname he was acquiring as "the Cross Country Killer," and that was a troubling matter to deal with for some of the law officers who were looking for him. If it was true, as they suspected, that at least three women died at his hands in less than six weeks, there was every reason to believe that if he wasn't run down and stopped immediately the grisly death toll would continue to rise.

America's Most Wanted, the popular Fox television anti-crime series hosted by John Walsh, began researching a segment on the suspected serial killer. Since first airing in 1988, tips called into the show's toll-free hot line and to police agencies as the result of the program had already led to the apprehension of more than 400 fugitives. Ten of them were on the FBI's famous "Ten Most Wanted" list. Local police in Los Angeles, Jackson, and Tampa circulated photos of the suspect and flyers with his picture and other information to fellow law enforcement agencies and to the press. His picture and description began increasingly appearing in newspapers and on television shows across the country, but the reports were most heavily concentrated in California, Ohio, and in the southern states.

In Van Nuys, Rein Keener couldn't escape the awful rush of stories that continued to resurrect unwanted memories of her chilling brush with destiny. Every time she watched and listened to the tearful or choked-up statements of a father, mother, brother, or sister talking about one of the dead women the barroom hustler was believed to have killed she thought of her own family. It could have been their faces on the screen, talking about her.

Homicide Detective Sergeant George McNamara of the Tampa Police Department told reporters that authorities were doing everything possible to notify the public about the murder suspect's past, his violence, and the methods he used to meet women. "He is a violent, killing individual. We need to get him off the street before he kills again," the experienced investigator told the Los Angeles area's *Daily News.*

Aware of Rogers's background as a roustabout and occasional grab-joint food peddler when he wasn't setting up or dismantling rides, police put carnivals and fairs high on their list of locations to look for him. Eight different carnivals were working the Tampa Bay area when Tina Marie was killed, and within the first twenty-four hours after Rogers's photo and description were released to the press, nineteen people reported spotting him at one place or another. None of the tips bore fruit.

No one inside the It'll Do who may have observed him enjoying himself and having a good time could have had any idea that he was in so much trouble. When he boasted to a waitress that he served time in prison for murder, she blew it off as bar talk from a guy who was looking for attention. She figured correctly, but there was more than a kernel of truth to what he was saying. It was true he was an ex-convict, and although he wasn't imprisoned for murder, he was a hunted man who was a suspected multiple killer. Presumably, a man in his position would be under terrific emotional pressure, but he was behaving as if he didn't have a care in the world, drinking, shooting pool, and dancing.

About the only obvious sign of emotional distress was the beginning of a rash on his hands. The disorder tended to pop up, often accompanied by a nasty gut ache, when he was in trouble or under serious pressure. But it wasn't something that strangers were likely to notice.

He did most of his dancing with Andy, and when they weren't snuggled up against each other on the dance floor or lining up bank shots and combinations at the pool table, he was showering her with sweet talk while she sat at the bar, smiled and sipped her Miller Lite through a straw. It was her favorite drink, and the straw was one of those little touches that was classic Andy. Along with her good looks and foxy personality, the idiosyncrasy helped set her apart from some of her friends.

Bartender JoAnne Allen felt good for the vivacious redhead. Andy wasn't a woman known for taking up with strangers, but her companion was so good-looking and charming that he was hard to resist. Ms. Allen later told a news reporter that she remembered thinking, "Wow, she found someone nice." Andy was well known in Podunk bars. She was not only a good customer, but her primary profession was barmaid. It was a job she was good at, and she was hoping to get hired at one of the saloons so she could go to work and get back on her feet financially. Andy was smart, quick with a joke, and even faster with a smile. If she couldn't get people to feel good and smile back, she figured she wasn't doing her job. Everyone who knew her, it seemed, liked her.

She was good-hearted and so trusting that even if someone had a thick wad of money secretly tucked in the pocket of their blue jeans and told her they were broke, she would take their word for it and buy them a drink. The popular barmaid with the sunny disposition quit her latest job early in October because she didn't like working nights. Basically, however, she merely moved to the other side of the bar. Podunk watering holes still provided her primary source of recreation. It was where her friends were.

The night was still young when the lovebirds left the

It'll Do, and moved on to another bar in the lively military town. A Touch of Class was a busy honky-tonk where thirsty off-duty airmen from the nearby Barkesdale Air Force Base with a taste for cold beer and country music occasionally mingled with local civilians. It's a redneck bar in a rough section of Podunk known as The Strip, according to local police who patrol the area, doing their best to keep bruised heads and broken beer bottles to a minimum and the body count down. Andy was a regular there and stopped in about every day or night. It was one of her three favorite saloons, along with the It'll Do, and Mr. Bill's, all of them in Podunk.

But the couple's mood changed at the new watering hole. Andy was seated on a stool at the end of the bar with a fresh Miller and a straw in front of her, while Rogers stood alongside her when they started to argue. Bartender Vicki Henry noticed what was going on, but the spat didn't seem to be anything serious. It wasn't the sort of disagreement that was flaring into loud threats or active violence. It was all verbal, and Andy was a grown-up who knew how to take care of herself. She was a scrappy little woman, and with her dander up and the neon lights behind the bar highlighting the rich orange and yellow hues in her hair, she looked as hot and spicy as Cajun cooking.

Whatever the couple's differences were, the trouble was apparently patched up, at least temporarily, because they wound up together later that afternoon in the one-bedroom apartment at the Port Au Prince. Rogers was loaded, and lurched inside to sleep off the drunk. The apartment was upstairs, over a Mormon church.

When Andy's twenty-nine-year-old roommate returned home late Wednesday night the bedroom door was closed. She figured Andy was inside and didn't want to be disturbed, so she settled down on the couch for the rest of the night. The next morning when she woke up, the door was still closed, and inside the bedroom it was as quiet as death.

It was still early when Andy's former boyfriend showed up, looking for her. It was too quiet inside the bedroom, and Teresa was concerned about her friend. The man and the woman tapped on the door, then opened it and peered inside.

Andy's naked body was wrapped in a pile of bloody blankets and sheets, and sprawled on top of the water-bed. She had been repeatedly stabbed with a big knife or some other sharp, heavy object in an attack so savage that deep slashes ripped through the bed's thick plastic bladder, and the floor was awash in water.

Alerted to the horrific discovery, the Bossier City Police converged on the apartment and secured it as a crime scene. Photographs were taken from various angles of the woman on the bed; doorknobs, drinking glasses, and other common objects the killer may have touched were dusted for latent fingerprints; and at last the corpse was released to the parish coroner, loaded onto a gurney, covered with a sheet, and wheeled outside to a waiting ambulance for the trip to the morgue.

Police and pathologists eventually determined that Andy's left chest and upper abdomen were ripped with three ragged stab wounds. A knife or similar object was plunged six more times into her left upper back. The body of the once-beautiful woman looked like it had been worked on by Jack the Ripper.

Although the time of death was still to be determined more exactly, the chilling possibility hung heavily in the air that the killer may have carried out his foul work inside the bedroom, then padded quietly through the darkened apartment past the sleeping woman on the couch and out the front door. The shaken roommate later described a few objects, including her purse and her Power Rangers pillow and Little Mermaid blanket, that were missing from the apartment.

Homicide investigators quickly focused on Rogers as a strong suspect in the slayings. The burnt-orange pickup truck, registered in his name, was parked in front of the apartment. The Hinds County, Mississippi, license plates had been removed, and police speculated he may have switched them to the Festiva. Once again police tapped into NCIC computers, and matched the information from the vehicle registration with that of the Ohio drifter who was being named on a rapidly burgeoning number of fugitive warrants as a murder suspect.

A witness was also located who reported seeing a man who looked like Rogers loading a battered old gray and white cloth-covered suitcase and some other objects into a white Ford Festiva outside the apartment early the morning Andy's body was discovered. Further confirmation was obtained later in the day by employees and customers at the local bars where he was seen drinking and romancing the victim. A criminal complaint was filed and another warrant was issued by a judge in Bossier City, naming him as a murder suspect.

The latest slaying linked to the muscular blond ratcheted up the fear and alarm that was rapidly spreading across the country. Four women, all redheads or with red highlights in their hair, had died violently in one ghastly forty-two-day period in California, Mississippi, Florida, and Louisiana. Three of the the four were murdered or were discovered dead in one dreadful blood-drenched week between November 3 and November 9. All the slayings apparently occurred at the hands of the same man, who was feared to be raging across the country like a mad dog in a ghastly sex and murder orgy.

The suspected killer was so out of control that he wasn't even making a serious effort to hide his identity. Even though he was expert at using false identity, he hired motel rooms in his own name, and used his true name while he was romancing his victims and meeting their family and friends. He openly boasted to strangers he was wanted for murder, and his truck was left behind after the latest killing, providing police with what appeared to be a rock-solid clue placing him in the immediate area where the crime occurred.

That behavior was especially disconcerting to law enforcement professionals with the FBI and other agencies who specialized in tracking serial killers because it was an indication that he was apparently running amok on a blood spree and the murders would continue until he was captured or killed. The work of most serial killers is marked by periods between slayings that may be a few days, weeks, months, even years. If Rogers was the killer of Mark Peters and of the four women, as police suspected, he was drastically cutting down the time between slayings.

He was behaving as if the slaying in California whetted his appetite for murder, and he was moving fast. The drifter's mobility accounted for one of the major problems in putting a halt to the murderous binge. If he had confined his killing to a specific area or region of the country covered by closely cooperating police jurisdictions, as many serial killers do, he would almost surely have already been captured. But the murders were committed hundreds of miles from each other, and by the time a body was found in one state police believed he was already in another state luring a new victim.

Professionally speaking, in terms recognized by law enforcement, psychologists, psychiatrists, and others who specialize in the sociopathology of such psychopaths, he was considered to be more of a spree killer than a serial killer. Serial killers typically take cooling-off periods between slayings to savor the memory and pleasures of their latest murder while homicidal urges build up. Most of them carefully plan their crimes.

Once a spree killer is on the run, however, a blood lust takes over and he goes berserk. During one dreadful three-month period early in 1984, a South Florida man went on a kidnap, rape, and murder spree that cost the lives of eight young women in five states. Another was repeatedly stabbed but survived, one woman was raped and tortured in a motel room before escaping, and a California teenager was inexplicably released after she was kidnapped and taken along on part of the cross-country murder tour.

The bloody killing orgy of Australian-born Christopher Wilder wasn't stopped until he was shot to death with his own .357 Magnum during a struggle with a police officer in New Hampshire a few miles south of the Canadian border. Wilder was a classic spree killer who continued to glut himself with murder and rape while managing to stay just ahead of thousands of police officers who knew his name, what he looked like, and were tracking him through a dozen states.

Now, more than a decade after Wilder died, police feared another sex-crazed spree killer was on the loose and leaving a trail of burned, or chopped-up, blood-drained female bodies behind him. He had to be stopped.

Chapter Seven

THE CHASE

EVERYWHERE THE FAST-MOVING fugitive went, grief, shock, and loss were left behind him.

In Southern California, Sandra Gallagher's friends and family said their final good-byes to the woman who had dreamed of one day becoming a country music star. A few miles away at McRed's, Rein Keener was trying to deal with a profoundly heightened sense of her own mortality. The redheaded bartender was deeply shaken after her narrow escape from the homicidal madman.

Maria Gyore returned to California from Hungary and walked into a nightmare. If what police were saying was true, the brutal lover she fled halfway around the world to get away from had turned on other women in her absence, strangling and slashing the life out of them.

In Jackson, Linda Price's family gathered with their friend, Kevin Smith, at the apartment on Rainey Road after police completed their crime scene investigation, and began removing the treasures she'd so lovingly decorated it with. The doll collection, china cabinet, family pictures, and Harley-Davidson mementos were distributed among family members to become cherished keepsakes of the woman whose ghastly death left such a gaping hole in their lives.

Linda's private little love nest was drenched in gloom, as if the footprints of all the homicide detectives, evidence technicians, and coroners' assistants who had walked through it still lingered invisibly on the floors. After the family was through, cleaners moved in to vacuum the floor, scrub down the bathtub that had held the body, and tidy up so that no visible traces remained of the woman who died there—or of her blond Rhett Butler.

In Florida, after pathologists completed their autopsy on the body of Tina Marie Cribbs, she was cremated. She was so dreadfully mutilated by her killer that cremation seemed to be the best thing to do. Her friends attended a memorial service at the local VFW hall, then took the urn with her ashes back to the Showtown USA. They set the urn on a table and had a drink in her memory.

Most of Tina's friends agreed during the extended toasts that her good nature permitted her to be lured to her death. She had no romantic interest in her suspected killer, but was merely doing a favor for a friendly stranger. If they were correct, she made the same fatal mistake that doomed Sandra Gallagher more than 2,000 miles across the country only five weeks earlier when she left a barroom to drop a stranger off at his home.

Cindy Torgerson, one of the group of friends drinking with Tina at the Showtown USA, told a newspaper reporter of the chilling brush the group of women had with the suspected killer. "He was picking us out like oranges," she said and shuddered. Tina, with the orange highlights in her hair, was the one he plucked.

In Bossier City, Andy Sutton's thirty-one-year-old brother, Willie Jiles, spoke to reporters through a haze of anger and shock. He said he hoped his sister's killer would be returned to Louisiana, a state with the death penalty. Jiles also publicly offered to personally meet with Rogers any place and any time. Then no one would have to worry about jail sentences for his sister's killer.

At the It'll Do, at Mr. Bill's Lounge, where Andy was also a favorite, and at other local Podunk watering holes, employees and patrons were eyeballing strangers with more caution or suspicion than they ever had before. If a stranger ordered a drink for a good-looking woman who was by herself, in many bars, there was a good chance it would be refused. Women, including employees, were scared and they had good reason to be.

"This man is very, very dangerous," Bossier City Police Department spokesman Mike Halphen cautioned reporters. "He knows now that we know who he is. He has nothing to lose now. He'll kill and kill again until we catch him."

In Jackson, FBI Agent Hal Neilson warned: "He is armed and extremely dangerous." The agent said inquiries and tips were being received from several other states, and being checked out along with reports of sightings of the fugitive. Information about Rogers was also forwarded to the Bureau headquarters in Washington, D.C., and a federal warrant was sworn out for his arrest on a charge of unlawful flight to avoid prosecution. Neilson said he believed it was likely Rogers would be placed on the FBI's famous "Ten Most Wanted" list.

FBI agents in Texas were also checking out the Houston area, and farther south in Corpus Christi, where the fugitive's sons were living with foster parents. There was concern he may have traveled to the Lone Star State to see his boys. From Corpus Christi it's only a short sprint down U.S. 77 to Brownsville and the border with

Mexico. Rogers was no international traveler and had no facility with the Spanish language, but police were aware that almost any foreign country can be appealing to a desperate man who is scared and on the run.

Police mug shots of the fugitive, along with detailed descriptions of his appearance and method of operation, were distributed to major national news agencies and to the local media in areas where he was suspected of committing murders or might possibly show up. His travel with carnivals was pointed out, and other police agencies and the media were advised that he sometimes used the alias James Edward Peters.

Sightings of men resembling Rogers were reported to police agencies in a half-dozen states. A brief flurry of concern was set off in Mansfield, Louisiana, about thirty-five miles directly south of Shreveport and Bossier City, when a customer and an employee at a convenience store reported seeing a man there who looked like the bearded blond drifter. Forty-eight-year-old David Slay told police he was working at the Snacks store Sunday night when a husky young man walked in and bought a couple of soft drinks. Slay said before the long-haired man left he looked around the store like he was checking things out. The suspicious stranger drove away in a dark blue or black Ford pickup truck with Mississippi license plates. Mansfield police interviewed Slay and also talked with their brother officers in Bossier City but failed to turn up any other leads to support the suspicion the blond stranger was the serial killing suspect.

A couple of days after Andy Sutton's body was found slashed to bits on her waterbed, the segment on Rogers was aired on *America's Most Wanted*. Producers of the Washington, D.C.–based syndicated show rushed the short segment onto Saturday's program so they could get a picture of the fugitive and a description on the air in hopes of shortening the manhunt. More than 400 telephone calls were logged from viewers reporting sightings and offering other tips after the show aired, far more than normal, but none of the information led to an arrest.

Inside Edition and *A Current Affair* also began looking into the story and preparing broadcasts. Newspapers, especially those in areas where Rogers was linked to killings, and in Southern Ohio where he grew up and spent much of his adult life, gave the story prominent daily coverage. The articles, along with television and radio broadcasts linking him to a cross-country murder orgy, were becoming increasingly alarming. A major investigative piece in Jackson's *Clarion-Ledger* reported that he was described as a serial murderer who used "a machete against three of the nine people police say he's suspected of slaying." Three of the female victims believed killed by Rogers were said to have been stabbed, then slashed with a machete. The message was clear. He was considered to be an extremely dangerous man who butchered his victims.

Unaware of, or uninterested in the devastation and grief he was leaving in his wake, Rogers was heading for familiar territory. He had always been pursued by his own personal demons, and now an army of police from a dizzying array of jurisdictions in cities and states, topped by the nation's premier law enforcement agency, the FBI, was on his trail. Apprehension and fear built up as he steered the little white Ford Festiva northeast, flying across the highways back toward the comforting hills and jagged crags of the Appalachians.

Tensions were especially high in the fugitive's hometown. Hamilton Police were on the lookout for him, and carried copies of his mug shots with them to use for comparisons in case they saw someone who looked like him. Former neighbors, acquaintances, and old girlfriends were nervously glancing over their shoulders, expecting to see him at any moment. One of his former common-law wives was so scared she took a leave of absence from her job so she could lay low until he was caught or killed. It would be like him to return back to his old stomping grounds, with his tail between his legs, looking for sympathy and help. There was good reason to suspect the fugitive was making a dash for his home ground. There was a saying around Hamilton that anyone who got their feet wet in the Miami River always found their way home when they were in trouble.

The local newspaper, the *Journal-News*, published a story on the manhunt, quoting Pratt as saying he doubted Rogers would return to his hometown. The HPD media chief acknowledged, however, that the police department was fielding "all kinds of calls" about local sightings of the fugitive. None of them panned out. The news story concluded with the admonition that anyone who saw Rogers should telephone 911. He was "considered to be armed and dangerous," it added.

Rogers's distraught mother appeared on local and national television, appealing for him to surrender. "Glen, babe, if you hear this, please give up. Please. I love you," she urged in one appeal. Mrs. Rogers also told reporters her son telephoned her a few days earlier and said he knew the police were looking for him, but he hadn't done anything wrong. He denied that he killed Peters or anyone else, and was afraid he was going to be shot to death or would be captured and spend the rest of his life in prison.

In interviews with reporters who telephoned her or hurried to the modest little white clapboard house with the redbrick columns supporting the front porch, she claimed he was innocent of the crimes he was being blamed for and was being used by police as a "patsy." He was the most caring of all her children, she said. "They have no proof. He just happened to be in the area."

Rogers telephoned his mother in September, a few days after Sandra Gallagher's murder to tell her he was in trouble and police were looking for him beause they thought he may have killed a woman. He told her he didn't do it, but was being framed.

Neighbors who lived near Mrs. Rogers's neatly kept two-story house weren't convinced he was the innocent victim of a police frame-up, or that he was harmless. They peered nervously out their windows every time they heard a car pull up or footsteps on the sidewalks. And they made certain when they went to bed at night that their doors were locked and the windows shuttered.

Hamilton police made the rounds of all of his known haunts in the city, questioned informants, and listened to street talk. They wanted to know immediately if the local bad boy who had suddenly become a national bogeyman returned to his old haunts. About 6:30 one night while Rogers's face was plastered all over the news someone ran through a busy Hamilton department store yelling, "Glen Rogers is in the store. I saw Glen Rogers." There was a rush for the exits, and the store cleared out in minutes. If Rogers was in the store he would have had all the privacy he could have asked for to do his shopping. He would have had it all to himself—but he wasn't there.

At McRed's, Rein Keener was scared to death. Her growing unease and fears had turned to sheer dread when she received a chilling telephone call several days after Rogers was thought to have cleared out of the San Fernando Valley. A man called her at the lounge, and in a voice that sounded an awful lot like her former admirer, growled: "You'll pay for this." Then the phone clicked off at the other end. The redheaded bartender's hand trembled so badly after taking the call, she could hardly put the receiver back in place.

Soon after that, she got herself a shiny pistol. She was no Annie Oakley, but she was genuinely scared. She also knew which end of a hogleg was the business end, and it was comforting to have it around in case she needed it. Rein also had some friends in the Los Angeles Police Department, and they temporarily moved into her home.

Nevertheless, despite all the safety precautions, she still couldn't feel completely safe. The bartender was spooked. The mere sound of a rolled-up morning newspaper suddenly slapping down on the front steps could cause her heart to jump in her chest. She had trouble sleeping at night. When she closed her eyes, she saw the blue-green eyes of Glen Rogers staring back at her. The eyes didn't look dreamy, like they were described by so many love-smitten women. They were the befuddled, spacy eyes of a homicidal maniac. They were frightening and evil.

Even carrying a pistol and surrounding herself with police officer friends didn't totally chase away the fear. His face still showed up too regularly on television, and while she was at work much of the talk from regulars and casual drop-ins focused on Rogers and the cross-country manhunt. Rein was talking about directing her legal career into criminal law. She was thinking of becoming a prosecutor, like Marcia Clark. The Rogers case wasn't quite a media reprise of the O. J. Simpson case, but the homicidal drifter was a focus of intense interest, especially at McRed's. And it was a subject that wouldn't go away. Rein's fears wouldn't be silenced for good until the frightening man she had rejected and angered was captured or dead.

Across the country, the long-haired blond man blamed for creating all the fear and havoc pulled the Ford Festiva off Interstate 75 at the Lake City exit in East Tennessee. Moments later he stopped the car against a fence at the rear of a parking lot and checked into the Lamb's Inn Motel. It was early Friday evening, about dinnertime, and heavy storm clouds were moving in fast over the ridge. The fugitive had made an exhausting drive, the last few miles of the trip through the Cumberland Mountains. During his three-day stay in Lake City, he continued to use the alias stolen from the son of his former benefactor and landlord in Hamilton and signed his name on the guest register as James Peters.

While police agencies around the country were beating the bushes for him, he laid low in the sleepy mountain hamlet and behaved himself. Lake City is a quiet mountain community of about 2,500 people approximately a twenty-minute drive north of Knoxville, and thirty-five minutes from the Kentucky border. It provided the perfect hideout.

The little town is in the Cumberlands less than a one-hour drive from the Great Smoky Mountains, and the storms that blow up can move in fast and furious. The first night Rogers stayed at the Lamb's Inn, high winds blew the wood fence at the back of the motel onto the little white Festiva, scratching the paint and leaving a few new dents. The next morning the motel owner and his nephew, night clerk Derrick Johnson, helped him lift the fence off the car. When the owner offered to pay him for the damage and suggested filing a police report, the hotel guest refused. He smiled, shook his head, and said the damage wasn't that bad.

His attitude fit in well with the reputation he began building for himself from the time he checked in. He was affable, friendly, and exceedingly polite. He did his drinking at the nearby First and Last Chance Bar, tucked away huge breakfasts of bacon and eggs, with grits, gravy, toast, and lots of hot coffee, and he tipped well. About the only thing different from his usual persona was his appearance. His shirt and pants were sweat-stained and a bit rumpled, the toes of his cowboy boots were scuffed and dusty, and his hair looked like it hadn't been washed and combed for a while.

The fugitive paid his motel bill by the day, in cash, and finally checked out at about noon Sunday. In less than an hour, the hatchback with the brawny man at the wheel crossed the state line into Kentucky. At about one o'clock Monday afternoon Rogers was driving along Kentucky Road 52 in western Lee County when he spotted a sheriff's car, and pulled off the highway at the first exit.

Diana Smith and Amy Brandenberg were working in the office at the Youth Haven Bible Camp when the dust- and dirt-covered white Ford Festiva pulled into the parking lot and stopped. A solidly built bearded man with blue eyes that stared wildly out from his face and long dishwater-blond hair that was pulled back in a po-nytail slid out of the compact car and loped into the office. He was dressed in rumpled blue jeans, a striped open-necked workshirt over a white T-shirt, and had cowboy boots on his feet. His distress and agitation were obvious, and he looked like a man with the devil on his heels. The shaken stranger told Ms. Smith that he wanted to talk with a preacher. Rogers was belatedly taking his mother's desperate advice.

The Bible Camp was only two miles from the dilapidated cabin where Mark Peters's remains were found in 1994, and some people in Lee County knew that Rogers was a suspect in the old man's suspicious death. But the secretary had never heard of him, and didn't know what he looked like.

Ms. Smith said she was sorry but there weren't any clergymen around just then who could talk with him. The man grunted his disappointment, then turned and walked out the door. But he was so obviously terrified that her coworker followed him outside to the car to see if there was anything else that they could do to help him. There was nothing they could do. Ms. Brandenberg watched while he climbed into the car, started the engine, and pulled slowly out of the drive, back onto the highway.

The police car that had spooked him was driven by Lee County Sheriff Junior Kilburn, with a plainclothes state police detective riding in the shotgun seat. The two lawmen were investigating a case that had nothing to do with Rogers, and were unaware of their close brush with the most wanted fugitive in the country. Nevertheless, Rogers's time, options, and freedom were rapidly running out. He was badly shaken. The tables had been turned, and he was a predator on the run.

A few miles down the road, Rogers pulled his car to a stop in the front drive of a neatly kept green and white mobile home. Edith and Clara Smallwood were distressed when their suddenly notorious cousin showed up at the door to their weathered trailer on the south side of Old Landing Road, just down the ridge from the old Rogers farm. Anyone standing in the front yard and looking up toward the ridge could see the dilapidated structure of weather-grayed wood that was the cabin where Mark Peters's pitiful remains were found tied to the chair.

Rogers's eyes were red and tears were running down his cheeks into his beard while he stood, weaving unsteadily, on the tiny plywood front porch at the front of the trailer talking to his second cousins. The women had helped him before when he was down on his luck, buying him food and cigarettes, but the trouble he had gotten himself into this time couldn't be cured by a handout.

"Glen, why don't you give yourself up?" seventy-two-year-old Edith pleaded.

"I don't know what to do," he blubbered. He was scared and confused. Rogers told his elderly cousins he loved them better than anybody, and the things that were being said about him in the press weren't true. "I just wanted to tell y'all 'bye, and I love you, because I know when they catch me they're gonna kill me." He never asked to go inside, and the awkward confrontation lasted about ten minutes before he finally turned and stumbled back to the car on legs that were egg-noodle limp and as trembly as Jell-O. The last thing he said to sixty-four-year-old Clara and her sister before he climbed into the dusty Ford was, "Pray for me." Moments after choking out the desperate plea, he guided the car out of the driveway and back onto the road. He was headed toward Richmond.

As soon as he was out of sight, his cousin Edith picked up the telephone and dialed the Kentucky State Police. It was a few minutes after 2 P.M. The women loved their rapscallion cousin, and it hurt to tip off the police, but it was a call that had to be made. He was so desperate and frightened it was hard to tell what he might do, and she was concerned for his safety. Importantly, as well, if the things that were being said about him were true, he wasn't merely involved in little-boy orneryness. He was dangerous, he was hurting people, and he had to be stopped.

Kentucky State Police troopers, sheriff's deputies from Lee, Estill, and Madison Counties, and a motorized posse of officers from cities and towns along the winding mountain highways beginning about twenty miles southeast of Lexington began converging on the area. Every police agency in that part of central Kentucky from two- and three-man departments to the State Police were on the alert for the man whom Mississippi detective Chuck Lee had described to the press as ". . . the most dangerous individual in the United States." Lee added, "It's turned into a game for him."

The "game" began veering to a dramatic conclusion when an unmarked car with a Kentucky State Police officer at the wheel spotted a white Ford Festiva traveling west along Kentucky Road 52 in Estill County and fell in behind it. Detective Robert G. Stephens, a twenty-four-year veteran of the KSP, had overheard a radio dispatch from the State Police Post 7 in Richmond that a white Ford Festiva driven by a murder suspect had just left Beattyville.

Stephens, who was in plainclothes, radioed in the information about the car to Post 7. Moments later the dispatcher confirmed the Festiva fit the description of a car owned by Tina M. Cribbs, a woman who was murdered in Florida. Mrs. Cribbs had carried Florida tags on the car, not Tennessee plates, but everything else fit. The car was believed to be driven by Glen Rogers, who was wanted for investigation of murder in four states.

When Stephens pulled up beside the vehicle for a closer look, the long-haired driver reached over to the passenger seat, popped a can of beer, and chug-a-lugged it. Then he rolled down the driver-side window and flung it at the police car. Beer splattered against the side of the cruiser, and the can bounced off and tumbled to the side of the road. Stephens radioed the KSP post in Richmond and said he was in close pursuit of the suspect, who had tossed a can of beer at him. The state trooper had a copy of Rogers's mug shot with him in his car, and there was no doubt in his mind who the brazen beer drinker was.

A few minutes later at the eastern town limits of Irvine, a twenty-five-year-old small-town rookie cop who was parked beside the state highway noticed the Ford. Charles Cox didn't know who the driver of the Ford was, but he recognized the driver of the unmarked car as a state police officer. He pulled onto the highway and followed the two cars to a spot just past a bridge spanning the Kentucky River, then turned on his siren and flashing red lights.

Throughout the long drive all the way from Bossier City, Rogers was careful not to exceed speed limits. But the rules changed when the guy in the plain car pulled up next to him, and the police car fell in line behind him a few minutes later with a wailing siren and a flashing light bar. He pressed down on the accelerator and sped away. According to a court affidavit Stephens later filed, a couple of times Stephens pulled his vehicle up alongside the speeding Ford, only to have the driver swerve and try to run him off the road.

Other police cars joined the chase as the driver of the Festiva led them along the steep, winding road halfway to Richmond in Madison County. At times they reached speeds of up to one hundred miles an hour, as the caravan progressed up and down the mountains. The pursuit had covered more than ten miles, when the speeding cars neared Waco, a tiny mountain settlement of about 400 people approximately seven miles east of Richmond in Madison County. Police set up a roadblock in the middle of the main drag, in front of the Richmond Bank.

Local resident Paul Rogers, who is no relation to the suspect, was in town when the roadblock was set up and he watched the action. When he saw the police cruisers blocking the street and uniformed cops pulling shotguns from racks and taking up positions around the barricade, it was plain that whatever was about to take place was deadly serious business.

Glen Rogers's adrenaline was pumping in overdrive; blood was rushing from his skin to the muscles and the brain, his pupils dilated, and wild light flashed from his eyes. He weaved right through the roadblock, pumping the brake and slowing to about thirty-five miles per hour while he steered the compact onto a gravel strip at the side of the road next to the guard rail. Then he shot through a tiny gap in the barricade of police cars and barrels with all the steady expertise of a Burt Reynolds *Smokey and the Bandit* stunt driver. A customer at the A & B General Store watched in eye-popping amazement while KSP Trooper Ed Robinson squeezed off one quick blast with a shotgun at a tire, then scrambled with other officers to get out of the way. The shot hit one of the rear tires, but it didn't stop the fleeing man. It just made it a little more difficult for him to steer.

Stephens and another officer, Sergeant Joey Barnes, who had joined the pursuit in another car, hurtled past the roadblock only a few yards behind the fleeing Ford. Ironically, Barnes was a former Florida Highway Patrol trooper stationed in Zephyrhills, a prison town just north of Hillsborough County and Tampa, where Tina Cribbs was killed.

In Richmond, Post Commander Captain Charles Bowman was in radio contact with his troopers and he was concerned that the situation was deteriorating. The bizarre caravan was only about five miles from Richmond, and rapidly closing in on the heavier populated countyseat town. He told the troopers the car had to be quickly stopped.

The Festiva made it another two or three miles down the road before Barnes at last drew up even with it, and eased his heavier police cruiser over against the driver's side. The agonized sound of metal crunching against metal ripped the air as both vehicles veered off the road. Then the Ford stopped as abruptly as if it had struck a brick wall. The pursuit ended just outside the northeast edge of the sprawling Blue Grass Army Depot.

Barnes, who was bumped and bruised, slid out of his cruiser and joined Cox and other officers converging on the stricken vehicle with their service revolvers in their hands. Behind them, other police cars screeched to stops and parked at crazy angles on and off the highway. Squad car doors opened and more officers slid out to crouch behind the protective metal, with their service pistols in their hands. But there was no shooting. Although police were warned that Rogers was believed to be armed, there was no obvious sign of a gun in the car.

The driver of the battered and dirt-smeared compact was seated, securely buckled in place in the front seat, with both hands still gripping the steering wheel while his distinctive blue-green eyes bulged in fear and stared straight ahead. His hands were so firmly locked in place that an officer had to pry them loose so he could be pulled outside.

The brutal alcoholic blamed for butchering women and holding a nation hostage while sowing fear and grief across a half-dozen states didn't put up a fight when he was pulled out of the car and shoved facedown on the dirt. While his arms were pulled behind him and cuffs were clamped around his wrists, he was as emotionless as a zombie. Then he was pulled to his feet and marched to a police car. Officers loaded him inside almost exactly a half hour after he lurched away from the mobile home of his elderly cousins.

A television reporter had time for a single, quickly shouted question. "Glen, did you kill the women?" he yelled. "No," Rogers replied. Just before a trooper pushed his head down and loaded him into the backseat of a cruiser moments later, he growled: "One-on-one, talk to me in person, alone."

There was no trace of the smooth-talking dandy who had entranced and lured women with his smooth pick-up lines, crisply clean and pressed, carefully selected costumes, and his distractingly soulful eyes. He was di-sheveled, sweat-soaked, reeked with the odor of stale beer, and was uncharacteristically quiet while he slumped in the backseat of the police cruiser during the twenty-minute drive to Richmond.

The battered little Ford believed to have been driven across at least six states by the fugitive was left behind under secure guard until it could be transported to Post 7. Officers peered around inside for a gun or other possible weapon that might be lying in plain sight while they were dragging the lumpish, unresisting suspect from the vehicle. A gray and white suitcase with orange designs on the corners was stuffed between the rear seat and the hatch and was visible from the windows, but it wasn't touched during the arrest.

Richmond was the Madison County seat, and the courts and the jail were located there. This time when Rogers was led into the booking room to be finger-printed, photographed, and processed into the Madison County Detention Center, he would be beginning a long stay behind bars. The specific jails and prisons might change, but the quality of the security and nature of the environment would be the same—or stricter. There seemed to be little doubt he would wear manacles and spend long days in courtrooms.

No amount of street savvy or lucky breaks tied to an overworked criminal justice system would change that. His freedom was ended; now he was about to face the life-or-death fight of his life.

Chapter Eight

A NEW LOOK AT OLD CASES

PEOPLE WHOSE LIVES WERE touched by Rogers reacted with sighs of relief, celebration, and amazement when news of his dramatic arrest was flashed to the nation via television screens, radio broadcasts, and newspaper headlines.

The chronic bad boy from Southern Ohio was big news, the new "Ted the Troller" Bundy, Son of Sam, and Nightstalker all rolled up into one evil, blood-crazed lunatic whose homicidal cross-country killing spree was at last brought to an end. That was a relief to many people, especially to many of his former neighbors in his hometown.

Rogers's mother was relieved her son wasn't hurt. "Thank God, he's caught and safe," she said.

Chief Fluckiger's relief that Rogers wouldn't be showing up in Hamilton, possibly endangering local citizens and causing more trouble for local police, was tempered by other considerations. He found himself publicly defending his year-old decision to call off Nugent's trip to Los Angeles to talk with Rogers, following his arrest for torching his girlfriend's closet. "I've been in the business for a long time, and I've never seen an attorney allow his client to talk, unless you've got an airtight case or they're looking for a plea bargain," he told the hometown *Journal-News*.

The bar at the Whistle Stop Inn, one of Rogers's favorite hometown watering holes, was decorated with his photographs clipped from newspapers during the manhunt and after the arrest. One of the bartenders said during the manhunt she was scared to death he would walk in, acting like nothing had happened.

In Van Nuys, Rein Keener reacted with a whoop of joy and tears of relief when a picture of Rogers on Channel 2 was flashed on the television screen behind the bar at McRed's. She cradled her head in the palms of her hands, while she stared at the film showing Kentucky State Troopers leading the handcuffed fugitive to a police cruiser. Moments later she dashed outside and hung a big handwritten sign on the entrance to the lounge: "THANKS TO THE 'POLICE.' SERIAL KILLER CAUGHT. 11/13/95 12:20 P.M., KENTUCKY."

It was almost exactly 2:20 P.M. Eastern Standard Time in Kentucky when Tina Cribbs's battered hatchback lurched to a stop and police surrounded the driver to haul him away. Twenty-five hundred miles across the country, the relieved bartender was operating on local Pacific Time. The crowd at McRed's could have cared less, however, about such esoterics as time zones.

They were already exchanging hugs and high-fives, ordering fresh drinks and offering toasts to celebrate the capture when the willowy barmaid returned inside. She was just in time to watch her boss post a sign of his own on the mirror behind the bar: "GLEN ROGERS CAUGHT. LADIES ½ PRICE ON ALL DRINKS." Then the bar crowd settled down to watch the capture replayed on television footage. It was repeated throughout the day, and it was more popular than sports.

Similar signs were going up and mini-celebrations launched in barrooms across the country, which Rogers had visited at one time or another—and at other saloons where people were simply inclined to join in the celebration.

Jeannie Fuller, one of Tina Marie Cribbs's friends from the Ramada Inn, was in a mood for revenge when she was asked by a reporter about her reaction to Rogers's capture. "I hope he gets castrated," she said.

In Dossier City, Teresa Whiteside was watching a film of Rogers being taken into custody, when she spotted her Power Rangers pillow and Little Mermaid blanket inside the beat-up little hatchback. Then she got together with Andy's brother, Willie Jiles, and some other friends and family members at the It'll Do to talk about the woman who meant so much to them and about the man accused of her savage murder. Mourners met again several days later and organized a fund-raiser to buy a headstone for Andy's grave. Spaghetti dinners were served for three dollars per plate and donations were accepted during the afternoon event at the Coach's Place bar.

In Jackson, Mrs. Wingate was at work when Detective Lee telephoned her about 2 P.M., and told her the man sought as her daughter's killer was captured in Kentucky. "They caught him, they caught him," she shouted. Later family members got together to monitor television news reports of the capture, and Linda's sister, Kathy Carrol, recognized Rogers's face the moment he looked up toward the camera outside the car. "It was a mean look he had on his face," she told a reporter. ". . . I'm happy. I'm very happy that he's caught. Praise the Lord."

In Winchester, Anna Means was shocked and dismayed when the image of the handsome charmer whom she had invited into her home was flashed on the television screen and identified as a suspect in a string of brutal murders of women. "He was a good person. Everybody liked him here," she told a newspaper reporter. "Seeing him on TV, that's not the Glen Rogers I know."

Law enforcement authorities in jurisdictions all across the country and as distant as Alberta, Canada, didn't share her surprise or dismay. Since the early hours of the manhunt, they had been pursing their lips and blowing the dust off old case files on unsolved homicides to look at the possibility the violent fugitive may have been involved.

There was nothing unusual about members of cold-case squads and other homicide detectives checking unsolved murder files for similarities to high-profile murder cases. According to FBI statistics compiled for 1994, the year Mark Peters died so mysteriously in a remote mountain cabin, 23,305 murders and cases of non-negligent manslaughter occurred in the United States. Even though that represented a five-percent drop from the previous year, the national murder rate of nine per 100,000 people was about average.

Many of the slayings are the work of people who have killed before, or who kill again. Los Angeles Police Detective Stephen Fisk told the *L.A. Times* he believed Rogers had killed others. "I think we're going to be amazed by all the bodies we find behind this guy."

But the Hamilton, Ohio, bad boy turned up the heat and made sure that the attention of homicide investigators all around the country was focused on him when he apparently let his Hamiltuckian tall-tale–telling get the best of him during a four-hour interrogation by KSP Detectives Stephens and Floyd McIntosh. McIntosh was lead investigator in charge of the Mark Peters case.

The captive was driven for questioning directly to KSP Post 7 on the southeast side and the eastern bypass that loops around the city of Richmond. One of sixteen State Police posts in Kentucky, Post 7 is on the sprawling campus of the Eastern State University, across the highway from Kentucky's Criminal Justice Training Center. Local police officers from cities, towns, and county sheriffs' departments throughout the state train at the center, learning the basics of police work and keeping up on new techniques. The KCJTC is also located on the college campus. The KSP has its own training center at the Kentucky State Police Academy in Frankfort, the capital city.

At Post 7, Rogers was marched inside between two husky state troopers, and taken into a spartanly furnished interrogation room toward the rear of the building. He was surrounded by law enforcement professionals, and two of them were alone with him in the room, which was equipped for recording interrogation and statements on either audio, video, or both. The rumpled prisoner was facing one of the most important confrontations of his life. In police parlance, they were about to take his pedigree.

The Hamilton troublemaker was a mess. The adrenaline rush set off by the blast of excitement and fear that carried him through the wild police pursuit along the mountain roads after he was spotted by Stephens had subsided. But all the violence of the past few weeks, his nonstop boozing, and the steadily building pressure of the hellish cross-country odyssey had exacted a devastating physical and emotional toll. Rogers was drained and empty when he agreed to talk with the experienced police interrogators.

An FBI agent also joined in the interrogation for a while. In addition to Rogers's apparent violation of federal law by fleeing interstate to avoid arrest, the agent was also concerned with the possibility the captive may have been involved in a bank robbery. On the Thursday before the arrest a man said to resemble Rogers barged into a nearby small-town bank and robbed it at gunpoint. (Rogers was quickly eliminated as a suspect.)

The officers began reading him the so-called Miranda warning, named after a kidnap-rapist in Arizona who won a precedent-setting U.S. Supreme Court case that makes it more difficult for police to obtain confessions. The warning read to Rogers outlined his rights under the Fifth Amendment to the U.S. Constitution, including his right to remain silent, a reminder that any statement he made could be used as evidence against him, and that he had the right to an attorney, either hired by himself or appointed by the court if he could not afford private counsel.

There is none of the old third-degree or KGB-style threats and bullying in proper police interrogations today. Since the landmark *Miranda vs. Arizona* was decided in 1966 and was backed up by subsequent U.S. Supreme Court rulings and interpretations, criminal suspects must be handled with kid gloves. If they're thirsty, they're given a nonalcoholic drink; if they say they're hungry, someone sends out for a cheeseburger and fries, or an order of Kentucky Fried Chicken; if they want to smoke, they're provided with cigarettes. Importantly, suspects, including Rogers, are advised that even if they waive their right to have a lawyer present and consent to an interview, they can change their mind and stop talking at any time.

Outside the interrogation room, telephones were ringing with calls from reporters all across the country, and other journalists were hurrying to the police post looking for interviews and firsthand descriptions of the chase and the capture. They especially wanted to know what was happening to the man accused of being the mad-dog killer who raged across the country leaving a trail of dead redheaded women behind him. Captain Bowman told the anxious newshounds that the suspect was "co-operating to some degree." Trooper Ed Robinson, one of the officers who was involved with the chase, was more blunt and told reporters: "He's been talking his head off back there."

A good deal of the things the murder suspect had to say had a barnyard smell to it, and the hard-faced cops had heard the same kind of stories before from other people during questioning. That was the way it tended to be with some people, especially during the early minutes, or hours, of confrontations in interrogation rooms. Eventually, if they kept at it, there was a good chance at getting at the whole truth, or enough of the truth to help piece together a believable story once it was combined with other evidence. The secret was to keep the suspect talking, and Rogers was a good subject to work on. He loved the sound of his own voice.

Inside the spartanly furnished room, Stephens advised him they were checking him out as the suspected killer of five people. Authorities had five bodies, the detective pointed out. Rogers looked at McIntosh, smirked, and said it was more like seventy bodies. Then he laughed.

The disturbing possibility raised by Rogers's own boast that he might be one of the nation's most prolific serial killers made national news after WTVQ-TV in Lexington discovered the statement among information supplied by Stephens in an application for search warrants filed with the Madison District Court. WTVQ broadcast the story, and within hours it was flashing across the country.

Authorities at KSP Post 7 received requests for information about Rogers from more than 200 law enforcement agencies in the United States and northeastern Canada. Calls were made to the post from as close as Versailles and Henderson, Kentucky, and from states as distant as California and Maine.

"There is the possibility that he has committed several heinous crimes," Captain Bowman told reporters at a hurriedly called press conference. "Now he's in custody, and I think a lot of people around the country can rest a lot better."

Police in Port Hueneme, California, about sixty miles up the coastline from the suburban Los Angeles sprawl, were among the callers. They were taking an especially close look at the shocking murders of three women killed during a nine-week period in 1993 for possible ties to Rogers. There were some striking similarities in the Port Hueneme slayings to the four more recent murders of women Rogers was suspected of committing, but there were also some glaring dissimilarities.

Among the most intriguing parallels between the Port Hueneme slayings and the more recent cross-country murders were indications they both may have been part of murder sprees. Of the three women murdered in the coastal city two years earlier, the slaying of forty-four-year-old Cynthia Burger seemed to offer the most obvious similarities to the manner in which victims in the latest killing spree died.

Ms. Burger, who worked as the customer service manager at a car dealership owned by her parents, Gold Coast Acura, was strangled and raped, and her body was dumped in her bathtub. Then her two-story condominium on Outlook Cove was set on fire. Firemen found the body, still clad in a nightgown, floating facedown in the half-filled tub on August 5, 1993. Sandra Gallagher was strangled and left in a burning pickup truck.

Both Linda Price and Tina Marie Cribbs were slashed to death and left in bathtubs. Andy Sutton was slashed to death on a waterbed. In all five murders, the killer or killers took pains to eliminate foreign hairs, fibers, and other potentially valuable trace evidence either with fire or with water.

Thirty-two-year-old Norma Rodriguez was the first of the Ventura County murder victims to die. The mother of two young boys was strangled in the living room of her home on June 1, while her three-year-old slept undisturbed in a nearby bedroom. Her estranged husband discovered the fully clothed body when he stopped at the house to pick up their sons. Neither of the children were harmed.

The other victim, eighty-seven-year-old Beatrice Bellis, was raped and stabbed to death with her own kitchen knives inside her home in a senior citizens' complex on June 27. The body of the frail, deaf woman was found lying on her bed in her rumpled, bloody nightgown.

Although Mrs. Bellis was much older than the other victims in Port Hueneme or the other women Glen was suspected of killing in the cross-country murder spree, she fit another important aspect of the profile of people he was known to prey upon. She was much weaker than Rogers, and unless she was armed with a gun or some other lethal weapon would have been unable to defend herself in a physical confrontation with a strong young male. None of the three Port Hueneme victims, however, were redheads, accounting for an important difference compared to the profiles of women Rogers was most often attracted to.

The unsolved murders were especially troubling to the Port Hueneme Police because homicides occur there so rarely. Years sometimes pass without a single slaying. Investigators asked for samples of Rogers's DNA so they could make genetic comparisons with the victims.

The police in the eastern Los Angeles suburb of Ontario were also among the agencies to contact authorities in Kentucky for DNA samples or reports to match against evidence in a year-and-a-half-old murder there. The victim was Judith Kennedy, a fifty-five-year-old grandmother and the neighborhood Avon lady. Her body was found in March 1994 dumped in her bathtub. She was stabbed to death. Her missing 1987 Ford Taurus was recovered a month later in upstate California, abandoned in a grocery store parking lot. In the City of Angels, police said they were looking at the unsolved murders of a half-dozen women for possible connections to the notorious serial-killing suspect.

Rogers's identification as a suspect in the string of redhead murders, followed by his dramatic arrest and his unwise boasting, also piqued the interest of police in southern Ohio in unsolved murders there. He was barely in custody before newspapers around the country were printing stories that a Hamilton teenager murdered in 1993 may have been his first victim.

Sixteen-year-old Kelly Lynn Camargo was last seen alive by friends on August 23 as she was getting into a car with a stranger outside a bar in Fairfield, a southern suburb of Hamilton. Her family and friends never heard from her again, until her partially decomposed body was found by hikers on September 5 in a woodlot near the small town of Camden in adjoining Preble County several miles north of Hamilton. Mark Peters was reported missing two months later.

Preble County Sheriff Tom Hayes told reporters that his investigators were especially interested in Rogers as a possible suspect because both he and the girl were from Hamilton and he was known to pick up "his victims" in bars.

Hopes of linking Rogers to the Camargo killing were dashed, however, when a records check in Kentucky disclosed that he was in jail in Winchester during the period between the times that the girl disappeared and her body was found. He was locked in the Clark County Jail on August 9 after his assault on the fifteen-year-old boy and he wasn't released until September 7, two days after the remains were recovered. But public disclosure that he couldn't have murdered Kelly Lynn didn't discourage police in other jurisdictions in Ohio and elsewhere from continuing to take a long, hard look at Rogers and his activities.

One of the cases the Hamilton Police were looking into was the grisly stabbing death of Emerson Skinner in October 1994. The seventy-seven-year-old man lived only two blocks from one of the homes Rogers had occupied, and he was killed on the anniversary of Mark Peters's disappearance. Detective Nugent was quoted in the Cincinnati *Post* as pointing out that Skinner was stabbed, "and Glen Rogers's M.O. is with a knife, and with fire, and with his hands. He likes to choke 'em and stab 'em."

Nugent's observation fit in with what experts have learned about most serial killers whose motivations are more closely aligned to sex and control than to robbery. During all of Rogers's fighting and brawling, and, if police and prosecutors were correct about his murder spree, guns were never his weapon of choice. He stabbed, slashed, choked, kicked, punched, and bludgeoned. Studies by criminologists have shown that a classic serial killer can obtain sexual pleasure from feeling the contortions and watching the fear-twisted face of victims turn red, then blue, while listening for the last gasp of life to leave the body as they're strangled to death. They love the feel of a sharp blade slicing through flesh and scraping against bone. Guns are too impersonal. Classic serial killers get up close and personal when they butcher, torture, and maim.

Springfield Township Police were especially interested in the possibility of a connection to a baffling local crime when they learned that some of Rogers's suspected victims were from areas he visited during his days traveling with carnivals. Rogers was known to have worked carnivals in Louisiana, Mississippi, Alabama, and Florida, but may have ranged through areas of the Midwest and as far north as Minnesota.

His days as a carnival roustabout were apparently over forever when police and journalists began working to reconstruct his travels. Springfield Township Police hoped to pin down his employment and whereabouts in May 1987 when William and Juanita Leeman were found murdered at their suburban home just outside the northern border of Cincinnati. Nearly a decade later the grisly knife slayings were still unsolved.

The body of the fifty-three-year-old homemaker was discovered lying just outside the house on Adams Road at about 10 o'clock on Wednesday night, May 13. She was stabbed and her throat was slit. Police followed a trail of blood from Mrs. Leeman's body inside the house to the bedroom, where they found her husband. He was also slashed to death, apparently minutes after he and his wife returned to their home and surprised a burglar inside. His wallet and her purse were missing.

The shocking double murder occurred during the middle of the annual Mt. Healthy Heritage Days Festival, which was in full swing a few minutes' drive from the Leeman home. Springfield Township Police speculated the killer was a transient, and during the investigation learned that some carnival equipment was stored in nearby Northbrook. Adams Road formed a direct link between the two communities and anyone transporting equipment from the storage area to the festival site would have driven past the Leeman house.

One more curious anomaly connected with the mystery also took on special significance years later when it was learned that a suspected serial killer had worked the carnival circuit. Pennsylvania psychic Nancy Czetli was hired by members of the dead couple's family in 1992 to investigate the five-year-old unsolved murders. Springfield Township Police investigators cooperated by providing her with crime-scene photos.

Ms. Czetli studied the photos and determined that the killer was a tall, broad-shouldered man with gray eyes and blond hair. He was a loner, who was likely to have an alcohol or drug problem that led to violence and difficulties holding a job, she added. Authorities weren't aware of it at the time, but a local drifter from Hamilton in adjacent Butler County fit the psychic's amazing description in almost every respect. The husky blond was a vicious alcoholic who couldn't hang onto a permanent job, and almost everywhere he went he got into minor scrapes of one sort or another. Women, booze, and trouble were the three constants in his life.

After Rogers's arrest, homicide investigators dug out evidence collected at the scene of the old slaying, including fingerprints and a palm print, and contacted authorities in Kentucky for help in making comparisons with his prints.

Speculation was also aired in law enforcement circles and in the press that Rogers may have been involved in the death of Carrie E. Gaskins in the town of Bethel, a few minutes' drive southeast of Cincinnati. The bloody corpse of the thirty-year-old mother of two was discovered by her twelve-year-old daughter, Cherrie Estep, in their apartment in the Clermont County hamlet on January 20, 1992. The woman had multiple stab wounds in the chest and her throat was slit. Bethel was miles from Hamilton, but Rogers was driving a cab in his hometown around that time and it wasn't unusual for him and his fellow cabbies to pick up or deliver fares in such distant areas. Ms. Gaskins was a brunette with reddish tints in her hair.

More importantly, Clermont County Sheriff's officers said they determined after talking with witnesses that Rogers and the woman knew each other, and may have had a romantic relationship. A sheriff's investigator drove to Hamilton and talked with some of the people who knew Rogers, including his former employer, Doug Courtney. The detective was especially interested in anything that might help track down specific information about fares the suspected killer drove to Clermont County.

Directly across the Ohio River from Cincinnati, police in Covington, Kentucky, also pulled out their files on the July 1994 disappearance of forty-year-old Diane

Washington, to give them a close look for any possible links to Rogers.

In Columbus, homicide investigators dragged out the files on one of their most perplexing unsolved cases, the 1994 murder of Ohio State University coed Stephanie L. Hummer. The near-nude body of the eighteen-year-old girl from Cincinnati was found in a field about two and a half miles from the college campus on March 6 after a crew member spotted it from a passing train. The only clothing on the body were a bra, tennis shoes, and socks, and investigators theorized that the girl was abducted from an alley near the campus, driven to the murder site and forced to walk into the field before she was struck on the head with a heavy object and strangled.

Stephanie wasn't a redhead, didn't frequent the type of low-class Ohio bars Rogers hung out in, and other aspects of the slaying didn't fit his usual mode of operation, but Columbus is only about one hundred miles northeast of Hamilton, a comfortable two-hour drive, mostly along interstate highways, and Rogers was carefully checked out as a possible suspect nevertheless.

About the same time, police were also checking the possibility that a glamor and automotive photographer with local ties might have been involved in the freshman honor student's slaying. A few days after Rogers's arrest, Charles Rathbun was charged with the murder of Linda Elaine Sobek, a lovely blonde model and former cheerleader with the Los Angeles Raiders National Football League team.

Stephanie's father, Daniel Hummer, told reporters he was anxious to learn exactly where both Rogers and Rathbun were when she was murdered. "I look at these characters and I look for some similarities with Stephanie's [case] and I look for some differences, and I see both," he was quoted by the Associated Press. "I ask myself, 'Is this the character?' If it is, it would help a lot of people." Rathbun was ultimately dropped as a possible suspect in the OSU student's baffling slaying, but was convicted of the model's murder.

But Stephanie's father was typical of many parents of children who are victims of unsolved murders. Whenever a local murder is solved or a high-profile case emerges somewhere else in the country that seems to have similarities to their own family tragedy, they are apt to wonder if there is a connection.

In Shreveport, the manhunt for Rogers and his arrest left Mrs. Huggins thinking about her daughter's mysterious death, and wondering if their paths might have crossed at the Holiday in Dixie festival. Caddo Parish Sheriff's Department spokesmen said Rogers was not a suspect, but Lori Mae Bonneau's mother couldn't ignore or forget troubling coincidences, such as the work connection and her daughter's red hair.

Just as they did following Rogers's apprehension, police responded to Rathbun's widely publicized arrest by dragging out their old unsolved murder files to look for a possible connection and similarities to the model's slaying. If investigators were correct, the two accused killers shared at least one aspect of their techniques. They targeted women, and gained their trust before killing. Curiously, the two men arrested only a few days apart each had strong Ohio and California connections, lived for awhile in Hollywood or West Hollywood, had light-colored hair, were both in their thirties, and had previously experienced serious troubles with the law.

Both Rogers and Rathbun were checked out as possible suspects in another shocking Midwest murder, the savage sex-and-torture slaying of a petite flight attendant at the Hilton Airport Inn in Romulus, Michigan. Forty-one-year-old Nancy Jean Ludwig was apparently overpowered as she opened the door of her room in the hotel near the Detroit Metro–Wayne County Airport and shoved inside. The naked body of the 105-pound suburban Minneapolis woman was found the next afternoon by a hotel maid, lying facedown on one of the twin beds. A gag was still in her mouth, and her throat was slit. Police uncovered evidence she was bound with a rope, then raped at least once on each of the beds. Rathbun ultimately was dropped as a possible suspect.

Romulus police investigators got in line with other agencies looking for DNA samples or test results on Rogers, so they could make comparisons with evidence collected at murder scenes.

Closer to home in Kentucky, state police and local Henderson County investigators were taking a hard look at a bizarre abduction and disappearance for possible ties to Rogers. Henderson County abuts the Ohio River, and it was a typically hot and sultry late summer day on Saturday, August 26, 1995, when Heather D. Teague headed for the beach to sunbathe. The twenty-three-year-old beauty from the town of Clay in adjoining Webster County stretched out on a chaise longue placed on a ribbon of sand on the south side of the river known as Newburgh Beach. Sunbathers, swimmers, fishermen, and anyone else using the beach can peer across the wide river and see the town of Newburgh, Indiana.

A man on the Indiana side of the river was scanning the Kentucky beach with a telescope when he saw a stocky gunman with bushy brown hair and a beard suddenly emerge from a thick woods. The gunman stalked over to the petite brown-haired woman sunning herself, pointed the gun at her, then wrapped a beefy hand in her long brown hair, and dragged her across the sandy riverbank into the bushes. The confrontation, in the middle of a sunny afternoon, with other sunbathers, swimmers, and boaters only a few yards away, was over in about twenty seconds.

Kentucky State Police and Henderson County Sheriff's deputies later described the woman's abductor as about twenty-five to thirty years old, six feet tall, 210 to 230 pounds, with brown bushy hair and a beard. About a week later investigators drove to the trailer home of Marvin Ray Dill, in the fly-speck settlement of Poole a few miles south of Henderson, to serve a search warrant. Dill was a construction worker with a record of drug and other arrests, and was a prime suspect in the abduction. He fatally shot himself while officers were still outside.

Although the bearded Dill was at the top of the list of suspects in the disappearance of the green-eyed beauty, after Rogers's arrest investigators turned their attention to the accused serial killer. Even though his hair was blond rather than brown, he had other strong physical similarities to the gunman spotted through the telescope.

Early in 1996 Rogers was linked as a possible suspect to an even more celebrated murder case, the so-called crime of the century—the slayings of Nicole Brown Simpson and Ronald Lyle Goldman.

William Pavelic, a private investigator for O. J. Simpson, reportedly revealed that he had talked with one of Rogers's former friends who claimed the onetime housepainter admitted to him that he committed the murders and framed the former sports hero. Although Simpson was cleared of criminal charges by a jury verdict following his celebrated trial for the double slaying, when Pavelic's stunning disclosure was made the retired football star was still mired in a wrongful-death lawsuit filed by the families of the murder victims.

According to a story in the *New York Post*, a man claimed Rogers told him that on the night of the murders he was hiding in the bushes outside Nicole's Brentwood condo when Goldman showed up at her front gate. Rogers met Nicole while they were trying on sunglasses at a Rexall drugstore in Brentwood and was involved with her for a while, according to the story. But he began to stalk her after she dumped him to return to her ex-husband.

"I killed them and made it look like O. J. did it to frame the . . . nigger," Rogers reportedly told his friend. When the man asked what happened to the knife, if he indeed committed the murders, Rogers reached down, pulled it from his boot, and offered to let him touch it, according to the story. The *Post* also quoted a defense investigator as saying he uncovered "incredible coincidences" between the twin murders in Brentwood and the gory knife slayings Rogers was already charged with committing.

One of the most chilling similarities between the Simpson-Goldman murders and most of the slayings Rogers was accused of, was the use of a heavy cutting instrument to stab and slash victims. Investigators were also intrigued when they learned that Rogers painted a house a few minutes' walk from Nicole's condominium about three months before the double killing there.

Stories that were equally strange cropped up during the investigation, the trial, and the aftermath of the murders on South Bundy Drive, and most were quickly discarded by authorities. The concept of Rogers as the killer was intriguing nonetheless, and several factors piqued brief press interest in the hypothesis: Rogers was a ladies' man, and Nicole was going through a period of her life when she was experimenting with a variety of lovers; he was living and working in the Hollywood area as a housepainter shortly before the murders occurred; and, most importantly, two of the women whose murders he is charged with committing were so viciously stabbed to death with knives they were cut to the bone.

On the other side of the coin, however, there were some glaring differences in the Brentwood murders and in the slayings Rogers was accused of:

- The killer of Nicole Brown Simpson and Ron Goldman was apparently a stalker who lay in wait for them, and that wasn't believed to be Rogers's style.

- Rogers was attracted to women with red hair, red tints in their dark hair, or who were strawberry blondes. Nicole was a natural blonde, with no red tints in her hair.

- O. J. Simpson's blood and DNA were found at the crime scene, but there were no similar discoveries to tie Rogers to the townhouse.

- Rogers always left the state in a hurry following the deaths of the women he is accused of killing, as well as after Peters's death in the Kentucky cabin, but he remained in the Los Angeles area for months after the double killing in Brentwood.

- According to investigators, Rogers committed his murders in privacy, had sex with the female victims, and didn't bother to use gloves. The Simpson-Goldman murders occurred in a courtyard a few feet from a well-lighted public street; there was no indication the female victim was involved in sexual activity; and the killer was believed to have worn gloves during the slayings.

Although Pavelic was cautious about claiming to have solved the controversial murder case, he said he and his colleagues were looking into the allegations of a Rogers-engineered frame-up. He pointed out that any leads that could help clear Simpson's name were being pursued. Detectives with the Los Angeles Police Department were unimpressed by the disclosure, however. In press statements they branded the allegation as "silly" and "ludicrous."

Published reports that Simpson's defense attorneys would argue in the civil suit that Rogers committed the double slaying never materialized. When Simpson was asked during an interview on Black Entertainment Television about the reports Rogers might have been the killer of Nicole and Goldman, he said he and his attorneys laughed at the suggestion. A bit later it was reported on the syndicated television show *American Journal* that Rogers's talkative bar buddy failed a polygraph test when he was questioned about the alleged confession. Press interest in Rogers as a potential suspect in the Brentwood murders quickly faded.

Early in 1996, about the time many Americans were digging old green neckties and scarves out of trunks and closets in preparation for St. Patrick's Day, a multijurisdictional force of Kentucky State Police, Kentucky National Guardsmen, and a special search team dispatched from the FBI Academy in Quantico, Virginia, gathered at the Old Rogers Place near Beattyville.

Kentucky State Police had been contacted by a tipster who claimed that more bodies were hidden on the farm. The informant was unable or unwilling to provide information about the exact location of any bodies, other details were hazy, and it wasn't even the first time a tipster had talked to police about a secret grave Rogers was purportedly linked to.

In December, a few weeks after Rogers's arrest, a confidential informant told Butler County Sheriff's officers that a body was wrapped in plastic and buried under a shed in Somerville, where the suspected serial killer lived for a while as a boy. Five detectives drove to the tiny settlement at the northern border of the county with support personnel and tore up the concrete floor of the shed, then excavated the earth underneath. Momentarily it appeared that the Rogers case was about to take a ghastly new turn, when they uncovered a strip of plastic, then turned up a pile of large bones. The remains were in the exact location specified by the informant.

The rush of excitement soon dissipated after closer inspection of the remains indicated they were probably animal bones. Laboratory testing later confirmed what Butler County authorities already suspected. When the caravan of investigators drove to Somerville, they were on a wild-goose chase; the remains were not human.

The story about a secret graveyard at the Old Rogers Place near Beattyville sounded like another yarn that was too fantastic to be true. But like the report of a human body buried under the shed in Ohio, it had to be checked out.

Rogers may have been only reveling in the attention he was getting and spouting off when he boasted during his interrogation about being responsible for seventy bodies. He had popped off before about being a serial murderer, boasting to friends in California that he killed eight people, and trying to impress Linda Price's family and friends in Jackson by repeating boasts of his killing prowess. But nobody knew for sure if it was all merely more Glen Rogers bluster, and it seemed that if there were other victims in addition to the five he was already suspected of killing, some of the bodies might be buried under the roughly sloping hillsides of the isolated Lee County farm.

"Legally, morally, and ethically we need to follow up the leads," KSP Sergeant Tony Young told reporters. "Before this chapter of Glen Rogers comes to an end, this is a lead that has to be followed up."

"If you definitely found one, you've got to believe the possibility of there being others," David Jones, director of the Kentucky State Medical Examiner's Office added.

Ironically however, there were still no charges against Rogers in connection with Mark Peters's death. On the one hand police described Rogers as a suspect in the suspicious death that apparently occurred at the abandoned farm; on the other hand they referred to the ongoing process simply as a "death investigation," rather than as a murder probe.

State Police decided soon after the tip was received to conduct the search, but held off several weeks because of bad weather. When the weather finally cleared and warmed up, about two dozen heavily bundled-up men at last gathered at the farm once more to look for bodies.

The forty-acre spread was divided into 100-foot squares for the search. Along with the FBI team, which was equipped with ground-penetrating radar and other state-of-the-art gear to detect underground anomalies in order to avoid unnecessary digging, the searchers were also assisted by a dog especially trained to sniff out human remains.

While the teams moved along their assigned grids and spread out over the rocky farm, red flags were placed on spots where there were indications the ground may have been disturbed. The dog and the FBI teams followed up and gave special attention to the flagged areas. On March 12, two bone fragments that appeared to be human were recovered near the cabin where the major portion of Peters's decomposed remains were found during the earlier search. It was the second day of the latest canvases of the rocky farm.

The bone fragments were transported to the KSP Crime Laboratory in Frankfort for analysis, to determine if they were part of Peters's remains or were from someone else. State Forensic Anthropologist Emily Craig later disclosed that the bones were believed to be those of Mark Peters. She cited the size, location, and weathering patterns as leading to the deduction, but recommended in a letter to Lee County Coroner Emmitt Daugherty that DNA analysis be conducted in order to positively confirm identification.

The search of the isolated farm was ended and it was just beginning to look like public interest might begin turning away from the possibility the suspected serial killer had dumped bodies in makeshift graves at the isolated farm when his older brother, Clay Rogers, made a television announcement.

Clay told an interviewer with WLEX-TV that the searchers should look harder. He claimed the family farm was a cemetery for victims of unsolved murders going back as long as twenty-five years. It was a chilling concept, and despite the police searches the disturbing idea of the Old Rogers Place existing as a secret graveyard was certain to linger and become part of the local folklore of Lee County.

But the purple mist-shrouded mountain crags, deep ravines, and quiet hollows of Kentucky have always been steeped in ghostly lore about premonitions, apparitions, and other mysterious creatures of the night. Stories of the supernatural, of ghastly "haints" seen riding the ridges on horseback whenever there's a full moon, of phantom black dogs, of death tokens delivered by an owl hoot, and other supernatural mysteries are as natural to many of the mountain folk as breakfasts of bacon and grits.

A tale about a rocky old farm on the outskirts of a little mountain town as the repository of an army of the restless dead wouldn't be all that unusual.

Chapter Nine

CONFESSIONS AND COURTROOMS

"A lawyer has no business with the justice or injustice of the cause which he undertakes, unless his client asks his opinion, and then he is bound to give it honestly. The justice or injustice of the cause is to be decided by the judge."

Dr. Samuel Johnson

ROGERS STOPPED TALKING TO his interrogators after they began pressing him for details about exactly how the four women who died during the murder spree were killed. Rogers admitted knowing some of the victims, but he didn't confess to committing any of the murders during the seven-week period police were convinced he was raging across the country on a killing spree. He said he decided he should talk with a lawyer.

By that time the experienced homicide detectives had flattered, cajoled, wheedled, and chatted with the bedraggled prisoner for four hours. The serial murder suspect spoke freely about some of the women he met during his crazy-quilt wanderings across the country while he was the subject of an intense manhunt.

Although Stephens and McIntosh garnered a huge amount of information that was vital to the investigation, they were still far short of squeezing a confession from Rogers. But once he asked to talk with a lawyer, his conversation with the two Kentucky State Police investigators was permanently ended. Both the bedraggled serial murder suspect and the detectives were aware of his constitutional protections under the Fifth Amendment in the Bill of Rights to speak with a lawyer. The basics of those rights were spelled out in the Miranda warning read to Rogers before the beginning of the interrogation. And no criminal defense attorney would be likely to allow the officers to resume their talks with his or her client.

It was shortly after 8 o'clock on a mid-autumn evening and there was barely any traffic on the bypass outside the police post when Rogers was handcuffed again, loaded into a state police cruiser, and driven to the nearby Madison County Detention Center at 107 West Irvine Street in downtown Richmond. The state police officer at the wheel of the cruiser guided it through a sally port at the rear of the modern bilevel redbrick building behind the Madison County Courthouse, and dropped off his prisoner. The sally port is an important security feature, and when a vehicle is driven inside the doors automatically close behind it. When prisoners are being delivered to the jail, it is only after they close the port that car doors are opened.

The detention center, constructed and opened on January 1, 1990, to replace a nineteenth-century structure across West Irvine, was built on a gentle slope so that from the front, which faces Main Street, it appears to be a single-level structure. But most of the activity is centered at the rear of the building, where the street dips and both stories can be clearly observed. The sally port is there, prisoners enter and leave from there, and attorneys use an entrance there as well. The modern structure is a local Richmond showpiece, and local law officers, officers of the court, and inmates have their own special nickname for it: "The Madison Radisson."

After the exhausted shaggy-haired prisoner was handed over to the custody of jailers, he was run through the booking process. A photographer snapped mug shots of him looking directly at the camera and from the side, and a full-length shot was taken of him as he stood against a background marked to show his height; fresh palm and fingerprints were taken; and personal information, including his name and date of birth, were recorded. Finally he was directed to strip to his underwear and turn over his clothes, which were later picked up by a state police officer. Then he was issued a dark green jail jumpsuit, a pair of flip-flops, given an armload of fresh linen, and locked up in an isolation cell on the first floor. Prisoners keep their own underclothes.

The jail was constructed with cells on both floors, with the second level designated for most minimum-security prisoners. Maximum-security prisoners, and inmates who are considered suicide or escape risks, or for some other reason need special surveillance, occupy first-floor cells. A section on the first floor is also set aside for female prisoners.

As an occupant of one of six cells designated for special watch, Rogers was personally observed by a jailer every fifteen minutes. The deputies on duty in the isolation wing are stationed about fifteen feet away from the cells, and four times an hour, around the clock, a deputy walks to each of the occupied cubicles, pulls up the flap covering a small opening in the solid metal door, and peers inside.

The cells and other facilities at the detention center are state-of-the-art, or as nearly so as they can be in a period of such rapid change. Rogers's cell was equipped with a bunk, sink, and a lidless commode which he could flush himself by pushing a button. Like other cells in the 140-inmate capacity jail, it was also equipped with its own shower, pay telephone, and television set programmed with cable and HBO, which he could control himself. There is no censorship of the available programs, and Rogers was permitted to watch film clips of his apprehension and arrest when they were repeated on television news shows.

Nevertheless, the roughly ten-foot-by-ten-foot cell was dismally restrictive and depressing. A solid metal door barred the front of the cell, and the back wall was constructed of cement blocks reinforced with steel. Solid cement and steel also separated it on the sides from other cells. It was an unpleasant place to be for anyone who might have had claustrophobia, or for someone like Rogers, who had spent his adult life as a rolling stone.

He was held without bail on preliminary charges, including two counts of wanton endangerment and a single count of receiving stolen property. The stolen property charge was tied to Mrs. Cribbs's Ford Festiva.

Rogers didn't go right to sleep, however. Shortly after he was booked, he talked with a pretrial release officer assigned to interview new prisoners and obtain information about their criminal records, other personal history, bail-bond eligibility, and to determine if they need a court-appointed attorney. The pretrial release officer works for the local courts and is on twenty-four-hour call. When the interview was completed, it was obvious that Rogers would need a court-appointed attorney. He was near broke, and indigent.

A pair of homicide investigators from the Clermont County Sheriff's Department in Ohio also showed up at the jail to question the new prisoner about the knife slaying of Carrie Gaskins. While Rogers met with Lieutenant Dennis Stemen and a partner, a jail employee telephoned Erwin W. "Ernie" Lewis to tell him what was going on. Lewis was an assistant public advocate and director of the local Department of Public Advocacy, whose office on West Water Street a few blocks from the detention center and the courthouse would provide the court-appointed attorney. He immediately telephoned the Ohio lawmen and his client at the jail, forbidding them to continue with the interview.

Tuesday, the day after Rogers's arrest, he had his first meeting with Lewis, his court-appointed attorney. The occasion was the suspect's arraignment on the preliminary local charges. As the senior and most experienced of the five full-time lawyers with the public advocates' office, Lewis was telephoned from the courthouse and given one hour to meet with his new client at the detention center before representing him at the arraignment.

Rogers was rapidly becoming a part of Kentucky's folklore, the dark counterpart of earlier figures like sharpshooting frontiersman Daniel Boone; sixteenth president Abraham Lincoln, who guided the nation through the heartbreak of the Civil War; and the tragic Floyd Collins, who inspired an enduring ballad when he died in 1925, after he was trapped in a cave he was exploring with friends. The young Kentuckian lived for eighteen days, pinned under a boulder while rescue crews worked feverishly to free him, and curiosity seekers flocked to the cave by the thousands, setting up food tents, hawking popcorn, peanuts, cotton candy, and souvenirs.

No one was pitching food tents or souvenirs in front of the Madison County Courthouse, and there was no "Camp O. J." like the lot rented and set up by television reporters in Los Angeles to park mobile units and trailers, install electronic equipment, and string telephone lines during the recently completed Simpson trial. But the media converged in force on Richmond, the Kentucky State Police Post, the detention center, and especially on the Madison County District Court for the modern-day desperado's arraignment on the preliminary local charges. On Main Street near the center of the action on Tuesday morning, a shopper could peer out the window of about any store and see a fleet of TV mobile units and out-of-town vehicles carrying logos of news organizations or license tags issued to car-rental companies. Most of them were cruising or parked close to the entrances of the "Madison Radisson" and of the courthouse, which both front on Main Street.

Ironically, Rogers never set foot in the old nineteenth-century courthouse for the arraignment. The proceeding was conducted via closed-circuit television between the courthouse and the detention center. A special room was set aside in the detention center for the camera. When Madison County authorities began handling all first court appearances that way in 1988, they were the first jurisdiction in the state of Kentucky and one of the first in the country to do so.

Television reporters, lacquered hair glistening with spray and notepads in their hands, nevertheless competed with radio and print journalists and with members of the curious public for seats inside the cramped third-floor courtroom on the Tuesday after the notorious suspect's capture. The courthouse, constructed with three stories and a full basement, has four huge white columns at the Main Street entrance.

About sixty people moved between the columns and filed past a huge boulder just inside the front door. The approximate five-foot-high chunk of stone, which was uprooted from northern Madison County near the Clark County line and moved to the courthouse years ago, has the name of Squire Boone carved into its surface. The eighteenth-century frontiersman marked the stone when he first moved into the area to establish Fort Boonesboro, so his younger brother, Daniel Boone, who was following behind, would know he had been there.

The crush of reporters, photographers, and a handful of curious residents from the area jammed into the courtroom to listen and to stare at the closed-circuit television screen during the arraignment. The room was so crowded that a television cameraman knocked the clock off the wall while he was leaning over to get a good angle. The spillover from the crush of reporters, cameramen, and sound operators watched from a Madison County District courthouse annex.

The hearing was brief and simple. Madison District Judge William G. Clouse advised the defendant of the local charges against him, and reviewed his constitutional rights. Rogers replied to the judge's questions in a soft but audible monotone. One time he asked the judge to speak up.

The defendant did not enter a plea to the charges, and declined to waive his right to fight extradition. Judge Clouse ordered him held without bond, and scheduled a preliminary hearing for 3 P.M., Tuesday, November 21.

Lynn Clontz, Rogers's thirty-four-year-old stepniece, who used her maiden name during contacts with the media, lived in nearby Berea, Kentucky, and had hoped to visit with him Tuesday. She was advised by jail authorities that she couldn't see her notorious relative until his normal visiting day, on Thursday. So she mailed him a card, assuring him of her love and support. Ms. Clontz's stepmother was the defendant's sister, Clara Sue, and she had known him since she was nine years old and he was eight. In comments to a reporter for the *Clarion-Ledger* she was defensive of her uncle and said, "The Glen I grew up with didn't have a violent nature. I think it's been blown way out of proportion."

Lewis also had a message for the press. He announced that Rogers would not talk with police, prosecutors, or the media. "At this time he's not going to talk to anybody," Lewis declared. "And once he's made that assertion, nobody can talk to him in the police department unless he initiates it."

No one at KSP Post Number 7 was surprised. Lewis was an experienced, no-nonsense litigator. He knew the ropes, and when he was appointed by the courts to handle the local charges against Rogers, he also took on defense responsibility for the critical extradition process that was just a few days down the road.

The local charges were comparatively minor when judged against the various counts of murder Rogers was facing in other states. But there were enough of them, and they were serious enough, to keep him behind bars long enough for authorities in California, Mississippi, Florida, Louisiana—and Kentucky—to do the necessary sorting out. The first of four anticipated murder warrants from out of state had already been received at the courthouse by fax machine from Louisiana. In the highly unlikely event that bail was permitted on the local charges, or Rogers somehow managed to win an order for his release through some other means, the Louisiana warrant would serve as a detainer and keep him locked up.

Soon after exchanging information with Sergeant Glenn Sproles, the lead detective in the Bossier City case, KSP Detective Robert Stephens was contacted by Detective Julie Massucci of the Tampa Police Department, by Detective Mike Coblentz from the Van Nuys Division of the LAPD, and by Detective Chuck Lee in Jackson. Both Lee and Coblentz had already obtained arrest warrants for Rogers, and Massucci and her colleague, Randy Bell, were working closely with the prosecutor and the courts in efforts to move the Tampa case forward as expeditiously as possible. The prisoner's troubles were piling up and the net was rapidly closing.

Three days after Rogers's capture, a Madison County Grand Jury returned indictments against him on two counts of wanton endangerment and one count of first-degree criminal mischief. It was contended in the indictments that the lives of Detectives Barnes and Stephens were put at risk during the chase, accounting for the twin counts of wanton endangerment. The other charge was tied to at least $1,000 in damages inflicted on Barnes's police cruiser at the conclusion of the chase. The preliminary charge of theft was dismissed, and would become a matter for authorities in Tampa to deal with.

It went virtually unnoticed during the commotion, but the eight-year-old drunk-driving charge in Richmond that Rogers skipped out on was still on the books and also lurked in the background. There appeared to be little chance that authorities would resurrect the charge, which was insignificant compared to the newer, more horrendous offenses he was accused of in other states.

Russell pointed out to the press, however, that the

Rogers affair was a tremendous burden on the local law enforcement and court system, and Kentucky officials were anxious for him to be moved and put on trial in another state where the charges were more serious. All three of the counts tied to the car chase carried a maximum penalty of one to five years in prison on conviction. They were similar to charges Rogers's court-appointed attorney had dealt with many times before. Like everyone else who was involved, Lewis knew, of course, that the local charges didn't pose the most critical danger to his client. The issues of life and death would most certainly be decided by other lawyers and judges, in other courts, in other jurisdictions.

Lewis's dress and style were severe and unemotional, giving him the sober look of a dedicated accountant. He was a small-town defense lawyer, not a multimillionaire legal superstar who preened and showed off on courtroom cameras in $2,000 suits and perfectly fitted rugs. He wore a neatly trimmed, jet black Van Dyke beard and mustache, and a shiny patch of skin at the top of his head stretched straight up the middle Samurai-style and tended to shine and reflect light from courtroom cameras. Ernie Lewis was one of the busiest criminal defense lawyers in East Central Kentucky.

The public defender's office headquartered in Richmond represents indigent clients in a broad area, encompassing Madison, Clark, Rockcastle, and Jackson Counties. It is a vast area of flatland, mountains, and a rugged strip of dense woods that is part of the Daniel Boone National Forest extending from Winchester on the north through Richmond, then almost straight south along U.S. 75. The national forest sprawls along the southern end of the jurisdiction, where U.S. 75 is bordered on the west by Rockcastle County and to the east by Jackson County.

It is a huge territory to cover with a total population of roughly 110,000. About half the people in the quad county area live in Madison County or Clark County, which is the second most heavily populated, and has a larger population than Rockwell and Jackson combined. During the fiscal year ending July 1, 1996, the period when Rogers wound up with Lewis as his attorney, more than 2,200 clients were represented through the Department of Public Advocacy in Richmond.

The five staff attorneys were supported by two office workers, an investigator, and by volunteers, including a law clerk and a paralegal. Nevertheless, they had a big cud to chew. The public defenders operate a bit like the old-time circuit judges who "rode the circuit" on horseback or in carriages from one courthouse, town hall, or saloon to another to mete out justice across a broad territory that might include several counties. Lewis and his legal sidekicks make their rounds of the courthouses and jails in the quad county area dressed in darkly conservative suits and ties and driving their own cars.

Local motels and bed-and-breakfasts in Richmond quickly filled with newspaper reporters and television news crews, along with members of the print and electronic tabloid press. Tabloid TV producers were aggressively recruiting anyone who had almost anything at all to do with Rogers or with the people who became his presumed victims.

While her brother was still on the run, Clara Sue Rogers taped a show for *A Current Affair* that was broadcast on the day of his capture, and said he told her police would never catch him unless he wanted them to. He vowed to kill himself before surrendering, and told her he had a gun and was saving the last bullet for himself. "He wasn't going to spend the rest of his life [on] death row," she said. Tacking on an especially ominous note to her remarks, she added that he told her it was "too late to stop and that . . . we've only scraped the surface. And that you'd find a whole lot more dead people." She said her brother told her he killed fifty-five people, and shot a highway patrolman.

Andy Sutton's roommate, Teresa Whitehead, appeared with Willie Jiles's fiancée, Beverly Chavez, on *Leeza*, and told a national audience: "I believe he [Rogers] killed my friend and had a chance to kill me. It feels like a nightmare you just can't quite wake up from." Mrs. Wingate and Linda's sister, Mrs. Marilyn Reel, also appeared on the same show. Willie Jiles and Bossier City Public Information Officer Mike Halphen were invited to appear as guests on *Rolanda*.

Guests on *Rivera Live* outraged some of Rogers's kinfolk when they referred to the accused spree killer as a psychopath. Although Clara Sue was still talking to reporters from her home in Monroe, a lickspittle settlement of a few hundred people about midway between Hamilton and Middletown, several of his relatives were beginning to signal to the press that they were fed up with all the negative attention.

After speaking freely to the media for days, Rogers's widowed mother decided she had had enough. She went into seclusion at her home in Hamilton. Reporters were no longer invited inside, where the walls, stands, and tables in the living room were dominated by pictures of children, grandchildren, great-grandchildren, and other family members; ceramic figurines; and dolls, including an image of Ringo Starr playing drums, and a beautifully kimonoed Japanese woman behind glass. When journalists drove to the house and walked onto the front porch, framed by two redbrick columns with an image of the American eagle overhead, they were confronted with a hand-scribbled sign on the front door that read: "NO TV NEWS REPORTERS, NO NEWS MEDIA. THANK YOU." The rebuff was reinforced by a two-word message on the "welcome" mat: "GO AWAY."

A shower of business cards had already been left off at the house from journalists and producers for her to sift through in case she changed her mind about talking. There was also a blaze of telephone calls to contend with, and talk-show host Geraldo Rivera sent her a telegram asking for an interview.

In Beattyville, Rogers's cousin, Edith Smallwood, told the local newspaper, the *Three Forks Tradition*, that she and her sister were merely doing their duty when they tipped off police to Rogers's visit. "You have to wonder if you would do it again knowing that these people won't leave you alone," she said. Then she and her sister left home for a while and headed for the hills to get away from the rush of reporters. A man who stayed behind at the modest trailer home told one reporter he was the seventy-fifth to stop by.

Some of the Smallwoods' neighbors were also becoming fed up with all the media attention being focused on their normally quiet little community. Opal Newman, owner of the Bear Claw Grocery, told a reporter for Jackson's *Clarion-Ledger* that two county sheriffs were in prison. Then the Rogers story became big national news. "It's been just one blow after another," she said.

On Thursday Rogers was permitted his first visit with family members, including his mother and stepniece. According to jail regulations, inmates whose last names begin with the letters "A" through "K" are allowed a single twenty-minute visit on Tuesdays or Saturdays. Inmates whose names begin with the letters "L" through "Z" are permitted visits on Thursdays or Sundays. There was some speculation in the press that Rogers's visiting day might be switched from the "L" through "Z" schedule to throw off reporters who hung around the jail when his relatives were expected to show up in hopes of obtaining interviews. The press was wrong about changing days. Jailers juggled the hours instead.

Along with visitors to other inmates, Rogers's family members walked through the front door of the jail, and crossed the lobby to the visiting room on the other side. When it was Rogers's turn, he seated himself in one of five seats on the jail side of a heavy, thick glass that separated prisoners from their visitors. No contact visits, which would permit an exchange of hugs, kisses, or handshakes—and frequently results in passing of contraband where touching is allowed—were permitted at the jail. Rogers and his guests were restricted to looking at each other and talking through telephones installed on each side of the heavy glass.

He and his fellow inmates were permitted to talk with as many visitors as they could jam into the twenty-minute period, but only two were allowed at the mirror with access to the phone at any one time. Rogers assured his relatives that he was being well treated.

According to jail regulations, Rogers and other prisoners were permitted twenty-minute visits once each week with family members or other approved visitors. Attorneys, of course, were allowed more generous access to the inmates. Lawyers and visiting clergy had their own entrance on the West Irvine end of the jail.

Rogers knew his way around a jail, and he was a

docile, courteous, and well-behaved prisoner. He got along with corrections officers he came in contact with, but inmates in isolation were firmly cut off from association with other prisoners. Even after he was moved into general population from isolation about a week after he was locked up, his contact with other inmates was minimal. He was assigned to another cell on the same floor, and given outdoor exercise privileges in a narrow yard facing the brick wall of the jail on one side and ringed with a barbed wire on the others. The yard is outfitted with a pair of backboards for playing basketball. Only once during his stay at the detention center was another inmate assigned to share a cell with him, and that was only for a day or two.

Rogers spent most of his time alone in his cell watching television, sleeping, mulling over his problems, or eating his meals. Meals were nutritious, but strictly institutional, and were delivered by a trustee who pushed a food cart along the corridors. The trustees shove the meals through a special slot in the cell door that is opened only when food is delivered and the trays are retrieved. The trustees are always accompanied by a sheriff's deputy.

Every once in a while, Rogers was led out of his cell and walked along the sterile corridors and hallways to a lawyer-client conference room at the back of the jail to talk with his attorney.

Despite Lewis's intimidating statements and presence on the scene, homicide investigators flocked to Richmond from police departments across the country, carrying bulging unsolved case files in briefcases and under their arms. When Lewis turned thumbs-down on interviews with his client, it hardly slowed the rush of detectives flying or driving to the Madison County–seat town with hopes of interviewing the prisoner and closing some long-standing homicide cases. By Wednesday, two days after the dramatic chase brought the manhunt to an abrupt close, homicide investigators from six states and from Alberta, Canada, were in town competing for scarce accommodations and clamoring to talk with the suspected serial killer. Two of the sleuths were from the Los Angeles County Sheriff's Department, and others flew in from Jackson, Bossier City, and Tampa. Most of the officers had to settle for comparing notes about investigations of unsolved crimes resurrected by the manhunt for Rogers and by his arrest.

Detectives from Hamilton were also preparing to make the trip, and although they were pessimistic about their chances of questioning the hometown boy, they planned to confer with investigators from other jurisdictions who were involved with the case.

It was easier for Lewis to enforce the proscription about talking with his client when he was dealing with law enforcement agencies than with the press. After the conclusion of the marathon Simpson investigation and trial in California that entranced a nation, Rogers and Rathbun were thrust into reluctant competition for the crime-story flavor of the month. The media was scrambling for information and there was very little that Lewis could do to keep a lid on a story that was boiling over with dramatic and lurid revelations.

One of the most explosive public disclosures occurred when WTVQ-TV in nearby Lexington obtained a copy of the affidavit signed by Detective Stephens quoting Rogers as boasting when he was told he was a suspect in five deaths that "it's more like seventy bodies." The affidavit was prepared and filed with the goal of obtaining a search warrant for Mrs. Cribbs's hatchback and the contents of the suitcase; and another warrant for search of Rogers's person to permit taking of blood, hair, and saliva samples from the suspect.

Stephens stated on the application that there was "probable and reasonable cause to believe that property or other things existed that showed evidence that Rogers had committed murder in at least four other states: California, Florida, Louisiana, and Mississippi." He included a capsule review of the homicides Rogers was suspected of committing in those states, and said his fellow officers in those jurisdictions were anxious to obtain samples to compare with blood or body fluids, hair and fiber, and also requested fresh fingerprints from the prisoner.

Similar requests for evidence to be gathered from Rogers were communicated to officials at KSP Post 7 from officers investigating unsolved homicides in many other areas as well, he wrote.

The veteran homicide detective also stressed that it was "extremely important, now rather than later," to collect a large number of hair samples. He said he was advised by Ed Dance, manager of the KSP Central Crime Laboratory in the state capital city of Frankfort, that the longer after the commission of a crime the more likely that hair may change color, length, and comparability with other hairs.

After details of Rogers's boast were aired by WTVQ, the story went nationwide, sparking an entire new round of finger-pointing at the drifter by police and the families of murder victims wondering if he might have been involved in their cold-case investigations and personal tragedies.

The interview with the lawmen at KSP Post 7 didn't account for all the talking Rogers did outside the courtroom. Listening to good advice was never one of the rambunctious prisoner's strong suits, not even when the counsel originated with his lawyer. While he was locked up, Rogers busied himself on the telephone calling family members and selected elements of the media.

He was apparently shocked by the fuss he kicked up with the wisecrack to Stephens and McIntosh about murdering seventy people. His Hamiltuckian tall-tale–telling finally backfired on him with a vengeance, and he was suddenly being pictured in the press and in the public mind as a ruthless modern-day Bluebeard, or a slavering vampire prince who seduced and lured innocent women to their doom. During his first weekend locked up at the detention center, Rogers made three calls to the media from the pay phone in his cell, in an effort to set the record straight.

One call was to his hometown newspaper, the *Journal-News*. After complying with a reporter's request to confirm his identity by providing personal details about himself, including a description of the tattoos on the fingers of his left hand, he said he was just joking when he bragged about killing all those people.

Like always, Rogers appeared to relish talking about himself. He said that when the detectives asked him about the four women he was suspected of strangling or stabbing, he wasn't familiar with any of the names. Rogers explained he wasn't good with names and had "no idea who's who." Then he explained that he wasn't allowed to say anything about the women.

Continuing in his typically exaggerated style, he told the reporter he traveled in bars all around the world and probably met "millions" of females and didn't kill any of them. His claims that he never killed anyone included Peters. The *Journal-News* ran the story in its Saturday editions, the day after the television broadcast in Lexington.

Another call was placed to the newsroom at WCPO-TV in Cincinnati on Saturday night. Earlier in the week members of the WCPO-TV news staff had requested an interview. All media requests for interviews were passed onto the inmate by jailer Ronald C. Dever, the elected civilian in charge of the operation and the thirty-three-member staff at the detention center.

"Yeah, I remember that I laughed because I thought it was funny," Rogers told a WCPO-TV reporter about his interview with the KSP detectives. "If he's going to ask me about a bunch of murders, I said, 'Well, what are you talking about?' I said, 'Why not?' I said . . . ask a stupid question, get a stupid answer."

The suspected serial killer said he didn't realize his response to the detectives was going to blow up that big. Then he laughed. Rogers also continued exhibiting his trademark braggadocio by boasting that he walked past FBI agents while they were looking for him in a Jackson motel. Before the comments were aired, reporters at the Cincinnati station checked the interview out with Rogers's brother, Gary, in Hamilton. Gary Rogers listened to a tape recording of the interview and confirmed it was his brother talking.

Rogers spread his interviews around, and surprised a local reporter for the *Richmond Register* by telephoning him at home from the downtown jail. Todd Blevins had a nasty head cold and so much trouble breathing he told his editor he had to stay home a couple of days and load his system up with medicine. He was stretched out half-conscious on the couch when the phone rang, and an operator asked if he would accept a collect call from Glen Rogers. The prisoner was using the pay phone in his cell, and Blevins, who was still groggy from the cold and the medication, mumbled that he would accept the call.

Rogers began the surprise interview by saying he wanted to tell his side of the story. He also stressed that he planned to fight extradition. Asked about his arrest, he said, "I guess it's a little bit of a relief."

Blevins wasn't at his best, and didn't ask all the questions he later realized he might have posed to his surprise caller, even though they talked for about twenty minutes. Rogers promised to write a letter to him at the *Register*, giving his side of the story. He said his niece would deliver it on Friday night, after her Thursday visit with him at the jail. Ms. Clontz would also be his spokesman, he said. "Lynn is solid. She's a firm believer."

Rogers said his lawyer told him not to talk to the media, so he couldn't discuss the the case. But he rattled on about other subjects, such as his treatment at the jail: they were very good to him; the mail he was receiving—most people who wrote to him were supportive. He lavished praise on his hardworking attorney, and said he didn't think he could have gotten a better lawyer. He said he wished Lewis could go with him to represent him in proceedings in other states. The conversation went on so long that it cost forty cents. When he got his telephone bill, the reporter put the forty cents on his expense account.

After Lewis read the brief story about the phone call, he headed for the detention center to have another serious talk with his exasperating client. Then he notified Blevins that he could forget about the letter. He said he believed he had convinced Rogers not to write it.

The local newshound nevertheless got a second

chance at the determined chatterbox when Rogers called back a few weeks later. By that time Blevins was feeling better, and got to the core of the matter in a hurry. "Did you kill anybody?" he asked. "No, I haven't," Rogers replied.

He made the second call because he was upset over a story printed in the *Bethel Journal*, which he complained quoted Lieutenant Stemen as accusing him of the Gaskins murder. Rogers told Blevins he heard of the little Ohio town but had never been there. He also denied reports that he knew the victim.

On the day the woman was stabbed to death, Rogers appeared in Hamilton Municipal Court, signing in at about 12:30 P.M. Ms. Gaskin was stabbed to death in her home in Bethel three or four hours before that, creating a time window that authorities in Clermont County claimed was sufficient for him to have committed the crime before driving back to Hamilton. Clermont County authorities still considered the accused serial killer to be a solid suspect in the local murder, however, despite his denial during the telephone call to the Richmond news reporter.

The prisoner even talked by telephone with a reporter for the tabloid television show *Hard Copy*. She faxed a note to him at the detention center asking Rogers to call collect, and it was delivered to him by a jailer along with other letters and faxes from reporters seeking interviews. Jailers saw to it that he received all his mail and faxes.

Rogers's response to the media frenzy may not have been all shock or disappointment at being depicted as a bloodthirsty ogre, if it was true he was a serial killer. Specially trained law enforcement experts, psychologists, and others with educational credentials in the field recognize that courting the press is typical behavior of many serial killers. They glory in the public attention which makes them feel important and allows them to relive their crimes.

After spending his adult life as a relatively obscure drifter, handyman, cabbie, and carnival roustabout, Rogers was suddenly someone that everybody in the country was interested in. His image was broadcast into millions of homes on television. Other photographs were on the front pages of newspapers and in magazines, along with stories exploring details of his life from his childhood to the present. He was solidly in the limelight and his picture and story were right there up front, beside those of people like the president, other world leaders, and Hollywood's most glittering stars.

When jailers delivered his mail, there were sometimes as many as twenty letters and faxes a day from reporters and producers pleading to talk to him. Talking was something he loved to do, and now when he talked everybody listened to what he had to say. Even his lawyer's warnings couldn't shut him up.

Lewis complained bitterly that people were camping in the little town and moving messages to his client in jail. The journalists were misleading him by telling him that his story wasn't being told, and they would be fair to him. It was a line that his client swallowed because he didn't know any better, the lawyer carped. The laid-back attorney was also experiencing his own problems with the media. For a while after the story broke, as many as thirty calls a day were being made to his office from journalists seeking to talk with him. The media attention exerted a massive drain on his time and the resources of the public defender's office staff.

Lewis talked to the media when it appeared to be appropriate, and when time permitted. He appeared with Madison County Attorney Robert Russell on a local television show called *Your Government*, that was broadcast on Sunday mornings by WLEX-TV, and offered a few insiders' comments on the case that was captivating viewers in Central Kentucky and in many other areas of the state and nation. Russell said he doubted that Rogers was responsible for murdering anywhere near the appalling number of seventy victims he once boasted of killing. At that time he didn't see any evidence or indication to back that up, the county attorney added.

Lewis reiterated that he was trying to convince his client to shut up and quit talking with the media. The lawyer was clearly getting fed up with Rogers's blabbermouth ways, and other news reports quoted him as saying he didn't know how to stop his client from talking with the press. If he could stop him, he would, Lewis insisted.

A new element was injected into the furor when a Hamilton lawyer journeyed to Richmond and spent more than three hours with Rogers at the jail. Then James Cooney, of the firm of Brever, Cooney, Beane & Lane, on Dayton Street, disclosed that he had been retained by Rogers to represent him on personal matters. If Rogers was named on criminal charges in Ohio, Cooney would defend him there. Cooney also had Kentucky connections, and was a graduate of the Chase Law School at Northern Kentucky State University in Highland Heights, just across the Ohio River from Cincinnati.

One of the first matters that the Hamilton lawyer addressed were the stories pointing at Rogers as the possible killer of Nicole Brown Simpson and Ron Goldman. Cooney said his client told him he met Nicole in a bar and they were acquainted but he didn't kill her. It was a story that was hard for some people to believe, regardless of whether he supposedly met Nicole in a drugstore, as he once said, or in a bar, as he told his attorney. Rogers and Nicole came from two widely disparate worlds.

While Rogers was reveling in the avalanche of attention and publicity, the investigation was rapidly progressing. Both the search warrant and the court order requiring him to provide the blood, hair, and saliva samples to compare with evidence at the murder scenes in other states were approved. KSP Detective Nolan R. "Skip" Benton served the warrant on Rogers at the detention center

Among items police were looking for, according to the affidavit, were knives or other sharp instruments, bloodstains, fibers, fingerprints, and palm prints from Rogers, and fingerprints of the last two murder victims killed during the reputed killing spree, along with any documents containing their names. The document also listed personal items believed to have been stolen from the women, including rings, bracelets, and watches, as well as food items including bottles of spices.

After the chase ended and Rogers was driven away, Mrs. Cribbs's battered and dusty Festiva with the broken headlight and broad new scrapes along the driver-side fender and door was loaded onto a flatbed truck and transported to the evidence room at KSP Post 7. Detective Benton headed the inventory search of the car and its contents, and observed a two-zipper gray and white cloth-covered suitcase between the rear seat and the hatch. He also removed a pair of tennis shoes that were lying in plain sight and were smeared with a rust-colored substance that appeared to be blood. The shoes were tagged with information noting the exact location they were found, the time, and Benton's name. Then they were locked up with other evidence.

Early Tuesday morning, the hatchback was again loaded onto a flatbed and Benton followed in a cruiser as the car, the suitcase, and the shoes were transported northeast to a gleaming new white building on Sower Road in Frankfort that is the KSP Central Crime Laboratory. In Building 100, at the conclusion of the forty-mile trip, Benton and evidence technicians from the police laboratory completed a meticulous search of the car. They carefully bagged or tagged and logged every piece of potential evidence found on the inside or outside of the vehicle, ranging from objects as large as the suitcase to strands of hair or fiber.

A police photographer snapped pictures of the exterior and interior of the car, of the suitcase before and after it was opened, and of individual pieces of evidence before they were picked up and tagged. Search of the car and of the suitcase in the back was disappointing, as far as any hopes may have gone of finding a knife, machete, gun, or some other obvious weapon. Although a report or two appeared in the press during the manhunt about fears that Rogers was armed with a gun, they were apparently unfounded. Except for a single pornographic magazine and a blue housecoat, most of the items listed in the inventory were unsuspicious personal effects that any man might be expected to carry with him on a trip. Three extra pairs of pants, seven shirts, ten T-shirts, fourteen clothes hangers, a safety manual from a contracting company, and a list of phone numbers and notes were taken from the car and suitcase.

On a more promising note, blood samples were discovered and collected from the interior of the car. An evidence technician also vacuumed the interior and collected hair and fibers. When the vacuum bag was emptied on a plain white surface, the hair and fiber samples were collected with tweezers and placed inside clear plastic envelopes, labeled, and set aside for later analysis.

Along with the suspiciously stained tennis shoes, they were turned over to crime laboratory technicians to be inspected and analyzed. An analyst specializing in forensic serology, the procedure of identifying and typing blood, semen, and other body fluids, was given the job of studying the blood samples and stains on the shoes.

The hair and fiber samples were turned over to other specialists to work on and make forensic comparisons. Hair is among the most common physical evidence found at crime scenes, and often offers the most valuable clues to the identity of a killer. At any given time there are about 300,000 strands of hair on the scalp of individuals who have not already suffered significant hair loss. It is constantly being shed, while new hair grows.

Importantly, sexual assault requires close contact between the attacker and the victim, and even the most careful rape-murderer is unlikely to notice the loss of a few strands of hair from his own person. In addition to normal hair loss from the scalp, pubic and other body hairs are often torn loose during sex and left on the victim or on sheets and other bedclothing. If Rogers murdered and had sexual relations with the dead women left behind during the cross-country rampage, the chances were excellent that he left some of his hair on their bodies or on the bedclothes. That was so, even though two of the bodies were dumped in bathtubs and washed, one was left sprawled on a punctured waterbed, and the other was burned.

A single strand of hair subjected to forensic analysis

in a police laboratory can provide vital information about the identity of the owner. The color of the hair is an obvious clue, but it can also reveal the race, information about health, and detect traces of drug use. Drug molecules circulate in the bloodstream, seep into the hair roots, and stay there. Even a six-inch sample can become a road map to the drug history of the owner of the hair that is handily readable by chemists when it is inserted into a device called a mass spectrometer.

In the past few years, with the expanded role in forensic science of DNA, the complex chemical that forms tiny threadlike sequences of genes in the body's cells, foreign hairs collected at crime scenes have taken on more importance. Even if investigators fail to collect samples of blood, semen, or saliva from an attacker, his unique genetic code can be determined and pinned down by analyzing hair samples.

Crime laboratory analysis and comparisons of fibers found in Mrs. Cribbs's battered Ford, lifted from Rogers's clothing, or recovered at the murder scenes were also important to the combined investigations. Cross-transfers of fibers between victims and assailants are especially common in incidents of rape, other physical assault, and in homicides committed by strangulation, knifing, and other means where there is close physical contact.

Fibers and threads from clothing, blankets, rugs, and other common woven objects also have their own unique colorations and patterns that can be identifiable in meticulous detail during the laboratory process. Fiber analysis was expected to be especially important to the investigation and possible trials stemming from the slayings in Florida, Louisiana, and Mississippi. The fire inside Sandra Gallagher's truck cab in Van Nuys destroyed much of the trace evidence that might otherwise have been collected by investigators.

No information was immediately released to the public about possible match-ups of the stains on the shoes or the trace evidence with any of the murdered women in Mississippi, Louisiana, or Florida.

Detective Stephens served the warrant for samples of blood tissue and hair from Rogers on the suspect at the detention center. An important element of the personal search warrant provided for use of a "Kentucky State Police Male Sexual Assault Evidence Collection Kit," and Stephens subsequently collected: five full, ten-milliliter blood samples, which were drawn by a medical technician; approximately 100 samples of hair plucked from various areas of the suspect's head; samples of pubic hair obtained by combing; another 100 pubic hair samples from various areas of the groin obtained by plucking; 100 hairs pulled from various areas of his beard and mustache; twenty oral swabs; and twenty-five sets of inked fingerprints and palm prints.

Except for the samples obtained by combing the pubic area, technicians always pull hairs collected as evidence. The seemingly preferable method of cutting hair samples is avoided because the root structure is important in the analysis and comparison process. Samples were taken from various areas of Rogers's head because hair color often varies in the same individual. In obtaining the combed samples, technicians were required to use a paper towel and comb provided in an envelope enclosed in the kit. The recommended process calls for placing the towel under the buttocks, and then either the suspect himself or the technician moves the comb in downward strokes through the pubic hair. Any loose hair or other debris is caught in the teeth of the comb or falls onto the towel. At the conclusion of the procedure the comb was placed on the towel and the paper was carefully folded in order to retain any hair or other material, then placed in a labeled envelope provided with the kit. Finally, the envelope was sealed and the label filled out with the pertinent information. All the other hair samples were placed inside Ziploc bags, then sealed and identified by filling out an attached label. Separate bags were used for the head hair, mustache and beard, and for the hair taken from the pubic area.

The oral swabs were collected four at a time. A technician carefully rubbed the swabs over the mouth cavity and the gum lines, then allowed them to air-dry before placing them in envelopes, checking them off, and adding labels. After individual packaging was completed, the swabs, hair, and blood samples were placed inside the kit and kept under refrigeration until the evidence was distributed to analysts.

The techniques for obtaining various samples from the persons of suspects are meticulously proscribed in regulations, and any deviation in the system could lead to serious problems when the case moves into the courtroom. There is no room in the process for invention or creativity. Detectives and technicians have to be excruciatingly exact.

Stephens also collected the clothing and shoes Rogers was wearing at the time of his arrest, so tests could be made for bloodstains and blood spatters. Conventional biochemical tests were conducted on the blood by serologists at the state crime laboratory, to define the enzymes and type. DNA typing was carried out by biochemists in the FBI Crime Laboratory at Quantico, Virginia, to more specifically pin down the unique genetic code of the owner.

The results of the analyses and other tests, along with samples of the blood, were shared with other police investigating the slayings committed during the reputed murder spree, as well as with other agencies checking out possible links by the accused killer to unsolved homicides in their jurisdictions. Hair samples and fresh sets of fingerprints taken from the suspect were also shared with fellow police agencies.

A short time later homicide investigators from Kentucky and Ohio to Louisiana, California, and Canada began turning their attention away from the big-talking braggart and looking elsewhere for the answers to their old unsolved murders. Blood typing, DNA comparisons, and other tests on the samples firmly ruled Rogers out as a suspect in unsolved slayings from Canada and California to Ohio and Kentucky.

In Port Hueneme, the DNA test results definitely eliminated him as a possible suspect in the Burger case, the single slaying in the three local murders that seemed to offer the most promise of a connection. Detective Jerry Beck said he was disappointed in the blood test results, but some new leads were developed in the Ventura County slayings as a result of the media blitz generated by coverage of the Rogers story. Similar cases to the local bathtub murder were turned up in Malibu and in Los Angeles County. Beck said there was also nothing to connect Rogers to either of the other two unsolved slayings in Port Hueneme that occurred during the local murder spree.

The Kentucky State Crime Laboratory forensics reports brought similar reactions from investigators in other cities and states. Rogers was not the killer of Nancy Jean Ludwig or Stephanie Hummer. With the exception of the Gaskins slaying. Rogers was no longer a suspect in the slayings of any other women whose unsolved deaths it was once considered he may have been involved in.

On the West Coast at about the same time, Rathbun, the other celebrity murder suspect of the moment, was also cleared of any possible involvement in the Ludwig and Hummer slayings. Both men were featured in major writeups within a few weeks of each other in *People* magazine and the national weekly tabloids.

Information that Rogers was serving jail time when other crimes occurred, or had other solid alibis, cleared him in yet additional cases. He was eliminated of involvement in the Heather Teague abduction after local and state police compared notes with other investigators probing Rogers's activities. The young woman was still missing, and Dill was still the prime suspect.

There appeared to be little doubt that Rogers's injudicious remark to Stephens and McIntosh that "it's more like seventy bodies" was the incredibly stupid boasting of a lifetime gasbag. Depending on the outcome of murder cases he was already charged with, he might indeed go down in criminal history as a serial killer whose crimes stand out for their ruthlessness and brutality, but he would never be top gun. That dubious honor already belonged to another "Hamiltuckian."

Ironically, the modern American record for known slayings by a single killer, for the time being at least, still belongs to a seemingly mild-mannered little male nurse born in Rogers's hometown. Like Rogers, Donald Harvey's father moved from the Kentucky hill country when he found work in the Ohio factory town. Unlike Rogers, however, he was born in Mercy Hospital in Hamilton, and then moved with his family back to their roots in Kentucky. Like Rogers, he shuttled between states, and lived briefly in California.

During a sixteen-year murder orgy that didn't end until 1987, he killed more than fifty victims in eastern Kentucky and in the Cincinnati area, according to his own admission. A plea-bargain agreement kept him off Ohio's death row. Harvey's victims were patients and neighbors whom he killed while working at hospitals on both sides of the Ohio River, many with poison or by smothering them.

Early Tuesday morning, November 21, Rogers was routed out of bed, given a shower, and fed breakfast. Then he was cuffed and manacled, and placed in the back of a Sheriff's Department cruiser. The deputy at the wheel drove him across West Irvine Street to the Madison County Courthouse for his arraignment on the local charges.

Normally it would be a few minutes' walk from jail to the back entrance of the courthouse. But with his hands in cuffs and manacles, a belly chain, and his legs securely shackled, it was difficult for the prisoner to walk more than a few steps under his own power.

For once, the man the press was calling the "Cross Country Killer" wasn't in a talkative mood. After being helped out of the cruiser by a pair of stern-faced sheriff's deputies, he ignored reporters who shouted questions and shoved microphones toward his face. The shackled man stared straight ahead and kept his mouth closed while he awkwardly shuffled past the crunch of media into the back door and was taken up to the third floor by private elevator.

Armed sheriff's deputies were stationed outside and inside the courtroom. Rogers's niece Lynn was already seated inside the wood-paneled room in the first row of the spectator section when he was led to the defense table. With the pressure of the manhunt over and a few days' rest, Rogers was once more paying attention to his appearance. His hair, which had grown longer and tumbled over his shoulders in front and back, was neatly parted in the middle; and the baggy dark green jumpsuit was a surprisingly good fit and looked as if he may have pressed it military or jailhouse style by spreading it out under the mattress of his bed and sleeping on it. The sleeves of the jumpsuit were cut off at about elbow length, and showed off the long sleeves of the white T-shirt. Considering the circumstances, the defendant was about as neatly dressed as could be expected.

Before settling awkwardly on his chair, the securely manacled prisoner aimed a wan smile at his niece and blew her a shaky kiss. Madison County Commonwealth Attorney Thomas J. Smith, III, stood at the prosecution table on the other side of the courtroom conducting a last-minute shuffle through his files and notes on the case. Madison Circuit Court Judge William T. Jennings presided. Judge Jennings read the charges from the indictment to the defendant, and carefully explained the meaning of each count.

Lewis also briefly complained at the hearing about the questioning of his client at the jail by Clermont County Sheriff's Lieutenant Dennis Stemen. The court-appointed attorney said he wanted it pointed out in court that the meeting occurred without his knowledge or presence, even though Rogers had invoked his right to counsel and to silence. Lewis asserted that the Clermont County detectives violated his client's constitutional rights when they questioned Rogers on the night after his capture. He said he told Rogers and the deputies to halt the interview, but they continued asking questions anyway. "I think it's shabby and unprofessional," he carped.

Any information obtained during the interview would probably be thrown out of court before a trial, Lewis said.

Lieutenant Stemen told the press no rules were broken.

The lawyer also observed that he advised his client "about thirty times" not to talk, and said he would personally screen all future requests for interviews. He stated that he would deliver the requests to his client, but stressed that the prisoner would not be granting any additional interviews.

Speaking calmly, but in tones that were clearly audible in the spectator section of the courtroom, the suspect entered pleas of not guilty to the trio of charges tied to the police chase. During the brief proceeding, he didn't show any traces of the old cockiness he exhibited when he was trolling bars, talking to police and reporters, or tossing the beer can at the state trooper. He sat quietly beside his attorney, without any show of emotion, while he allowed Lewis to do the talking. At the conclusion of the ten-minute hearing Jennings denied bail and designated February 5, 1996, as the trial date. In the second row of seats an out-of-town reporter leaned over toward a colleague with the whispered offer of a ten-dollar bet that Rogers would never appear for a trial in the Richmond courtroom during 1996. The bet was rejected.

When the prisoner was escorted out of the courtroom to be returned to the detention center, he showed some of his old cockiness, turning to smile at his niece and raising a clenched-fist salute. Ms. Clontz appeared to be near tears. As the courtroom cleared she brushed off reporters' questions, slipped on a pair of sunglasses, and hurried from the courthouse.

Rogers's transparent show of bravado may have temporarily lifted his own spirits, but once he was back in his one-man cell at the detention center there would be plenty of time for the effect to fade. The brief proceeding barely hinted at the long hours that lay ahead of the prisoner and his attorneys in the Kentucky courtroom, and very likely in courtrooms in one or more other states.

Homicide investigators from other cities and from other states were still streaming into Richmond to compare notes in the case, and to take their virtually nonexistent chances to talk with the suspect. For a while, it may have seemed to Rogers and his lawyer that half the law enforcement agencies in the country were lining up to get a crack at the suspected serial slayer.

But in Kentucky, where he was brought to bay and captured, state police and authorities in Lee County were behaving like the death of the old man found in the cabin outside Beattyville was too complicated to deal with. They didn't even know how he died, and the man most people believed was responsible for his death was already in enough trouble in other states where prosecutors were anxious to win a death-penalty conviction or honest-to-goodness life-sentence prison terms that would put him behind bars for the rest of his days. But if everyone else failed to take Rogers permanently off the streets and out of the saloons, Kentucky could always reassess the evidence and their possible murder case against him. There is no statute of limitations for homicide.

Less than two weeks after his capture, Rogers spent a quiet, almost pleasant Thanksgiving Day at the detention center. It was visiting day, and his mother and stepniece walked into the detention center at 3 P.M., and talked with him for about twenty minutes. Along with approximately a hundred other inmates earlier in the day, he dined on a traditional holiday dinner of turkey, mashed potatoes, dressing, green beans, a roll, and pumpkin pie. His meal was delivered to him hot, in special trays that hold heat, and slipped through the food flap in his cell door.

Rogers had been locked up on holidays before, but this time it appeared he had little to celebrate or to look forward to except the dreary prospect of spending more time in courtrooms and behind bars.

Chapter Ten

EXTRADITION

WHILE ROGERS WAS COOLING his heels in the Madison County Detention Center watching himself on television and exasperating his lawyer by making collect calls to the media, events outside the jail were moving rapidly.

Law officers from the FBI and several states were holding a series of meetings in Richmond and in Louisville, continuing to exchange information, setting up a task force and parceling out responsibilities for the broad-ranging investigation into the reputed crimes of the so-called Cross Country Killer.

Lawyers, judges, other court officers, and the governors of five states were also busy, trying to avoid a dogfight over custody and jurisdiction of the suspected serial killer. They were working out the details over the pecking order: resolving the questions of extradition and who would get first crack at prosecuting Rogers for murder. In Frankfort, a spokesman for Governor Brereton Jones announced that the state with the strongest case against Rogers would probably be given the first opportunity to prosecute him.

The task of sorting everything out was occupying the time of a posse of crack homicide investigators and creating a blizzard of paperwork that showered courthouses and governors' mansions from Los Angeles and Sacramento to Bossier City and Baton Rouge, Tampa and Tallahassee, Jackson, Richmond, and Frankfort.

The process began when the first FBI agent walked into KSP Post 7 headquarters to join in the interrogation of the suspect, and it never let up. Rogers was even served with a warrant at the Madison Radisson from nearby Fayette County, charging him in the two-year-old case stemming from the reputed run-in with his fellow drifter in Lexington. The offenses he was accused of on the document were first-degree assault and first-degree robbery.

Two days after the capture of the serial-murder suspect, homicide investigators from several states met at Eastern Kentucky University to review and exchange evidence. Most of the focus at the multijurisdictional meeting was on evidence seized from the Ford Festiva, and on working out a game plan. For the most part the law officers steered away from the question of who would get the first shot at extraditing Rogers, and concentrated on shoring up their own investigations. The problem of who would first haul him into a courtroom to face murder charges was a matter to be answered by prosecutors, other attorneys, judges, and governors.

The five-hour skull session was the first of several that would be held in Kentucky by various members of the law enforcement and criminal justice professions to deal with questions surrounding the suspected serial killer. A few weeks later law enforcement professionals from California, Mississippi, Florida, Louisiana, Ohio, and other states met with Kentucky authorities in Louisville for a conference arranged by the FBI. Police, prosecutors, forensic experts, and behavioral scientists attended.

The purpose of the parley was threefold: to exchange information, to map out strategy for the expanding investigation; and to deal with prosecutorial questions, including priority for putting Rogers on trial for murder.

At the conclusion of the two-day gathering, there was still no decision about which state should go to the front of the line. The ball was bounced back to Kentucky's new governor, Paul Patton, and new Attorney General Ben Chandler. Patton and Chandler were sworn into office in December, following the November elections, and one of their first and most closely observed public tasks was dealing with the notorious Rogers case. It was up to Chandler and to the law enforcement authorities who attended the meeting to make a recommendation to the new governor.

The meeting produced more success determining the future handling and direction of the multistate investigation of the Rogers case. The FBI formally took over and the center of action moved from Kentucky to the Bureau's academy in Quantico, Virginia. FBI agents began coordinating the investigation from the academy, and established a toll-free 800 number for callers with tips on any of the known homicides he was accused of as well as other unsolved crimes he might be suspected of committing. Much of the evidence was also transported to the FBI laboratory for processing.

Under FBI guidance, investigators also began working out a comprehensive time line to track Rogers's movements across the United States. Tracking was set up to include any possible travels to Canada, Mexico, or other foreign countries by the suspect. The time line was expected to work both ways. It could be useful either in linking him to specific homicides, or in eliminating him as a suspect. Assignments were parceled out, with investigators from various jurisdictions assigned to specific duties in order to eliminate duplication and cut down on wasted time, resources, and effort.

A "rapid-start team" was established to develop, store, and analyze information. It was also agreed to take advantage of the federal government's national database, the Violent Criminal Apprehension Program (VICAP), to collect and analyze information. VICAP has functioned as a vital clearinghouse for exactly the type of investigation the conferees were involved in since it was set up at the FBI Academy.

Shortly after the meeting investigators showed up in Lake City and began questioning residents of the tiny mountain community who may have come in contact with Rogers while he was laying low at the motel. Most of the people who live in Lake City or nearby make their living in coal mines, or they commute the roughly twenty-five miles to Oak Ridge, where they work for Martin Marietta or in one of a scatter of other industries in the Knoxville suburb. For the most part they're hardworking people who mind their own business and would have no special reason to concern themselves with transients who spend a night or two in local motels. But a few of them had tidbits to share with the investigators, a couple more pieces to fit into the puzzle.

Lake City Chief of Police Jim Shetterly also checked out the motel room and recovered a few items of potential evidence, but the room had been rented out twice to other guests before local authorities learned the notorious fugitive had camped out there a couple of nights.

Other task force investigators were assigned to interviews or to run down leads in Hamilton, Bossier City,

Gibsonton, Jackson, and Van Nuys. Authorities were co-ordinating information about their investigations with each other in a cooperative effort to help in the decision-making process.

While FBI agents and state and local law enforcement officers were busy painstakingly piecing together evidence in the multistate investigation, the matter of extradition continued to receive priority attention from officers of the court and bureaucrats in several states.

Extradition can be a relatively smooth legal procedure, or immensely complicated. The Uniform Criminal Extradition Act was at the center of what was shaping up in the Rogers case to be a complex exercise in co-operation. The act is an agreement between states that permits movement of accused criminals back and forth from one jurisdiction to another.

Under normal circumstances, the state which already has the suspect in custody is given precedence in bringing him to trial. But the most serious charges against Rogers were not filed in Kentucky, and law enforcement and governmental authorities in the Commonwealth were prepared to take a place at the back of the long line forming to get a crack at him.

A cook's stew of legal options were available to prosecutors, judges, and governors in the five states that had the potential of sending the extradition process veering off into any one of various directions. Perhaps most importantly, Rogers and his lawyer weren't idle bystanders. Rogers's attorney stated almost immediately after his assignment to the case that he and his client would oppose extradition.

Lewis and his client were digging in for a tooth-and-nail fight to influence the ultimate decision in Rogers's favor, and to keep him out of states considered most likely to send him to death row. One of the most appealing options for Rogers would occur if the states played hardball with each other and two or more insisted on the first opportunity at prosecution. He could then select the state least likely to send him to death row, and waive his right to oppose extradition to that state while continuing to fight extradition to the others. Presumably, he would then be checked out of the Madison Radisson and flown to the state where he believed he had the best chance of escaping execution.

According to the terms of the federal extradition pact, prosecutors and police in the four states with immediate interest in pressing murder charges against the suspect had sixty days after Rogers's arraignment to send a synopsis of their evidence to the judge in Kentucky who was assigned to the case, in order to assist him in his decision.

Within a few days of Rogers's capture work on the preparation of an extradition request began in the office of Los Angeles District Attorney Gil Garcetti. Before the end of November it was delivered to the office of California Governor Pete Wilson in Sacramento, and forwarded from there to Governor Brereton Jones in Kentucky.

Authorities in Louisiana placed a close second to California in processing and delivering extradition papers to their governor. The Bossier Parish District Attorney said he believed they had a strong case against Rogers, and they wanted him.

Florida and Mississippi were lagging behind, but about a month after Rogers's arrest, a grand jury in Tampa returned a three-count indictment against him for first-degree murder, robbery, and grand theft in the slaying of Tina Marie Cribbs. Authorities in the Sunshine

State indicated that a formal request would be soon forwarded to Governor Lawton Chiles for an extradition order.

In Jackson, Chief of Detectives Jimmy Houston told reporters they were planning to file extradition documents with Mississippi Governor Kirk Fordice. FBI agents in Jackson faxed a copy of Mississippi's murder warrant to Kentucky on the same day they learned of Rogers's arrest.

Most of the concerned investigators and judicial authorities, along with many of the survivors of the murder victims who spoke out, were intent on seeing that Rogers got the death penalty. It didn't make much difference to them where he was put to death as long as he was made to pay the ultimate penalty as quickly as possible.

All four states where women were murdered during the spree provided for the death penalty in their criminal statutes. Two of those states, California and Florida, rank with Texas among the top three states with the largest number of inmates on Death Row.

Both California and Mississippi offer a choice of methods to the condemned of either death in the gas chamber or execution by lethal injection. The death penalty is carried out in Louisiana by lethal injection, and in Florida the condemned still "ride the lightning" in the electric chair.

Kentucky also has the death penalty on its statutes, although it appeared highly unlikely that Rogers had much reason to worry about the possibility of spending his final moments in the electric chair at the old maximum-security penitentiary in Eddyville. Detective McIntosh was still looking into the mysterious death of Mark Peters, but there was no talk of immediately filing murder charges in the case.

In 1995, when Sandra Gallagher was strangled and set afire in the cab of her pickup truck, California state criminal statutes provided the death penalty for treason, homicide by a prisoner serving a life term, train wrecking, perjury causing execution, and first-degree murder with special circumstances. But the Golden State had a record of long delays between the arrest and trial of capital-murder defendants, an average of three years.

In Mississippi, where Linda Price was slashed to death and dumped in a bathtub, the death penalty could be imposed for capital murder, the forcible rape of a child under fourteen by a person eighteen or older, and for air piracy. Capital murder includes the killing of a police or corrections officer, murder while under a life sentence, murder by bomb or explosive, contract murder, murder of an elected official, and murder during the commission of other felonies such as rape, robbery, kidnapping, arson, sexual battery, and unnatural intercourse with a child or nonconsensual unnatural intercourse with an adult.

If Jackson and Hinds County authorities chose to seek the death penalty against Rogers, the decision would be tied to evidence police said they had showing that he stole Linda's purse and jewelry. The case could be made even stronger if investigators were able to learn where the purse and jewelry were disposed of, Houston told local reporters. The whereabouts of the missing property was one of the loose ends detectives were still working to tie up.

Louisiana carries the death penalty on its statutes for first-degree murder and for treason, and by the end of 1995 had put twenty-two prisoners to death in the electric chair and the gas chamber at the state penitentiary in Angola since states resumed carrying out the death penalty in 1977 following a long hiatus created by a U.S. Supreme Court decision. Death Row in Louisiana is in Camp G, a scatter of single-story green buildings on the 18,000-acre facility known as "the prison plantation." The Death House, where prisoners are sent the day before execution, is two miles away, and the execution chamber is next door.

Florida permits the imposition of the death penalty for felony murder, first-degree murder, sexual battery on a child under twelve, unlawful use of destructive devices resulting in death, and capital drug trafficking.

On the surface the extradition contest over Rogers looked like the ultimate choice facing the suspected serial killer might not be *if* he was going to get the death penalty but *how* he was going to go. The contest was shaping up as a horse race. That may have been a development that would seem appropriate for a state that prides itself on its fine Thoroughbreds, but it could wind up wasting valuable human and financial resources by the time the Kentucky governor and the notorious prisoner reached the finish line.

It wasn't that simple a matter, however. Just because someone was murdered in a state that carried a capital-punishment statute on the books didn't mean prosecutors could seek the death penalty for the accused killer. Execution sanctioned and carried out by the state is the ultimate punishment, and authorities don't take the death penalty lightly. Capital-punishment states establish extremely narrow parameters outlining exactly which crimes and which criminals qualify for the death penalty.

After careful study of their case, authorities in California determined that the evidence didn't exist or couldn't be proven to qualify Rogers's prosecution for first-degree murder with special circumstances. Rape is a qualifying special circumstance, but if Sandra Gallagher was sexually assaulted, the evidence was destroyed when her body was charred in the fire. Consequently, the murder charges filed by Deputy District Attorney James Bozajian in the case did not include special circumstances, and the maximum penalty on conviction is twenty-five years to life in prison. Under the circumstances, it was the best the Deputy DA could do.

Authorities in Louisiana also decided they did not have sufficient grounds to seek a capital murder conviction and lethal injection for the accused killer of Andy Sutton. The Bossier Parish Prosecutor settled for filing charges of second-degree murder. "We can't show any robbery, rapes, or anything else, so it is not a capital case," Prosecutor Bobby Stromile told reporters.

Although there was serious talk for a while in Mississippi of filing capital murder charges, Hinds County authorities also eventually settled on charges that fell short of qualifying for the death penalty. By the end of December, Mississippi was also backing out of the extradition horse race, although authorities didn't totally scratch their entry. Houston said they planned to wait until Rogers was put on trial in at least one other state before getting in line for a chance to prosecute him for Linda Price's slaying.

It went unsaid, but Mississippi is a poor state with a population of about 2.5 million people that is even less than Kentucky's. The extradition process can be expensive, and a high-profile murder trial, which the Rogers case was sure to be, would be even more costly. Like their counterparts in every other state, authorities in Mississippi had to consider tight budgets and crowded court dockets. Detective Chief Houston apparently summed up the prevailing attitude among the Mississippi legal establishment when he told a reporter: "We're not going to get in a hurry. Everybody will eventually get a shot at him. After one or two convictions, it is a moot point."

Florida was the last state to file extradition papers, but when lawyers and state officials in Tampa and Tallahassee finally got the show on the road they took center stage. They asked Kentucky Governor Patton to send Rogers back to Tampa. They wanted to put him on trial for his life. A Hillsborough County grand jury returned an indictment against the accused killer of Tina Marie Cribbs for first-degree murder, robbery, and grand theft.

Houston had theorized in Jackson that Florida would probably wind up getting Rogers first because the state has the death penalty on the books and the justice system moves swiftly there. There was no question, as Lewis dug in his heels to fight that probability, that Florida was in the catbird seat. The decision wasn't a done deal. Other states still wanted to make sure they got their crack at the reputed mad-dog killer.

After careful study of the extradition requests from the three states still vying for custody of Rogers, the Kentucky State Attorney General formally recommended to the Governor that Florida should be selected. Chandler noted in his memo to the new chief executive that Florida had a strong case that was buttressed by witnesses who saw Rogers with the victim, and by evidence left at the Tampa 8 Motel. He also pointed out it was likely the accused killer would get the death sentence if he was convicted.

The governors of Kentucky and Florida were experienced politicians, so they decided to settle the matter by doing what politicians do. They cut a deal. On January 24, Patton agreed to sign an order to extradite Rogers to Florida. As his part of the executive agreement, Chiles, a crafty Southern politician and former U.S. Senator who won his second term as governor in 1994 campaigning as the "he coon," agreed that if Rogers escaped the death penalty in Florida courts he would give other states a chance to put him on trial for murder. If Rogers was put on loan to another state for trial, Florida would also pay half the cost for his prison care during that period. Florida was already paying half the cost of Rogers's incarceration at the Madison Radisson. Chiles additionally agreed that Kentucky could keep custody of Rogers if he was charged there with murder before being moved out of state.

Lewis immediately announced that he would file an appeal. He said he didn't want his client put on trial in Florida because it was an "avid death penalty state." At an extradition hearing before Judge Jennings in Madison Circuit Court the next day, Lewis was given one week to file a petition for a stay of the extradition. If Lewis failed to contest the warrant for extradition during that period, Jennings said the prisoner would be turned over to Florida. The judge issued the ruling immediately after the warrant was served and read to Rogers by Madison County Sheriff Cecil "Dude" Cochran. The hearing lasted barely fifteen minutes, but it was the beginning of another exhausting round of prolonged legal jousting over Lewis's last-ditch effort to keep his client out of the Florida courts.

Lewis filed a petition asking the local court to block the extradition on grounds that the punishment in Florida would be too severe if his client was convicted; Florida was the last state to request extradition; since no capital offenses were committed in Kentucky, Governor Patton had no basis for making a death penalty decision; and there were errors and omissions related to Rogers's identity in the documentation. The document had the wrong Social Security number, the wrong birth date, and did not include fresh fingerprints. The lawyer further contended that the governor never gave Rogers a chance to tell his part of the story, and instead relied on information from police and "the media circus." Lewis declared the decision was standardless and arbitrary.

Commonwealth Attorney Thomas J. Smith III responded to the legal barrage by accusing the public advocate of grasping at straws. In his written response, Smith also contended the governor and state attorney general had every right to take punishment into consideration when they decided to extradite the defendant to Florida.

He cited an earlier precedent-setting court decision, known among legal professionals as case law, that established a narrow list of four factors that must be considered when making an extradition determination: (1) Are the extradition documents in order? (2) Has the person sought been charged with a crime in the state seeking extradition? (3) Is the person named in the extradition request the same person who is resisting extradition? (4) Is the petitioner a fugitive from the state seeking extradition?

Judge Jennings set a hearing on the petition for Tuesday, February 6.

In the meantime, Lewis dropped another shoe. In late January, he filed a motion seeking funds to pay experts to determine his client's mental state, a process he claimed was necessary to Rogers's defense on the local Kentucky charges. The trial was still scheduled to begin on February 5, although it was doubtful a judge would ever gavel a court to order for the proceeding.

Lewis cited Rogers's long history of head injuries,

and both his and his late father's history of alcoholism, in asserting there was "a distinct likelihood that the defendant's brain has been damaged significantly, effecting [sic] his behavior, judgment and ability to remember.

"Based on this history, the defendant submits that a neuropsychologist, psychiatrist, and perhaps a neurologist (if later indicated by the evaluation) should be appointed to evaluate the defendant."

Lewis also disclosed his client's old prison diagnosis of porphyria, and noted that there were "indications that alcohol abuse exacerbates the symptoms" of the ailment.

"The defendant's history of porphyria raises serious questions about the defendant's ability to form the required mental state to commit the offenses charged in the indictment," Lewis wrote in the motion. "Further, acute porphyria in combination with the evidence of brain damage, alcoholism, and other psychiatric indicators require a complex evaluation of the defendant, including a doctor of internal medicine or endocrinologist and a psychiatrist."

Continuing, Lewis said his client tried to kill himself at least three times, and his history was full of "bizarre and volatile behavior, usually associated with being severely drunk." He listed several of Rogers's previous arrests; wrote that Rogers's mother had been hospitalized for a "nervous breakdown," and noted that when he was a child Rogers's brother injected him "with speed."

Then the lawyer pointed out that costs to taxpayers for the experts was expected to be substantial, and said it would represent a colossal waste of resources because the case should never go to trial. He argued that private experts should make the evaluations instead of staff at state facilities which carry out those duties for the Court or for the Commonwealth. The message appeared to be obvious. If the local charges were not dismissed, the taxpayers should be made to pay through the nose.

The filing of the new motion was a jarring development, especially among budget-conscious public officials who were aware of the soaring expenses of dealing with an unwanted prisoner who wasn't even charged with murder in Madison County. More time and money was already being spent on Rogers than any other prisoner locked up in the detention center, and bringing in a passel of high-priced shrinks and medical experts to peer into the hidden recesses of his alcohol-muddled mind would boost the costs astronomically.

Smith opposed the request. "They don't need it," he argued. "These are Class D felonies, the lowest of felony charges." Importantly, the Commonwealth was prepared to pass on putting Rogers on trial for the local Class D felonies stemming from the car chase.

On February 6, attorneys assembled in Judge Jennings's third-floor courtroom for the hearing on Lewis's petition to block the extradition. Outlining the defense argument, Lewis told the court, "The primary problem we see in the governor's warrant is that it's founded on the stated intention for Glen Rogers to receive the death penalty."

The lawyer asserted it was his position that although extradition is designed to allow the ready movement of fugitives between states, that in this particular case the governor "took into account which state could and would, and was most willing to kill, or to seek the death penalty against Glen Rogers."

The evidence of that was in the attorney general's recommendation where he stated that the paperwork of all three states seeking extradition was in order and each of the states appeared to have cases that could be pursued, the defense attorney declared. But neither California nor Louisiana planned to seek the death penalty, and that left only Florida, which wanted to execute Rogers.

Lewis's presentation was typically dry and crisp, and the only animation he displayed while he talked was created by occasional steepling of his fingers, motioning with the flattened palms of his hands, adjustment of his glasses, or an absent shuffle of documents lying in front of him on the defense table. But he liberally sprinkled his argument with the buzzword verb "kill" when referring to execution.

Rogers sat quietly at the defense table beside his lawyer, staring forward most of the time without any show of emotion. Occasionally, he turned his head to look at his attorney, but there wasn't a trace of a smile or a frown on his face. He kept his hands clasped in front of him on the table. His beard was neatly trimmed and his hair appeared to have grown several inches longer since his imprisonment, and flowed over his shoulders onto his back and chest. It was still carefully parted in the middle, and had grown darker near his scalp since he was locked up and his exposure to sunlight was severely limited.

The spectator section of the courtroom illustrated the fickleness of the media. Only about a half-dozen people, including Todd Blevins, the local reporter from the *Richmond-Register*, bothered to show up for the important proceeding. The remainder of the courtroom behind the barrier separating the players from the spectators was empty. The national press had broken camp in Richmond long ago and was away chasing other more current stories.

Continuing to assert that the possibility of the death penalty was an important factor in the governor's decision to choose Florida as the extradition state, Lewis said that in that case his client should have been permitted a hearing to argue his position. His client deserved a chance to say, "No, Glen Rogers is not the kind of person that ought to be executed," the lawyer declared.

Lewis talked about "media hysteria" that painted Rogers as a serial killer, and said consideration of the death penalty "contributed to that hysteria." He said the reality was that Rogers was a person with brain damage, and with the rare blood disorder, porphyria, which affected his metabolism, and symptoms which he counted off for the court on his fingers—dementia, seizures, and blackouts. While his lawyer talked about his mental quirks and physical infirmities, Rogers absently twiddled his thumbs and continued staring forward.

Lewis declared that mitigation was extremely important in death penalty cases, and contended he and his client were wrongly denied an opportunity to present their evidence of Rogers's brain damage and of his porphyria. He noted that the Commonwealth claimed he never requested a governor's hearing, and although that was true, the reality was that the extradition procedure ended immediately after his client's arrest. It was resumed later after a court hearing, and in the interim there was no ongoing extradition warrant procedure.

Moving on, Lewis addressed his contention that the governor's extradition decision was standardless and arbitrary. There is no standard in the extradition statute saying the governor should choose one state over another when more than one state is seeking custody. Consequently, he asserted, it was arbitrary and should not be enforced by the court.

The executive agreement between Governors Patton and Chiles accounted for the second major grounds cited by the lawyer in his argument to block the extradition. He contended the pact violated the extradition clause, and said he didn't believe the governors were allowed to make such an agreement. It was possible that a few years down the line extradition requests could be received from California, Louisiana, or Mississippi and one or both of the governors might no longer be in office. Lewis claimed the governors were trying to block the free flow of fugitives or prisoners between states by entering into the agreement.

He conceded that the extradition law permits Kentucky to ask as part of an executive agreement for the right to bring Rogers back to the Commonwealth. "What the statute does not allow is for an executive agreement between two states to bind other states; to bind Louisiana, to bind California, to bind future governors in seeking extradition of Mr. Rogers once the procedure in Florida is complete," he declared.

"And again, we think the purpose of that executive agreement was to say, 'Okay, Florida, if y'all succeed at killing Mr. Rogers, then he's not going to have to go anywhere else.'" The fact was, he said, that California, Louisiana, and Mississippi still had interests in extraditing Rogers to their states.

"So, what we're asking this court to do in this is to declare this executive agreement between the governor of Florida and the governor of Kentucky to be null and void and unenforceable," he declared. "And to the extent that this was part of the governor's decision to have Mr. Rogers extradited, we ask that the governor's warrant be declared unenforceable."

Lewis's repeated references to the murder suspect as

"Mr. Rogers," rather than as "the defendant," or even "my client," made it sound like he was talking about the genial host of a kiddie's television show. But there was nothing about the demeanor of the defendant either in the courtroom, or of his reputed bloodthirsty behavior during the six-week cross-country killing spree, that even hinted at such a pleasant demeanor and style. In the courtroom, he appeared flat and drained, looking for all the world like he was patiently waiting for everyone to stop jabbering so he could be led back to his cell and left alone.

Accusations that Rogers's due process rights were violated because of reputed procedural quirks tied to the manner in which the local charges and fugitive warrants were manipulated in order to keep him in custody, accounted for the third major point in the defense attorney's argument. Lewis contended the local charges were used to keep his client behind bars until "Florida finally, in the middle of January, was able to get its act together to seek extradition.

"We submit again . . . that what drove that was the desire to hold Mr. Rogers so the state that most zealously wanted to kill Mr. Rogers could get its papers together, get the request together and present it to Governor Patton."

Lewis's fourth point was based on his allegation there was insufficient proof of identity to justify issuance of the warrant for extradition because of the incorrect Social Security number and the wrong birth date and lack of other supporting documents in the paperwork prepared by Florida authorities. Lewis said he understood the Commonwealth attorneys had witnesses ready to explain the reason for the errors in the documentation, and to produce new fingerprint evidence. If that was so, he said, the new evidence should be presented to the governor and a new governor's warrant issued using the correct information.

The attorney wound up his meticulous but low-key presentation by asking the court to deny the extradition request, and not to permit his client to be turned over to Florida authorities. In the event the judge ruled against them, he said he wanted to clearly state that his client "does not want to be communicated with, interrogated, questioned on his way down there . . ." Rogers would "continue to assert the right not to be questioned that he's asserted from the moment he entered into this court, and in fact from the moment he entered into the district court . . ." Lewis declared.

Scott White responded for the Commonwealth, addressing each of the major points cited as grounds for the appeal, in the order they were presented by Lewis.

The attorney general's civil division chief declared there had been no statements by Chandler or by Governor Patton that it was their intention that Rogers receive the death penalty. Instead, he contended that severity of penalty available in states requesting extradition was one of the factors considered in determining what the attorney general's recommendation to the governor would be.

White also pointed out that prior court decisions confirmed that the state's chief executive clearly had the authority to make extradition decisions. Court decisions also upheld a governor's right to make extradition determinations without holding hearings to determine mitigating circumstances.

White pointed out that Rogers would not be deprived of any of his rights, and that once he was in Florida he would have available to him all the protections of the state and federal constitutions. "In other words, he is not convicted going down there and facing an executioner's chair within a matter of days," he said. "So to say that his due process rights are being trampled upon is just simply inaccurate and is a red herring.

Moving to accusations that the governor's extradition decision was standardless and arbitrary, White said Kentucky statutes did indeed establish standards for the process. "At the governor's request the attorney general shall investigate the extradition. That was done. In other words, we have just not taken the law at its word and said, 'Well, this looks awful fine and dandy, let's just send him off down South.' Instead, the attorney general's office examined the documents from the states seeking extradition, and made a recommendation. That is a standard that we feel we have met," he said.

The Commonwealth official defended the executive agreement between the governors of Kentucky and Florida, and said there were very good reasons for inclusion of the clause in the extradition documents. Rogers was still charged in Kentucky with felony charges, and although they were minor, the Commonwealth should have an opportunity to put him on trial for them "or any other charges that may be lodged against him based on further evidence that may come up." White was leaving the door open, it seemed, for possible prosecution at some time in the future for the mysterious death of Mark Peters.

If Rogers was convicted of capital murder in Florida and sentenced to death, however, it wouldn't make sense to return him to Kentucky for another trial, White said. "It's just not good judicial economy."

Turning to Lewis's contention his client was denied an opportunity for a hearing to present mitigating circumstances and tell his side of the story to the governor, White took off the kid gloves and aimed a bare-knuckle legal roundhouse at his opponent.

"Your honor, I don't know many lawyers that can't file motions," he said. "Mr. Lewis was certainly well aware that our attorney general's office and Governor Patton's office were considering extraditing Mr. Rogers to another state . . . In fact, I think that the week before it came out, Mr. Lewis, at least, I saw him on the news making comments about things we may or may not have been doing." The sentence structure was slightly fractured, but the message was clear: Lewis knew what was going on.

He added that if Lewis and his client wanted an opportunity to be heard on mitigating circumstances they should have written the governor, and he would have then decided if he wanted to schedule a hearing or not. It would have been the governor's call.

Addressing the final point, which he referred to as "the identity issue," White said the Commonwealth didn't need to show Rogers's Social Security number, his date of birth, or produce fingerprints. They all knew that the Glen Rogers accused of the murder in Florida was the man sitting at the defense table. White concluded by asking the judge to deny the defense request.

Judge Jennings first listened to three witnesses called by the Commonwealth to bolster their argument. Detective Randy Bell, who was one of the investigators representing Tampa at the Louisville conference, was the first to testify. Bell said he testified before the Hillsborough County Grand Jury that returned the Florida indictment against the suspected killer. The defendant used the names Glen Rogers and Edward Peters as well as Glen Edward Rogers, the detective said.

Asked to point Rogers out in the courtroom, Bell pointed at the long-haired blond man and said it was, "The gentleman sitting at the desk" with the white undershirt and green pants. Rogers's expression didn't change while the judge, other court officers, and spectators turned to look at the man being pointed out by the witness.

Lewis conducted a lengthy cross-examination, picking at the mistakes made on the affidavit for the extradition warrant that listed Rogers's date of birth and Social Security number. Bell explained he obtained the incorrect information from authorities in California, but pointed out that Rogers's criminal history records showed that he sometimes used the incorrect birthdate. NCIC reports also disclosed the prisoner's use of aliases and different Social Security numbers.

Cross-examination of the Tampa sleuth was marked by several objections from White, and all except one were upheld by the court. Jennings remarked a couple of times in his rulings that the defense attorney was moving into areas that were outside the limited purpose of the extradition hearing. "It's beginning to sound like it's becoming a discovery proceeding on the Florida case," he stated at one point.

Jennings overruled White's objection to Lewis's question to the witness, asking if he played a role in Florida's decision to seek the death penalty. When he was permitted to reply to the question, Bell declared: "All I am is a detective. All I do is gather the information and give it to the State Attorney. It's up to the State Attorneys to decide how they're going to go and what they're going to go with."

Detective Stephens and Tom Wintek, a KSP fingerprint analyst from Frankfort, were the other two witnesses, and were on the stand only a few minutes each. Stephens also pointed Rogers out from the stand, before testifying about running an NCIC scan and other information checks on him. The veteran KSP investigator confirmed that he turned up two different Social Security numbers, birthdates both for 1969 and 1962, and the names Glen Edward Rogers, Glen Rogers, and James Edward Peters. Wintek testified that he confirmed one of Rogers's fingerprint cards and other prints provided to him by Bell matched each other. He did not identify the source of the other prints during testimony.

After listening to all the hyperbole and legal nitpicking, the judge rejected the appeal. There were only four factors to be considered, he said: Were the documents in order? Was Rogers charged with a crime in Florida? Was the petitioner the person named in the request for extradition? And was Rogers a fugitive from the state seeking extradition? All the factors were satisfactorily answered in favor of the Commonwealth.

Addressing the question of identity, Jennings observed that when the Extradition Acts were first adopted by most of the states it may "have been a crucial issue back in 1960, way before the age of the speedy communication process we now have where photographs can be quickly transmitted by fax or computer all over the country, all over the world." But there was "no question" that Rogers was the person Florida wanted to extradite, he said. The discrepancies in the paperwork were "simply mistakes and don't affect his actual identity. Birthdates or Social Security numbers don't make a person's identity," the jurist declared. "The person is the person."

The remarks were delivered in a homespun manner, by a judge with a heavy Kentucky drawl, but they were on target and made good common sense—a rarity in many courtrooms around the country.

Addressing another point made by Lewis in his written motion and courtroom presentation, Jennings echoed White's argument that there was nothing in the statutes that required a governor to hold a hearing to consider presentation of mitigating circumstances. The extradition process was set up to be a rapid proceeding, and wasn't designed to be turned into something of an adversarial nature.

The judge's decision was not unexpected, and Lewis responded by announcing that he would take the matter before the Kentucky State Court of Appeals. "I don't think he should go to Florida because he's likely to face the death penalty if convicted," the small-town lawyer said. "Florida has demonstrated itself as an excellent killing machine." Ten days later Lewis took his case to the Kentucky State Court of Appeals.

Although it's part of the way the game is played, the prolonged legal jockeying was frustrating and troubling not only to authorities in Kentucky but to prosecutors in Florida, who were anxious to get on with the normal pretrial process there. Much of the evidence in Florida was "time-sensitive," and could be put at risk or compromised by too many additional delays, according to court documents filed by Smith in Kentucky.

The Kentucky Court of Appeals upheld Judge Jennings's decision. The higher court ruling was a crushing blow to Rogers's efforts to avoid return to Florida, but Lewis had been in legal dogfights before and he had other legal maneuvers in mind to delay his client's extradition. He packaged up a new motion appealing to the Kentucky Supreme Court to intervene, addressed it to the court in Frankfort, and dropped it in the mail Tuesday night. It was scheduled for overnight delivery.

But lawyers with the Commonwealth's attorney general's office had also been around the track a few times before, and they had some tricks of their own up their collective sleeve.

Chapter Eleven

BACK TO FLORIDA

GLEN ROGERS WAS ROUSED out of his bunk at the Madison County Detention Center long before sunrise on May Day morning. He was given a few minutes to clean up and dress, provided with some hot coffee, then turned over to four Florida police officers. It was 4:30 A.M.

Flanked by Florida and Kentucky State Police, the handcuffed man was escorted to the rear of the building, loaded into the backseat of a KSP cage car, and driven out of the sally port into the early-morning darkness of downtown Richmond. Rogers was on his way to Florida and a possible date with "Old Sparky" in the death chamber of the Florida State Prison near the town of Starke.

The driver of the police car drove his fellow law officers and their prisoner northwest on Interstate Highway 75 to the Blue Grass Airport in Lexington. They climbed aboard a private airplane at exactly 5:35 A.M. for the flight to Tampa. Peering outside the windows of the small airplane, Rogers took what may have been his last look at Kentucky just as the first rays of the new morning sun were beginning to stretch fingers of golden light over the rocky, rich green mountains and valleys to the east.

The Commonwealth attorneys had taken advantage of Lewis's decision to mail the new motion, instead of hurriedly driving to Frankfort and filing it there before the Supreme Court Clerk's Office closed at 4:30 P.M. Tuesday. By that time events were already in motion to have Rogers on his way back to Florida before the Kentucky courts' and clerks' offices opened for business the next day.

Scott White was in telephone contact with authorities in Florida within minutes after the Appeals Court decision was reported Tuesday afternoon. He advised them there was no stay in effect on Rogers's extradition, and if they wanted him they should pick him up at the jail before 8 o'clock Wednesday morning. "After 8 A.M., we didn't know what would be filed," he later told a reporter.

Although the surprise end to the five-and-one-half-month legal squabble was perfectly legal, it brought howls of outrage from Lewis in Richmond and from Rogers's new court-appointed attorney in Tampa. They loudly branded the move as "legal kidnapping." Commonwealth authorities and others with an interest in seeing an end to the delays in Rogers's extradition looked upon it as a neat maneuver. They merely outfoxed their opposition.

Lewis complained that he mailed his motion instead of rushing to Frankfort with it because Kentucky officials told him they wouldn't move ahead with extradition until the appeals process was complete. The action was "shabby" and made the attorney general's office look untrustworthy, he grumped. The chagrined lawyer said he felt like he hadn't been sufficiently vigilant, and was taken advantage of.

Smith conceded to reporters it was true he told Lewis the state wouldn't proceed with extradition while motions were pending before the appeals court. But no one said anything about waiting for subsequent appeals. White also chimed in, observing that the attorney general's office didn't and wouldn't agree to allow Rogers to delay his extradition months or years by filing endless appeals.

Kentucky is a thinly populated state and the legal community is small, so it wasn't surprising that Lewis picked up rumors late Tuesday that some monkey business was going on. He telephoned Smith and asked if the rumor that Rogers was about to be whisked away to Florida were true. Smith confirmed the story, so Lewis telephoned his client at the jail and told him to get ready for the move. Rogers took the news well.

Madison County authorities were relieved to see him go. Even though Florida was sharing costs of lodging for the Madison Radisson's reluctant guest, the price tag was still well over $2,000. That was only one of the expenses, and by the time the costs of police, judges, the prosecutor, pauper attorney, other court officers, clerical workers, materials, and equipment were factored in, the drain on the Madison County budget was horrendous.

Smith was tied up in one meeting after another, answering telephone calls from other prosecutors, police, or the press, and taking up valuable time he needed to devote to other affairs his office was concerned with. Lewis was tied up with similar demands. The Rogers mess was eating up human and financial resources that Madison County taxpayers would ultimately be presented the final bill for. If Lewis was sorry to see his client go, he represented a small minority among his neighbors.

The weather was Florida balmy, highways in Hillsborough County were afloat with snowbirds driving big cars with out-of-state plates, and Tampa Bay was sunspeckled and dotted with sailboats and motorcraft when Rogers was helped out of the small airplane. It was midmorning on May 1—May Day.

The prisoner was loaded in a waiting police cruiser and driven from the airport to Hillsborough County's Morgan Street Jail, where he was locked up among a motley collection of crackheads, drug dealers, stickup men, rapists, and other accused killers. He was just one more of some 2,300 men and women shoehorned into three jam-packed jails in the county. The Hillsborough County jails were much more crowded than the Madison Radisson, and there were so many inmates and so little space in fact that officials were under a court order to build another 512-bed facility. There were few frills, if any, in Rogers's new quarters.

The Morgan Street Jail where Rogers was confined with most of the other maximum-security inmates was the oldest of the three lockups and was typically crowded. The original three-story structure, which replaced an even more ancient jail, was built approximately thirty years ago, and a four-story annex was added a few years later. Although the official capacity of the jail was 508, on any given day it accommodated from 540 to 560 inmates. Overflow jailbirds slept on mattresses placed on the floor.

As a maximum-security prisoner, the effects of the crowding on Rogers were minimal, if they were felt at all. He was placed in a one-man cell, with a bed, lidless

.toilet, sink, and his own shower. Providing him with a cell with a private shower wasn't evidence of pampering. Jail authorities take every precaution they can to keep movement of inmates like the accused cross-country slayer to a minimum. Rogers, and others like him, are only allowed to move around outside their cells when it is absolutely necessary, such as visits with their lawyers, with family or friends on visiting day, and for minimal exercise periods.

Rogers was permitted to spend one hour, five days a week, in a narrow exercise yard. The yard was totally enclosed, with brick or cement walls and a thick glass roof over the top to let in the sunlight. Nevertheless, exercise periods are scrubbed during bad weather. There weren't even any provisions for weightlifting, jogging, or Richard Simmons–style workouts. At the Morgan Street Jail, Rogers exercised with his wrists securely fastened together in handcuffs, and his legs hobbled by shackles while he was closely watched by a sheriff's deputy.

Conditions in his approximately fourteen-foot-by-six-foot cell were only slightly more comfortable. Although he wasn't shackled while he was inside, his only contact with other convicts occurred when a trustee slipped his meals through a slot in the cell door. Like jailers at the Madison County Detention Center, a sheriff's deputy accompanied the trustee while meals were delivered and no unnecessary chatting was allowed.

The onetime vagabond lover's maximum-security home was a cell within a cell. To reach his cubicle, the trustee and jailers first had to pass through a locked solid metal door leading from the hallway into a room containing his barred cell. The side and rear walls of the cell are constructed of solid block and metal. Although

Rogers could control the water in his shower and wash-basin and flush his own commode, his activities inside the cell were severely limited. He had a small private TV set that he could control, but there are only two channels to choose from. One is an educational channel and the other offers religious programming. While Rogers was locked up at Morgan Street there would be no opportunity for him to watch himself on television when he appeared in court for hearings or at the trial.

Rogers also had telephone privileges, and was allowed to make collect calls after being escorted by a deputy about twelve to fourteen feet down the hallway from his cell to a pay phone. The deputy watched him until the call was completed and he was escorted back to his cell.

The day after the high-profile prisoner's arrival at the jail, he starred at his second closed-circuit televised hearing, and his on-camera performance lasted about one minute. While he sat in a special room at the jail, a judge at the courthouse ordered him held without bail. No court dates were set for the case, and Rogers didn't speak.

A week after Rogers's return to Florida he was given his first trip outside the jail. Sheriff's deputies escorted the cuffed-and-shackled inmate into the back of a van and drove him eight blocks south to the Hillsborough County Courts Building in the city center. He was the only inmate in the van. (In these days of political correctness, even the staffs at jails have been ensnared, and the use of terms like "guards," "wardens," and "convicts" are discouraged in favor of "deputies," "superintendents," and "inmates.")

Rogers was taken before Hillsborough Circuit Judge Diana M. Allen and asked for his plea to the first-degree murder charge. Rogers didn't speak as his attorney, Joan

Corces, an assistant public defender, responded for him: "Your honor, we stand silent," she declared. Judge Allen then ordered a plea of not guilty entered into the court record, and scheduled a pretrial hearing. Rogers would continue to be held without bond, the judge further ordered.

Rogers's new lawyer stated during the hearing that she planned to file motions challenging the court's jurisdiction over her client. She also said she would ask for dismissal of the indictment, which was issued by the grand jury while Rogers was still in Kentucky. And she reiterated the complaint over the manner in which he was whisked away from Kentucky before the State Supreme Court there could consider an appeal. She carped that it was a "legal kidnapping."

Tina Marie Cribbs's may also have been kidnapped, or at the very least forced into a motel room at knifepoint through some other threat. Semantics are important in courtrooms. "Girl" was one of the last of fourteen women, among forty-six people murdered in Tampa during 1995, and her slaying was among the most highly publicized. (Three police shootings were ruled justified, and four other people died at their own hand in murder-suicides and are not counted in the toll.) Unlike most of the victims, who were largely faceless as far as the national press was concerned, Girl's slaying became part of a major media event.

Before her pitifully mutilated body was lifted out of the tub and hauled away, experts in the social and biological sciences, along with reporters and other amateur analysts, were already busy looking for answers, trying to get into the mind of the perceived killer and learn why Tina and the other women all died so horribly. Even after all the psychiatrists, psychologists, neurologists, biochemists, and geneticists have had their crack at him, pieces of the puzzle will still be left over, impossible to fit into place.

If police accounts of Cribbs's murder are correct, there seems to be little doubt that Rogers's runaway alcoholism played a major role in the tragedy, although the details were still expected to come out in court when the first-degree murder case went to trial in Tampa. Rorschach tests on John Wayne Gacy, Jr., who tortured and slaughtered at least thirty-three young men and boys and buried most of them under his house in suburban Chicago, produced no symptoms whatsoever of violence when his system was devoid of alcohol. But after researchers fed him whiskey the inkblot analyses disclosed a man who underwent a Jekyll-and-Hyde change to sadistic sex killer.

At least three of the women believed to have been killed by Rogers died after he left barrooms with them. The exact circumstances leading up to Linda Price's death in Jackson are still being sorted out by police. But while they lived together, Rogers continued to drink as heavily as he ever had. And there is no question that he was extraordinarily violent when he was drinking, beating up on women and brawling with men.

There are important questions to be answered if Rogers and people like him are to be understood and identified before they kill, or before they kill so many. Was Rogers born with a predisposition to alcoholism, sadism, and violence? Acquaintances in Hamilton have said he loved to hurt women, and to see them in pain.

Did some kind of genetic programming occur in the womb? Or was he hot-wired for violence in infancy or early childhood? Rogers was trouble from early childhood and behaved like the proverbial ''bad seed.''

He concocted incredible lies, manipulated other people—especially females—boozed, skipped school, and got himself kicked out for good when he was in the ninth grade.

While researching this book, I had some opportunities to briefly peer into Rogers's troubled mind, but emerged from the experience with more questions than answers. During conversations with him while he was jailed in Tampa awaiting trial on murder charges, he showered me with classic Glen Rogers braggadocio. He sounded peacock proud of himself, and came off as more interested in demonstrating how he was outsmarting police, officers of the court, and everyone else around him than he was in shedding any real light on possible motivations for committing the darkling crimes he was accused of. He was also angling, in typical jailbird fashion, for money. He struck out completely, and I didn't fare much better.

Rogers continued his efforts to cash in financially on his reputed crimes when various groupies began corresponding or visiting with him at the jail. Like most accused serial killers and other high-profile criminals who have been the subjects of widespread press coverage, he was besieged by men and women attracted to his dark celebrity. But Rogers was no O. J. Simpson, and there were no million-dollar book contracts or big-money deals with trading card companies for him. The best he could do was try to take advantage of contacts with his newfound friends on the outside to peddle his autograph on index cards for thirty dollars each.

The "whys" of Rogers's reputed crimes and other misdeeds are intriguing questions. But the "what's" are the most crucial questions to be answered. What did Rogers do? Did he really murder Tina Cribbs and the other women, perhaps Mark Peters as well? And if he did, what can and should society do about it?

There's plenty of time for the sorting-out process. At this writing, Rogers still had many lonely days and nights ahead of him in the Morgan Street Jail, while lawyers on both sides of the case continued to file briefs, argue motions, interview potential witnesses, and tend to all the other matters that are such a vital part of pre-trial maneuvering. And things weren't going smoothly for him.

He didn't like his new lawyer, and a few weeks after their first meeting he tried to get rid of her. Rogers presented the court with a handwritten motion asking that she be dropped from his case because she works for the same state that wanted to execute him and wasn't spending enough time with him or working on his case.

"I have great fear . . . that the office of public defender and all of my court-appointed attorneys are predisposed as to my guilt," Rogers wrote in the five-page petition. "The state of Florida has already said they are going to kill me, when in reality they should be trying to learn the truth."

Ms. Corces also asked to withdraw from the case, complaining that her obstreperous client didn't listen to her advice and contacted the media whenever he wanted to spout off. He was up to the same old tricks that confounded and dismayed her predecessor in Kentucky.

Rogers appeared for a court hearing on the petition, wearing a bright orange jail jumpsuit and with his wrists cuffed in front of him. He told Judge Allen that he didn't even know what he was charged with. He asked his lawyer for a copy of the indictment, but was told she was too busy to send him a copy, to see him weekly, and too busy to work on his case, Rogers declared. Reiterating another complaint outlined in the written petition, he declared: "I'm represented by the same people who threatened to kill me."

When the judge asked the lawyer for her side of the story, she responded that she had eleven other cases to deal with, a trial, and other matters that were making demands on her time.

"A letter would have been fine to tell me they were still working on my case," Rogers retorted. The lawyer said she sent several letters to him at the jail, and cited the dates of the mailings.

The judge asked if he had any other complaints, and the bearded suspect said that was it for the time being. Judge Allen moved to bring the brief hearing to a close by remarking that she was satisfied with the defense attorney's explanations and believed he had appropriate counsel. Both his request to fire his attorney on grounds of incompetency and conflict of interest and Ms. Corces's request to withdraw were rejected. The jurist also scheduled a late October date for the trial, giving the reluctant duo of public defender and defendant a little more than three months to devise strategy and prepare a case good enough to keep him out of the electric chair.

But the stubborn prisoner had a final parting shot for the court. He told the judge he planned to file a motion to represent himself. "I can hardly wait," the judge retorted, peering soberly down at the hairy defendant in the rumpled jail uniform.

It seems unlikely that Rogers will wind up serving as his own lawyer, but if that occurs he wouldn't be the first serial murderer in the Florida courts to represent himself. Ted Bundy was also a narcissist who loved the limelight and took over his own defense. The "Love Bite Killer" was convicted of first-degree murder, and after ten years of filing and arguing appeals from death row he was finally executed in 1989.

Even if Rogers, acting as his own lawyer or with his court-appointed attorney, is unable to avoid a first-degree murder conviction, it could be years before he has a final date with "Old Sparky," the bulky wood and metal chair constructed with convict labor and first used in 1924. It might never occur at all. Despite Florida's reputation as a solid "death penalty state," the course of justice is frustratingly slow when it comes to carrying out the will of a huge majority of the American people by performing executions.

After the death penalty was reinstated in the United States following the U.S. Supreme Court's *Gregg vs. Georgia* decision in 1976, it was still three years before Florida carried out its first execution. By the end of 1995, however, thirty-six condemned men had taken their final stroll from a special holding cell on death row into the execution chamber. During that time, however, more than 300 inmates either were removed from death row after their sentences were overturned in the courts, had their sentences commuted, or died natural deaths.

By mid-July while Rogers was in court trying to dump his attorney, three hundred sixty men and six women were on death row near Starke or at the Broward Correctional Institution for Women near Fort Lauderdale. More than 100 of them had been on death row for ten years, and six men were twenty-year veterans.

On July 15, the erstwhile high-stepping good-time Charlie who spent much of his adult life roaming the country, boozing, and beating women, quietly observed his thirty-fourth birthday inside the Morgan Street Jail. There was no cake, no candles, and no Budweiser.

There were strong prospects he would spend many more drab and muted birthdays behind bars, either in county jails or in prison. The saga of Glen Edward Rogers was a long way from being over.

Chapter Twelve

THE TRIAL

EARLY IN MAY 1997, almost exactly nineteen months after Glen Rogers's capture during the dramatic car chase in Kentucky, he went on trial in Tampa for his life.

When Judge Diana M. Allen gavelled the Hillsborough Circuit courtroom to order, beginning Rogers's first-degree murder trial for the murder of Tina Marie Cribbs, the defendant was represented by a court-appointed private attorney who was prepared to present a predictable defense: Somebody else could have murdered the motel maid.

The tack chosen by the defense was not a big surprise to court watchers. In a motion presented in the case a few days earlier, Prosecutor Lyann Goudie disclosed that a jail informant claimed Rogers was scheming to get another murder suspect to take the rap for the Cribbs slaying. Jonathan "Rock" Lundin was accused of first-degree murder in the fatal stabbing of another Tampa Bay area woman, Janet Ragland, about a year after Mrs. Cribbs was killed. Lundin had worked with Rogers on the carnival circuit and was also a regular at the Showtown USA, who knew Mrs. Cribbs and her mother. He helped Mrs. Dicke look for her daughter the night the younger woman disappeared.

In the written motion the prosecutor declared that Rogers reportedly told an inmate that "Lundin was going to plead guilty in another homicide, and . . . was going to take the fall for Glen Rogers by saying that he killed Tina Cribbs." Goudie wrote that Rogers was quoted by the informant as saying "he was feeding Lundin with information about the crime scene and the evidence so that Lundin would be well-informed on evidence, circumstances, and on the case completely." Two other inmates were involved in the exchange of information between the accused killers, and efforts were made to enlist a third inmate to get a witness to testify about seeing Rogers by himself, and Lundin with a woman, according to the account.

Goudie and lead prosecutor Karen Cox stated in the motion that the accused killer tried to sell the scheme to Lundin by claiming the Rogers family had money, and convincing him that he would become famous by taking responsibility for the Cribbs murder.

The motion was filed after a surprise search at the jail ordered by Cox, and confiscation of boxes of documents from some of the inmates. No charges were filed in the reputed conspiracy.

The incident was only the latest of a series of peculiar events that had constantly swirled around Rogers since he was first singled out as a suspect in the grisly murder of Sandra Gallagher in California. If he was seriously brain damaged, as some experts insisted, it didn't appear to inhibit his fertile imagination and renegade behavior.

Almost as soon as he checked into the Morgan Street Jail, Rogers began peddling the idea to fellow inmates and to people across the country that someone else could have committed the Cribbs murder. A suspect in a federal drug case, whose cell was one of those searched, told authorities that Rogers claimed Mrs. Cribbs met a man at the motel named "Rocky" and left with him. But according to a deposition from another former carnival worker who knew Lundin, Rock was in Texas when Mrs. Cribbs was murdered.

Despite lengthy court-imposed orders sealing documents and banning comments from attorneys and police that prevented the local press from reporting in-depth one of the most notorious local murder cases in years, the defendant kept the telephone wires humming with calls to newspaper and television reporters, authors, male and female groupies, and to members of his family.

Incredibly, a few days before the beginning of the trial, Rogers interrupted a hearing on a petition by the *Tampa Tribune* to lift the gag order with a shouted denial that he was making telephone calls to the media. The surprise outburst occurred after a lawyer for the *Tribune* told the judge that Rogers telephoned an Ohio newspaper a few days earlier and professed his innocence.

"Your honor, I have not made one phone call to no news agency," Rogers roared in response. His startled defense attorney quickly shushed him, and the heavily shackled defendant remained silent throughout the remainder of the hearing. The *Cincinnati Enquirer* had already published a recent interview with him based on a jailhouse telephone call. He was notorious for playing by his own rules, and Cox asked that the gag order be extended to him or that his telephone privileges be taken away.

"Mr. Rogers gets on the phone . . . calls the media

and advances his agenda,'' she complained. The judge ruled against lifting the gag order against attorneys, and refused to extend the restriction to the defendant.

Immediately after Rogers was locked up in Tampa, he became the reigning superstar inmate at the maximum-security jail. While groupies vied with each other to get on his visitors' list, other inmates were also attracted to his sinister celebrity. According to court documents, one of the inmates drew a sketch, which Rogers passed off as his own and sold. One of the artistic inmate's other projects was called *The Evil-Ass Cookbook*, which included a recipe for human stew. Deboned fingers and toes, virgins' blood, and tears were listed as some of the ingredients.

An Illinois couple who deal in ghoulish mementoes from notorious criminals such as John Wayne Gacy, Jr., Charles Manson, and ''Nightstalker'' Richard Ramirez, offered his autographs on three-by-five-inch index cards on sale for thirty dollars each. Rogers thrilled other fans with clippings of his hair or beard.

Mary Dicke was dismayed at the dark celebrity enjoyed by the man accused of murdering her daughter, and resolutely attended the seemingly interminable hearings preceding the trial. Friends from the Showtown often attended the hearings with her, but she was also frequently accompanied by Tina Marie's son, Damien, and confided to reporters that she wanted the boy with her because he was ''the spitting image'' of his mother. She wanted to remind Rogers of the gravity of his crime.

When the trial began at last, a seat was reserved for Mrs. Dicke up front in the spectators' section. She had taken off work at the Showtown, where she had worked for years as a bartender. Rogers's mother; his brother, Claude, Jr., a Vietnam veteran and California real estate agent; and other family members were seated on the other side of the aisle.

Rogers sat a few feet away at the defense table next to his attorneys. The defendant's blond, shoulder-length hair was parted in the middle, and his distinctive beard and mustache were closely trimmed, accentuating the oval appearance of his face.

The defendant's attorneys were Nick Sinardi and Robert Fraser. The forty-eight-year-old Sinardi had a reputation as one of the Tampa area's top criminal defense attorneys, and was a former prosecutor with the Hillsborough county state attorney. The private attorney was named the previous July to represent Rogers because the state was seeking the death penalty. Fraser, his fifty-two-year-old defense colleague, was a former journalist in Hillsborough County who switched careers and became a leading attorney specializing in death penalty cases. He would be responsible for heading the sentencing phase of the trial for the defense if Rogers was convicted.

Assistant State Attorney Cox, a thirty-three-year-old experienced trial lawyer, and Goudie, her thirty-seven-year-old colleague who formerly served as a prosecutor in Brooklyn, N.Y., and in Miami, represented the state. Cox was chief of the State Attorney's Homicide Division, and Goudie formerly worked with Janet Reno in Dade County before Reno became U.S. Attorney General.

Although investigative reports disclosed that a confidential informant told police in California after the Gallagher slaying that Rogers telephoned him and said he had a "dead woman in a truck," Judge Allen ruled out any mention at the Tampa murder trial about Rogers's being a suspect in the killings of the other three women.

In opening statements Goudie outlined some of the evidence the prosecution planned to present, revealing that Rogers's black sports watch was found in the bathtub with the victim's body, and his fingerprints were lifted from her discarded billfold. She also publicly disclosed for the first time that after Rogers's arrest in Kentucky, police confiscated a pair of denim shorts stained with spots that matched his blood and the blood of the dead woman. Rogers sat between his lawyers, placidly staring at the jurors, while the prosecutor sternly declared: "We are all looking at a murderer."

Sinardi told the jury of seven women and five men that the case against his client was flimsy and constructed on circumstantial evidence. The evidence proved only that his client was a flirt and a thief who stole Mrs. Cribbs's car and billfold, but that didn't mean he stabbed her. She left the Showtown USA with another man, and Rogers drove off with her car after she failed to return, the lawyer said. Sinardi pointed out that when Rogers bought drinks at the bar and used his real name to rent the hotel room, it was behavior that didn't fit in with someone who was trying to get away with murder. "Mr. Rogers wasn't trying to keep a low profile," he declared.

Sinardi told the jury that the Tampa 8 Inn where the body was found was in an area considered to be "high crime," and was next door to another motel with a dangerous reputation. He also said he planned to challenge the expert who identified the blood spots on the denim shorts as coming from the victim.

The victim's mother, Mrs. Dicke, provided the most heartrending testimony of the trial, while telling the jury about the special bond between herself and her daughter and her desperate efforts to contact "Girl" on the night she disappeared. Testifying over portions of two days, Mrs. Dicke wiped tears from her eyes while she recounted telephoning her daughter thirty times that night, but never getting a call back. She also called police. "They said there was nothing they could do because she had not been gone long enough to report her missing," Mrs. Dicke told the jury. "I knew something bad had happened."

Mrs. Dicke also identified two sapphire rings and a heart-shaped watch that police found with Rogers when he was arrested, as belonging to her daughter. The personal items were easy to identify because she bought them for "Girl," and wore identical jewelry herself, Mrs. Dicke explained. She had also bought her daughter the white Ford Festiva that Rogers was driving when he led police on the wild chase through the mountains.

Later, Mrs. Dicke left the courtroom in tears after she learned for the first time that her daughter didn't immediately die after the vicious stabbing. Judge Allen had warned her just before former Hillsborough County pathologist Daniel Schultz was called to the witness stand that the autopsy evidence he was about to present would be grisly. Reeling with shock from the revelation, Mrs. Dicke told the judge: "I was told at the time of my daughter's death that she died instantly. She never knew what hit her."

Schultz testified that Mrs. Cribbs was conscious for some ten to twenty minutes after the vicious stabbing before she finally died. One of the stab wounds penetrated eight-and-a-half inches into her chest and punctured a lung. The stab wound to her right buttock severed a major artery. Her left wrist was also slashed, apparently as she tried to fend off the assault.

Some jurors were so repulsed and became so upset

during testimony about the discovery of the body, which included introduction of crime-scene photographs, that the judge ordered a brief break in the trial.

Another interruption occurred when KSP Detective Sergeant Joey Barnes testified that during the high-speed chase leading to Rogers's capture, cars and a school bus full of children were run off the road. The defendant's mother, Edna Rogers, startled the courtroom by shouting, "I object." Judge Allen quickly ordered the jurors from the courtroom. Then she laid down the law to Mrs. Rogers. "If I hear one more outburst from you, you will be removed from the courtroom for the remainder of the proceeding," she admonished the woman. Mrs. Rogers apologized.

Jurors were again sent back to their chambers when a highway rest stop attendant who testified about finding Mrs. Cribbs's wallet in a trash can, showed up in the courtroom wearing a T-shirt with the words, "Sho No Mercy" printed on the back.

Witnesses called by Sinardi included a DNA expert from the University of Alabama at Birmingham, who stated that the blood on the defendant's blue-jean shorts could have come from people other than Rogers or Mrs. Cribbs. A statistician also testified that the DNA profile was more common than prosecution witnesses indicated.

But Sinardi focused much of his defense on claims that police ignored other possible suspects. He submitted into evidence the criminal records of about twenty other people registered at the Tampa 8 Motel and at the neighboring Tropicana Inn.

At the conclusion of the seven-day trial, the jury deliberated eight hours before delivering a unanimous verdict of guilty to first-degree murder, car theft, and robbery. Wearing a blue suit and open-neck white shirt,

Rogers stood at the defense table, staring quietly at the judge while the verdict was read aloud. In the spectator section, his mother sat beside her eldest son, Claude, and one of the convicted killer's aunts, wiping tears from her face. Then she walked out of the courtroom.

On the other side of the aisle, Mrs. Dicke alternately watched the judge and stared at Rogers. Then she turned to the prosecutors, and told them, "You did a good job." When reporters turned to Claude Rogers, he stated the obvious, that the jury had made its decision. "It's just hard to believe that your own brother would be a serial killer," he added.

Friends of Mrs. Dicke and her daughter, who were watching television at the Showtown USA, cheered when the verdict was announced. Later that night at the Showtown, Mrs. Dicke thanked her friends for their support from the stage. Then, a few minutes before midnight, she placed a shot of tequila and a yellow rose on the well-worn bar in front of the stool where "Girl" had sat with her over drinks.

The next day, the jury and court officers returned with the defendant for the sentencing hearing, to determine if a recommendation would be made to the judge for life in prison without parole or death in Florida's three-legged electric chair.

At the same time Rogers's murder trial was underway, Florida was mired in a fierce debate over the death penalty and the future of "Old Sparky." While lawyers sparred during preliminary hearings in the Hillsborough Circuit courtroom over ground rules for the trial, supporters and opponents of the death penalty fought over the method of execution for convicted killers in the state. The controversy was precipitated early in 1997 after a sponge attached to the head of a killer who butchered an elementary school teacher with a knife was scorched during his electrocution. It marked the second time in six years that an imperfect execution occurred in the state.

In late May, a couple of weeks after Rogers's conviction, the Florida Supreme Court ordered executions put on hold pending a hearing on whether or not electrocution caused pain to the assorted serial killers, hit men, cop killers, and other murderers who were put to death. Substituting lethal injection for electrocution was being touted as the preferred alternative method of execution by forces opposing the electric chair. Most of the same people had indicated they were opposed to execution in whatever manner it might be carried out, despite overwhelming public support for the death penalty.

Claude Rogers testified during the penalty phase of his brother's trial about a childhood home life that was marked by alcohol and violence. The defendant's dead father was pictured as a mean-tempered alcoholic, who flew into rages, shooting up the neighborhood, smashing furniture, and breaking his wife's nose several times. According to the account, no love was shown in the home.

Mrs. Dicke also testified again during the penalty phase and talked movingly about her daughter. "It has totally destroyed my life," the distraught mother said of the murder. "She was all I had. I had lost my husband just before this happened to Tina Marie."

The jury deliberated approximately three hours, then reported a unanimous recommendation: death in Florida's electric chair.

A few weeks later the man labeled by the press as "the Casanova killer" appeared in shackles and a bright orange jail jumpsuit before Judge Allen for formal sentencing. As expected, she followed the jury recommendation and sentenced him to death. Rogers was silent during the proceeding, but as he was led out a side door of the courtroom he told television reporters he was "not worried about it, not worried at all."

THE WORLD'S FOREMOST AUTHORITY
ON SERIAL KILLERS REVEALS THE FBI'S
ULTIMATE WEAPON AGAINST THE NATION'S
MOST DANGEROUS PSYCHOPATHS...
THEIR OWN MINDS.

Face-to-face with some of America's most terrifying
killers, FBI veteran and ex-Army CID colonel Robert
Ressler learned from them how to identify the unknown
monsters who walk among us—and put them behind
bars. Now the man who coined the phrase "serial killer"
and advised Thomas Harris on *The Silence of the Lambs*
shows how he is able to track down some of today's
most brutal murderers.

WHOEVER FIGHTS MONSTERS

My Twenty Years Tracking Serial Killers for the FBI
Robert K. Ressler & Tom Shachtman